THE CLASSICS OF WESTERN SPIRITUALITY

THE CLASSICS OF WESTERN SPIRITUALITY
A Library of the Great Spiritual Masters

The Cloud Of Unknowing

EDITED, WITH AN INTRODUCTION
BY
JAMES WALSH, S.J.

PREFACE
BY
SIMON TUGWELL, O.P.

PAULIST PRESS

Cover art:
The artist, ANN DALTON, was born in Ossining, New York and now resides in New York City. A graduate of Pratt Institute in Brooklyn and Columbia University, she has done illustrations for the *New York Times, New York Magazine*, and several books. Her cover reflects her appreciation of the image of the inscrutable God presented in *The Cloud*.

Design: Barbini, Pesce & Noble, Inc.

Library of Congress
Catalog Card Number: 81-82201

ISBN: 0-8091-2332-0

Published by Paulist Press
997 Macarthur Boulevard
Mahwah, New Jersey 07430

Printed and bound in the
United States of America

Contents

THE EDITOR OF THIS VOLUME

FATHER JAMES WALSH, S.J., born in Lancashire in 1920, was educated at the Catholic College, Preston, Lancashire. He joined the Society of Jesus in 1938, took an honours degree in the Classical Languages and English Language and Literature at Oxford University, and was ordained a priest in 1952. After taking a doctorate in Ascetical and Mystical Theology at the Gregorian University, Rome, in 1957, he was appointed assistant editor of *The Month*. In 1961, he founded *The Way*, a quarterly periodical of spirituality, with Father William Yeomans, S.J., and remains its editor. He is also Vice-Postulator for the Cause of the English and Welsh Martyrs, and for the Cause of Mother Cornelia Connelly, Foundress of the Society of the Holy Child Jesus. His special study is fourteenth-century English Spirituality. He co-edited with Edmund Colledge, O.S.A. *Julian of Norwich, Showings* in The Classics of Western Spirituality series (which was based on their critical edition *A Book of Showings to the Anchoress Julian of Norwich*, published by the Pontifical Institute of Mediaeval Studies, Toronto, 1978), and *The Knowledge of Ourselves and of God* (Mowbrays Fleur de Lys Series 1961). He has published articles on Medieval Spirituality in the *Revue d'Ascétique et de Mystique* and *Archives d'Histoire Doctrinale et Litteraire du Moyen Age*, as well as contributing regular articles on spirituality to *The Month* and *The Way*. He edited and introduced the book *Pre-Reformation English Spirituality*.

AUTHOR OF THE PREFACE

SIMON TUGWELL is a Catholic priest, a member of the Order of Preachers. He did his early education at Corpus Christi College, Oxford. He has an M.A. in Classics and English and a Lectorate in Sacred Theology. Currently he is Regent of Studies in the Dominican study house at Blackfriars, Oxford, where he lectures and tutors in Theology and Ancient Philosophy. He has authored numerous books, including *Did You Receive the Spirit?* (Darton, Longman & Todd, 1972); *Prayer* (Veritas, 1974); *New Heaven? New Earth?* (Darton, Longman & Todd, 1976) and *The Way of the Preacher* (a forthcoming book to be published by Darton, Longman & Todd). Father Tugwell's articles have appeared in a considerable number of periodicals. A renowned preacher and retreat master, he has lectured in Europe, America, Africa, Australasia and the Caribbean. He has also been an occasional lecturer at the University of St. Thomas in Rome.

PREFACE

The Cloud of Unknowing is one of the gems of medieval English literature. Its anonymous author is a master of English prose, as well as a highly competent spiritual director, and his lively idiom and his shrewd, sensitive doctrine have combined to win for him, over many generations, a readership probably much wider and more diverse than he anticipated. But, in spite of his fears that all but the most carefully selected readers will misunderstand what he is saying, it is unlikely that many people have come to grief because of his book.

He writes, naturally enough, as a man of his own time, and what he says must be interpreted primarily with reference to contemporary sources and concerns. Father Walsh's learned Introduction and notes will help the reader to appreciate some of these.

But in a more general way, *The Cloud of Unknowing* belongs to the Church as a whole, and indeed to the whole sweep of Western thought and spirituality. Although its teaching bears the stamp of a highly original and creative mind, it draws on a multitude of traditions which have a long prehistory in and beyond the Church. Quite apart from the sources we can be reasonably sure the author actually used, we can recognize affinities with many of the influences that have been formative in the history of our culture, and it is the richness of these affinities that guarantees a certain universality in our author's appeal. Even though his own teaching is unique, he does not come to us as a complete stranger, talking in an alien tongue. Christians, although they may be surprised at some of the things he says, will nevertheless find that his message echoes things that they know already, and they will be able to acknowledge him as an exponent of an authentic Christian tradition. And even those who do not share his belief in Christ will find that his faith, far from cutting him off from the concerns of other men, gives him a particular insight into some of the problems that have been vexing us from the very beginnings of Western philosophy. Although he is quite innocent of any apologetic purpose, he does tacitly suggest a conviction that the fundamental aspirations of all men and women are fulfilled in union with the God who is revealed to us in Jesus Christ.

That we do have aspirations is taken for granted by our author, as by all early and medieval Christian writers. And he clearly shares the view, deeply imprinted on Western theology by St. Augustine, that it is through our aspirations that God draws us to himself. The most important mechanism of grace is that it forms in us a real will, a real desire, for God and for his will to be done. God *attracts* us to himself; he does not bully us or constrain us (except with the constraint of desire). The most typical evidence of grace being at work in us is not that we find ourselves aware of a duty, but that we find ourselves aware of a desire. This is why, with some important precautions, our author, like so many others, bids us follow our attractions and inspirations. Goodness is conceived of as being essentially attractive. This view, deeply rooted as it is in Greek philosophy, permeates Christian thought, and shows itself, for instance, in the assumption, shared by our author, that our Lord had quite outstanding beauty, and that those who follow him will become themselves attractive to their fellow men and women.

PREFACE

But our author is primarily concerned with those who are conscious of one very particular attraction: the attraction to contemplative prayer. He gives only the briefest of outlines of what he regards as the normal preliminaries to such an aspiration. There is no question in his mind about the need, in most cases, for the traditional practices of the spiritual life, such as meditation on the mysteries of the Incarnation and the Passion, and the attempt to live by Christian moral principles. It is by reading, thinking and praying that we approach contemplation (the scheme is quite traditional: it is found in Hugh of St. Victor, from whom it passes to St. Thomas and *The Nine Ways of Prayer of St. Dominic;* it is found in Guigo the Carthusian, from whom it passes to our author). But it is the final stage that is his special concern. He is writing for those who find themselves no longer satisfied with the "practices" of Christian piety; they are drawn by some mysterious further desire and must try to discover whether this desire is a genuine attraction to contemplation (in which case it may be presumed to come from God), or whether it is simply an affectation or mere intellectual curiosity.

The terms in which our author describes this desire are reminiscent of the way in which Plato describes the mysterious manner in which we are moved by an attraction we cannot identify, which beckons to us, hiddenly, in the everyday attractions we encounter in this life. (The theme was developed in a more modern guise by C. S. Lewis in his *Pilgrim's Regress* and *Surprised by Joy.*) "It is not a will nor a desire," says the author of *The Cloud,* "but something which you are at a loss to describe, which moves you to desire you know not what." This mysterious pull is a crucial factor in the famous erotic ascent of the Platonists. Plato points out how human love points beyond itself, and the neo-Platonists develop this to suggest that, beyond anything the mind can comprehend, it is *eros* that finally enables us to reach some kind of "contact" or even union with God.

This Platonist theme enjoyed considerable success in

Christian speculation. Many of the early Fathers, such as Origen and St. Basil, taught that it is through our response to the beauty that we see in creation that we are drawn to the invisible, incomprehensible beauty of God. In the West, this theme was developed by St. Augustine; in the Middle Ages it was expounded particularly by St. Bonaventure, who united it with St. Francis' well-known love of nature.

The author of *The Cloud* is clearly dependent, however loosely, on the Platonist tradition that our minds are defeated when we try to draw close to God; only love can take the final step, drawing us into the dark yet dazzling mystery of God as he is in himself. He also clearly receives this tradition through the mediation of the medieval Augustinian tradition which stresses the role of the will and of love rather at the expense of the mind. Unlike the Pseudo-Dionysius and St. Thomas, he does not seem to regard it as necessary for the mind to go to the limit of what it can do to approach the mystery before admitting defeat, nor does he see the final leap of love as being, precisely, an act of the *intellect* in love. But this does not necessarily mean that he is anti-intellectual, as he has sometimes been accused of being. All schools of Christian theology and spirituality, however intellectualist, recognize that it is an essential attribute of the healthy mind to be humble before the ultimate mystery of existence; similarly all schools of Christian theology and spirituality, however voluntarist, recognize that a certain mental clarity and seriousness are required if we are to situate the mystery correctly and not swoon prematurely and inadvisedly into an *O Altitudo*. The author of *The Cloud* is no exception. His writings show that he is very far indeed from being an irrationalist or primitivist. In the particular contemplative exercise he is describing, he does not see that learning or mental proficiency has any direct part to play; but he implies that he expects any contemplative of the kind he is writing about to be sensible and clear-headed in the extreme.

What we do not find in our author is any sign that he is interested in the lower reaches of the "erotic ascent." He

PREFACE

does not describe how we are attracted to God initially through our response to and reflection on creatures. At first sight, in fact, he seems to have a thoroughly negative attitude to creatures. During the practice of the contemplative "work" he is describing, he bids us put all creatures under a "cloud of forgetting." He regards it as being beneath our dignity to subject ourselves to creatures, as we do if we have any regard for them. And he seems to inculcate a real hatred of that particular creature which is ourselves.

We shall return later to this "self-hatred." For the moment let us consider what is meant by the "cloud of forgetting" under which all thought of creatures is to be trodden down. In the first place, it is important to notice that it is not creatures in themselves that are to be trodden down; it is the thought of them, and that only during the particular "work" of contemplation. And even thoughts of the attributes of God or of the mysteries of the Incarnation are explicitly included among the things that must be banished from our attention at such times, and the author admits that these are, in themselves, good thoughts, which, at other times, are valuable and important for us. It is, then, not because creatures are in any way *bad* that they are not to be the objects of our attention.

Though our author does not explicitly advert to the whole system of "erotic ascent," I do not think that his doctrine really contradicts it. Putting all thought of creatures under a cloud of forgetting does not necessarily mean any disparaging of creatures. It is, in the tradition of the erotic ascent, the creatures themselves that point us beyond themselves. We are respecting them for what they truly are in not lingering with them when they have served their purpose. The author of *The Cloud* is not interested in any speculation about the ultimate significance, theologically and metaphysically, of the material order, and in this he is unlike such philosophers as Proclus and such theologians as St. Irenaeus and, nearer his own time, Julian of Norwich. This is why he appears to be, as Fr. Walsh indicates, less optimistic about "sensuality" than Julian of Norwich. From the point of view of his own

PREFACE

particular purpose, to linger with the thought of creatures
would be to linger with the means instead of passing on to
the end. It would be like letting ourselves become fascinated
by medicines and then losing sight of the objective of becoming
healthy.

But there are hints that, in a different context, our author
might have spoken very differently about creatures and the
material order.

It was always at least a latent possibility within Platonism
that the ascent of the mind in love to the highest possible
union with God would be seen as resulting in a comprehensive
vision of all things, in which everything would be seen clearly
for what it is and appreciated as such, in the context of the
whole. This possibility is realized with particular fullness in
the late neo-Platonist, Proclus, who was one of the major
influences on the pseudo-Dionysius. And, through the Pseudo-
Dionysius, this all-encompassing holistic vision passed to the
theologians and other writers of the Middle Ages. It was particularly well-adapted to the synthesizing temper of the medieval mind, about which C. S. Lewis has written so well.
It found its most famous expression in the conclusion of
Dante's *Divine Comedy*. (There is a fascinating discussion of
the neo-Platonist background to this in an article by G. Quispel
in the Festschrift for R. M. Grant, *Early Christian Literature
and the Classical Intellectual Tradition*, ed. W. R. Schroedel and
R. L. Wilken, Paris, 1979.)

The author of *The Cloud* is certainly not concerned to
spell out the metaphysical implications of his doctrine. But
it is very suggestive that he recognizes, not only the obvious
danger of having too materialistic a view of spiritual things,
but also the danger of having too spiritual a view of material
things. The significance of this was indicated by Prof. John
Burrow in an article in *Essays in Criticism* 27 (1977), pp. 283–
298. In our author's opinion, it is of crucial importance that
we should not be confused about the structure of reality and
the differences there are within reality. The material order
is an expression of the spiritual order, and the unique con-

junction of the two in man is what makes man the most
"seemly" of all God's creatures. As a result of our proper
and passionate orientation toward God as he is in himself,
we should find that everything else falls into place, so that
we can see the truth of what creatures are in themselves
and respond to them accordingly. It is significant that our
author derives the most perfect kind of humility from contemplation of the mystery of God, and at the same time iden-
tifies humility as a readiness to "be what we are."

The ascent to the high point where God dwells in the
dark cloud of mystery, though it does involve a certain tran-
scending of creatures, does not annihilate them. Rather it guarantees that creation will be left intact in its own proper
integrity. It is very suggestive that the author of *The Cloud*,
having led us to the apex of all love, in God, and drawn
the necessary inference that our love for our fellow men and
women must be universal, like God's, insists that this does
not interfere with the ordinary preferences of our friendships.
God does not sabotage the workings of his world.

This means that it is mistaken to envisage God as being,
somehow, in competition with creatures for our attention.
He can only be seen as being in competition with creatures
if we have a wrong perception of creatures. Our aim must
not be just to transfer all our affectivity to God, but to reach
a state of "ordered love," in which all our affections fall into
place around our central love for God.

It is important to appreciate this point, because there
has probably always been a certain tendency to see our love
of God as nothing more than the transference to God of the
kind of love we might have for a human lover. This seems
to have been one element in the early Christian mystique
of celibacy, and it resulted in the widespread, more or less
articulate, heretical tendency toward encratism. In the apoc-
ryphal Acts of Judas Thomas, for instance, a young bride
opts for celibacy, with her husband, on their wedding night,
and explains: "The reason why I have set no store by this
transitory husband and marriage is that I am yoked in another

marriage. . . . I am coupled with a true husband" (that is, the Lord). In the Middle Ages this became a common feature of the literature of courtly love and of piety. Christ is presented as a "wooer," arguing his claim to be loved in much the same terms as any earthly lover might use. He is good-looking, rich, and aristocratic, and, above all, he is faithful. It is to him, then, that we can turn when we are wearied by the frustrations of earthly love. Thus Chaucer, at the end of his *Troilus and Criseyde*, bids young men and women love God, who will not let them down, rather than fickle human beings. As C. S. Lewis demonstrates in *The Allegory of Love*, this is a standard element in medieval literature of love.

Though there is plainly an element of truth in this picture, the danger is that it will lead us to try to *force* our affections to concentrate on God, without appreciating that our love of God is not, simply, exactly like the kind of love with which human lovers love one another. Something of this confusion seems to be present in the spirituality of Richard Rolle. He appears to have been a man of rather turbulent emotions and eager sensuality, who found, eventually, some kind of peace as a result of forcibly redirecting the whole energy of his affectivity toward God, which he did, at least in part, with the help of the kind of affective meditation on the Passion propagated by the Franciscan school. The result was a style of mysticism which was highly charged emotionally, and which set great store by felt consolations and paranormal phenomena, such as experiences of heat and angel-song.

The author of *The Cloud* is evidently very uneasy about all this sort of thing. He repeatedly warns us not to try to strain any of our faculties to achieve contemplation; it is a disastrous mistake to think that we shall attain our goal by forcing body or soul to operate in a way that is contrary to their God-given nature. It is dangerous even to try to think of nothing but God the whole time. When we are first drawn to the practice of the contemplative "work," we must only labor at it for a short time and then take our rest. The author is most insistent on safeguarding the spontaneity of this "work," which is the correlative in us of its nature as given to us by God. We must work with "zest," not violence.

Similarly the author is suspicious of any great display of emotion. He recognizes that we may be so moved by God that a strong emotional response is unavoidable, but he will not allow us to cultivate any such response artificially, and he would have us, as far as possible, avoid being demonstrative about our emotions. We should rather try to "hide" our love.

He is also suspicious of the imaginative decoration that is so characteristic of the spirituality of Rolle. In his view any picturing of heaven is simply going to distract us from our task. He would have approved of St. Thérèse dismissing the prospect of visions of angels, suggested by one of her sisters, with the blunt rejoinder: "You can't see angels on earth."

Although his terminology is different, our author seems to be fully convinced of the doctrine, so important in Greek philosophy and in the theology of the early Church, that the virtuous life (and the ideal life) is life in accordance with nature. The supernatural fulfillment of our life in no way violates our natural constitution. Our natural powers will help us toward our supernatural destination precisely in being allowed to fulfill their own functions. We shall turn ourselves into madmen, not mystics, if we try to bully our natural faculties into doing something they are not made to do. In any case, it is not, in the last analysis, the faculties that are capable of realizing our highest ascent to God. It is only our "naked being" which can approach the "naked being" of God. Like the German mystics, especially Eckhart and Tauler, and like Proclus before them, the author of *The Cloud* believes that the possibility of our contemplative union with God resides, not in our faculties, but in the mysterious and elusive depth of our own souls, which even we ourselves cannot comprehend. Like St. Thomas, he calls this our "being" (*essentia*), the "I" which we know only from its acts (*I* see, *I* think, *I* feel), but which is not identical with its acts (I am not simply my seeing, my thinking, my feeling, etc.).

PREFACE

It is the union of our naked being with the naked being of God that anchors our whole life. Apart from such union, there is bound to be something slightly contrived and artificial about all our behavior. Even our piety, even our virtues, will be slightly strained and unconvincing. But if we are enabled by God to approach him with the depth of ourselves in the mystery of his own transcendence, then our lives will become natural and well ordered.

This is why the author of *The Cloud* is convinced that true contemplatives are naturally and easily well-behaved and sensitive, and why he regards it as superfluous to give them lots of rules about their external actions. They will spontaneously behave in an appropriate way, and need no other guide to determine such things as how much they should eat or talk or sleep. They should be "heedless" in such matters. This, surely, is the true freedom of the children of God, and this is the "life according to nature" desired by the philosophers; this is also the life of spontaneity dreamed of by so many of our contemporaries. It is also legitimate to connect our author's doctrine of "heedlessness" with the old monastic doctrine of freedom from anxiety, and with Eckhart's doctrine of acting from the ground of our being "without any reason why."

We can see now why the author of *The Cloud* is so wary of any attempt we may make to conform ourselves to any pattern of holiness or mysticism. Such ape-like imitation (the simile is his) can never produce the reality of contemplation, or of anything else. True contemplation arises from a depth which we cannot manipulate. All we can do is try to avoid interfering with it, should it arise. Until then, we must use our ordinary faculties which we can, to some extent, control, in ways that are appropriate and sensible.

But all this still leaves us with one major problem. If it is our naked being which must approach God, why does our author speak so appallingly of the pain and obstruction caused precisely by our consciousness of our own being? Why does he say that "he who knows and feels that he exists has a very special experience of sorrow"?

Once again, it is important to notice that it is not our being, as such, which gets in our way, it is our *awareness* of our own being. The author explicitly rules out any desire to "unbe." We should be glad to exist, even while suffering so bitterly from the consciousness of our own existence.

But what is this strange sorrow caused by the feeling of our own existence? In part, no doubt, it is the awareness of how inextricably sin is mixed up with our existence. It is not uncommon for people to feel that, beyond whatever actual sins they may be conscious of, there is a deep root of sin, and that it is this which they really long to be rid of. It is the awareness of this that prompts the reaction of compunction, which is so characteristic of early monastic spirituality, and which then plays an important part in the spiritual literature of East and West, and which shows itself most obviously in the gift of tears so often reported in the lives of the saints and so earnestly desired and recommended in a multitude of texts.

But even this is not enough to account fully for the language of *The Cloud*. Without wishing to postulate any direct influence, I would suggest that it might be helpful to consider, as indicating the kind of thinking underlying the words of *The Cloud*, a neo-Platonist doctrine, taken up in the Middle Ages by Eckhart, and rediscovered in modern times by some of the Existentialists, that it is precisely our "existence" as independent subjects that is our original "fall." It is our standing-out (*ex-sistentia*) from the primordial wholeness and oneness of all things in God which breaks our union with him. As long as there is an "I" which confronts God, there is no real union with him. He is not an "object" which can be apprehended by us; he is *the Subject*. This is something that has been rediscovered by some modern theologians through their encounter with Hinduism (cf. Bede Griffiths, *Return to the Center*, especially page 25, and Henri le Saux,

Sagesse Hindoue, Mystique Chrétienne, especially page 111). Any self-consciousness of ourselves as existing *over against* God, contemplating him or loving him or whatever, is the very denial of union with him. We must, in Eckhart's striking phrase, strive to be as we were before we were created. Only so are we really one with God.

It is good that we exist; our existence is part of the richness of the world of God's making. But our consciousness should be so totally united with God that there is no room left for any separate consciousness of ourselves. If there is to be any awareness of ourselves, it must be as "object," not "subject"— object of God's gaze, as part of (though even that is an inadequate expression) his total seeing of himself and, in himself, of all that he has made, not subject of any vision of our own. The contemplative does not "see God"; he enters into God's seeing. The abolition of any clear notion of God in the cloud of unknowing thus goes with the abolition of any clear awareness of the knowing subject. Our being must approach God in such nakedness that it is clothed not even in itself. Only so can it perform the "nothing" in the "nowhere" that our author recommends. Only "nobody" constitutes no obstacle to this work.

As Proclus teaches, there is in us, underneath, as it were, our psychological and mental powers, a "no thing," and it is this that is drawn to that "no thing" which is God.

It is certain that our author had not read Proclus, and it is unlikely that he had read Eckhart; and it is not clear that he had made any deep study of Proclus' disciple, the pseudo-Dionysius. But he too realized that, if God is to be all in all, there is no room for us as a separate center or focus of existence. It is God's business, not ours, to safeguard our distinctness from himself; it is our business to accept, insofar as we are able, the gift which enables us to be, by grace, what he is by nature. It is only God who can fully know God, and if we would attain to genuine contemplative union with him, we must shed all that we mean by "ourselves," leaving only him to know and love himself in us. But this

PREFACE

"self-naughting," though it means that we must lose our consciousness of ourselves, is actually the way that we *become* ourselves.

Maybe our author was being unduly cautious in suggesting that most people ought not to read his book; but he was perfectly right to insist that if we are going to read it, we should read it carefully and as a whole. With the confidence of genuine expertise, he is going to lead us into deep waters. If we wish to follow him, we must be prepared to be taxed to the limit. But if we have the courage and the ability to follow him, we shall not find that our effort has been in vain. It is with great pleasure that I present to the reader this new and lucid translation of one of the masterpieces of Western literature and spirituality.

Simon Tugwell, O.P.
Blackfriars, Oxford

FOREWORD

Many years' acquaintance with *The Cloud of Unknowing* has convinced the present editor that any true appreciation of this work depends on the knowledge of its author's background: that is, of the spiritual climate in which he writes, and of the sources essential or helpful to this environment. The author's other works are simply elucidations of, or preparations for, a better understanding of *The Cloud* itself. They will be presented together in a subsequent volume of this series. Most important among them are two letters written to the same addressee as is *The Cloud:* on prayer, and on privy counsel (or counseling), which we have frequently modernized as *Private Direction*. These are probably his last extant works. Prior to these, but following *The Cloud* chronologically, is his paraphrase of the most frequently employed Latin rendering of the *Mystical Theology* of Denis the Areopagite (the Pseudo-Dionysius): the version made by John Sarracenus from a copy of the original Greek text. The *Cloud* author entitles his paraphrase *Deonise hid Divinite*, which we have entitled, *Hidden Theology*. His remaining works consist of a third letter—*Discrecioun of Stirings (Discernment of Impulses)*—and two other translations, highly different in form. The first is a free and

FOREWORD

synthetic paraphrase of Richard of St. Victor's *Benjamin Minor*, which is an allegorical and didactic treatise on the preparation of the heart and mind for the graces of contemplative prayer. The *Cloud* author calls his version *A Treytyse of the Stodye of Wysdome that Men Clepen Beniamyn (The Pursuit of Wisdom)*. Finally, the little work which he calls *A Tretis of Discrescyon of Spirites (Discernment of Spirits)* exhibits a strong dependence on two sermons of St. Bernard of Clairvaux, from a collection called *De Diversis—On Various Topics*.

Two other points need to be stressed. First, frequent allusion has been made to the work of the thirteenth-century Carthusian, Hugo de Balma, much of which is an extended commentary in Latin on the mystical theology of the Pseudo-Dionysius. The late P. Dubourg, S.J. made available to us his critical edition of this work, which has yet to be published. It has, therefore, not been possible to do more than offer English translations of relevant passages without references to the original. Secondly, all other citations in English from various Latin sources are my own.

ACKNOWLEDGMENTS

It would hardly be possible to name all those who have helped me in this work, either directly or indirectly, through correspondence and discussion. Many of them have a place in the bibliography. I do wish, however, to thank especially Father Edmund Colledge, O.S.A., a valued collaborator in so many published works, and Miss Denise Critchley-Salmonson, a devoted and conscientious editorial assistant to *Way Publications* and their editor over more years than she would, perhaps, care to count. I also owe particular gratitude to Miss Lena Cooper, who has managed to decipher the often-undecipherable in typing the manuscript. Finally, I would like to acknowledge the friendly prodding of Paulist Press and the editor-in-chief of this series.

INTRODUCTION

To search once again through the tangled mass of hypotheses advanced during the last century and a half concerning the content, sources and authorship of *The Cloud of Unknowing* might seem a futile exercise. However, the several recent attempts to pan-syncretize the author's method of contemplative prayer, and to tear it loose from its traditional roots and Western monastic context, encourage such an effort. For example, Ira Progoff, of *Intensive Journal* fame, has this to say: "We realize that the references to the Bible, to Jesus, and to the nature of God have only a transitory significance...."[1] Such a statement is so extraordinary in its historical naiveté as to put one in mind of the literary critic who drew a detailed comparison between Homer's *Iliad* and Tolstoi's *War and Peace*. One thinks of historical scandals of the dimensions of the Piltdown Man, and of extravaganzas like the Great Mushroom hypothesis to explain the Qumran discoveries. This is not to deny that we shall find Neoplatonic elements in *The Cloud*, or that *imageless* contemplation, and certain techniques that aid the stilling of the senses and the

---

1. *The Cloud of Unknowing* (London, 1959), p. 27.

1

faculties, will illustrate points of similarity between the masters, of, for example, Zen Buddhism or John of the Cross. But this is not to say much more than that there is no natural comparison between the finite and the infinite. Progoff and other modern editors are simply not competent to proffer comments on Christian works such as *The Cloud* without doing serious violence to the treatise, unless they accept seriously the statement of a historian like the late Professor Maurice Powicke:

> Only those who accept the dogma of the divinity of Christ as the central fact in a long process of divine revelation can escape bewilderment in the contemplation of the spread of Christianity, which has been so unlike other religions in its claim to penetrate and control the whole of life.[2]

THE AUTHOR

Undoubtedly, the most intractable problem that has exercised serious students of *The Cloud* is the identity of its author. Dr. Phyllis Hodgson, the author of the most definitive text to date, has handily summarized the various hypotheses advanced over the centuries,[3] and particularly in recent years.[4] Once the attribution to Walter Hilton is effectively disposed of, as most students believe that it has been, and especially

---

2. "The Christian Life," in *The Legacy of the Middle Ages* (London, 1926).

3. A fifteenth-century Carthusian, James Grenehalgh, who worked in the *Scriptorium* of the Sheen Charterhouse, took it for granted that its author was Walter Hilton, the author of *The Scale of Perfection:* Cf. Phyllis Hodgson (hereafter referred to as H.), *The Cloud of Unknowing* (London, 1944). However, Grenehalgh, and others after him, believed Hilton to be a Carthusian, (H., p. xi). As we shall see, there is a certain amount of internal evidence to support the claim for Hilton's authorship.

4. Dom Justin McCann argued tentatively that he was a secular priest; Evelyn Underhill, a strictly cloistered monk, whose order could not be determined, but not a Carthusian. H. herself argues that he was some sort of solitary; whilst Helen Gardner favours his being an anchorite (H., p. lxxxiii).

INTRODUCTION

by Helen Gardner,[5] the content and the context of the book, in the opinion of the present writer, leave us with the simple alternatives: that he was a Cistercian who had retired to the regulated hermitage, or—and this is by far the strongest conjecture—that he was a Carthusian priest. It has been suggested that too much weight has been given, in arguing for his priesthood, to the blessing he imparts to his addressee at the very end of the treatise. Two points, however, are worthy of notice here. First, there is the actual form of the blessing:

> I beseech almighty God that true peace, sane counsel and spiritual comfort in God with abundance of grace be always with you. . . .

Its invocative nature is clearly quasi-liturgical in character, with its references to peace and grace; whilst its form is consciously or unconsciously Pauline.[6] Second, by the last decades of the fourteenth century, it was becoming less and less frequent to separate regular spiritual direction and auricular confession. To these arguments may be added what the author has to say in Chapter 37:

> For those who are truly exercised in this work have more regard for the Church's prayer than any other. And they perform them in the manner and according to the rubrics ordained by the holy fathers who have gone before us.

As we have remarked in the note on this passage, the author is clearly speaking of the communal liturgy and chanting of divine office in the monastic choir. The reference to "the holy fathers who have gone before us" ought to be given its full weight. In fact, there is no monastic rule that gives

---

5. Cf. *Medium Aevum* XVI (1947): 40–41.
6. Cf. 1 Corinthians 16:23–24; Ephesians 6:23–24; 2 Thessalonians 3:18; Titus 3:15; Philemon 25; 2 Corinthians 1:2–4.

so much weight and pride of place to the Divine Office as
does the *Consuetudines Cartusiae* of Guigo I. It constitutes the
first twelve chapters of the "customs" and the rubrical detail
is formidable.[7] One would be hard put to it to find the *opus
Dei* treated with such care and at such length in any effective
rule of this date.[8] Nor can it be objected that the author
is referring only to his addressee. Not only does he constantly
associate himself in detail with the person (or persons) to
whom he addresses his treatise, but he speaks of the "holy
fathers who have gone before *us*." It has been objected, with
a certain inconsistency,[9] that the author couches his treatise
in the conventional genre of a personal letter. More serious
is the observation that the *Letter on discernment of impulses*[10]
is written for someone who is not bound to any religious
rule. The latter argument, however, takes it for granted that
this letter, like those on prayer and privy counsel, along with
The Cloud itself, are all addressed to the same individual. This
is obviously true of *Prayer* and *Privy Counsel* and, with certain
qualifications, of *The Cloud*. But there is no evidence, apart
from its content, that the third letter is written to the same
disciple; whilst the prologue to *The Cloud* makes it clear that
the author expects his works to be read or listened to by
others.

There are two other objections worthy of consideration
against the thesis that the author was a Carthusian. The first
is that the author, in defiance of the Carthusian ethos, is
concerned to defend himself with vigour against actual detractors of the contemplative method that he calls the work

---

7. Cf. "Edition critique des *Consuetudines Cartusiae*," in *Aux sources de la vie
cartusienne* (Grande Chartreuse, 1960, private printing), 4, pp. 60–93.

8. The earliest extant MS of the *Consuetudines* is of the eleventh century,
ibid., p. 1.

9. Several critics have pointed out that the prologue is couched in the form
of a general *caveat*, and that the personal references, along with the *envoi*, are no
more than a literary convention. On this point, see infra, p. 9.

10. Cf. H., "A Pistle of Discrecioun of Stirings," in *Deonise Hid Divinite*
(London, 1955), pp. 62ff.

of his book: and this not simply in general and according to the conventions followed by the medieval disciples of the Pseudo-Dionysius in his *Mystical Theology*. It would appear that between the time the neophyte had received *The Cloud*, and its sequel, *Privy Counsel*,[11] the book had been the object of severe criticism:

> I hear some folk say (and I am not speaking of illiterate men and women but of very learned theologians) that what I write to you and to others is so difficult and so profound, so subtle and so unfamiliar that it can scarcely be understood by the cleverest or most intelligent man or woman alive. . . .[12]

His defence is that it is an "easy exercise, through which the soul of the most ignorant man or woman alive is truly made one with God in loving meekness and perfect charity."[13] The same point is made in similar terms by another outstanding medieval Dionysian and also a Carthusian, Hugo de Balma,[14] with whose work our author was obviously familiar.[15] Some critics, however, have alleged that a work open to such criticism or given such publicity would hardly be likely to have received a Carthusian *imprimi potest*, or even that a Carthusian author would have been acquainted with such criticism. Whether or not the actual date of *The Cloud* is too early for involvement in the Wycliffite controversy— and this is the opinion of the generality of scholars—a matter to be discussed later on, England in the fourteenth century was a time of extraordinarily lively theological controversy,

---

11. This will be published in a subsequent volume, under the title *A Letter of Private Direction*, along with the other treatises attributed to our author.
12. From *A Letter of Private Direction*.
13. Ibid.
14. Cf. infra, p. 19.
15. Cf. infra, p. 20.

with the inevitable affective and anti-intellectual reaction.[16] Though the antagonists were Benedictines and Friars, Emily Hope Allen has drawn our attention to the treatise in defence of Richard Rolle, by the hermit Thomas Basset in the last decades of the century, against the criticism of a distinguished and learned Carthusian priest.[17]

It is not that one would wish—or have the temerity—to impugn the studied opinion of a scholar such as Dom André Wilmart, who has written of the early Carthusians:

> These men, austere and discreet, founded their hermitages so that they could live in silence among the shadows, occupied in meditating upon eternal truths. We do not expect self-revelation from them.[18]

The point is rather that it was not possible to involve oneself in the medieval spiritual teaching ascribed to Denis the Areopagite without being involved in the long drawn-out theological discussions of the time concerning the nature of the Beatific Vision,[19] quite apart from interest surrounding *The Divine Names* both before and after Saint Thomas's celebrated Commentary. And when all is said and done, the *Cloud* author still remains anonymous.

Though a century and a half will pass before we find the prior and proto-martyr of the London Charterhouse, Saint John Houghton, appealing for books from his brethren on

---

16. W. A. Pantin emphasises the reaction in fourteenth-century England "against the excessive intellectualism and excessive sublety of scholasticism": cf. *The English Church in the Fourteenth Century* (Cambridge, 1955), pp. 132–35.

17. Cf. *Writings Ascribed to Richard Rolle* (New York and London, 1927), p. 529.

18. *Auteurs spirituels et textes dévotes du moyen âge latin* (Paris, 1932), p. 272; cf. J. Walsh and E. Colledge. *The Ladder of Monks and Twelve Meditations by Guigo II* (New York and London, 1978), p. 11.

19. For the involvement of English theologians, such as FitzRalph, Uthred of Boldon and Adam Easton, see Pantin, op. cit., pp. 151–54, 165–81.

the continent, this was no late development. Though William of St. Thierry, in his famous *Epistola Aurea* to the Carthusian brethren of Mont-Dieu, will take it for granted that the Carthusian will need no other book for study than the scriptures,[20] it is abundantly clear that, not only at the *Grande Chartreuse*,[21] but at several other Charterhouses, a well-stocked library seems to have been taken for granted. A fascinating example is the late medieval catalogue of the house at Salvatorberg, printed in the *Mittelalterliche Bibliothekskataloge*,[22] with its detailed description of one manuscript after another, and its special sections on mystical theology—*Diversi libri pro theologia occulta divinissima, que dicitur mistica*—covering some seventy printed pages.[23] One would not have to argue, as does Richard Methley, that the author of *The Cloud*, were he indeed a Carthusian, would have had to be a professional theologian before he entered his Charterhouse.

One final objection to Carthusian authorship is the weight given to the matter of bodily sustenance, or rather to the indifference he and his disciple should have towards it:

> ... you must trust steadfastly that God will give you, without your attending to it, one of two things: either an abundance of what is necessary, or strength in body and spiritual patience to put up with the lack of them.
>
> I say this in refutation of their error who maintain that it is not lawful for men to devote themselves

20. *Epistola ad Fratres de Monte Dei, X,* 31; P.L. 184, 307–54. English trans. W. Shewring, *The Golden Epistle of Abbot William of St. Thierry to the Carthusians of Mont-Dieu* (London, 1930), p. 16. It should be pointed out that the treatise is addressed in particular to "the younger brethren, and to the novices who come to you ..." (Shewring, p. 3).

21. For the literature to which Prior Guigo II had access, see *The Ladder of Monks,* pp. 21–38, 54–76.

22. München, 1928.

23. Ibid., pp. 298–366.

to the service of God in the contemplative life, unless they are assured beforehand of having what is necessary for the body.[24]

The revised Carthusian Statutes of 1368, which attempted to restore the primitive poverty of the order,[25] coincided with the formation of an English Carthusian Province.[26] The first community, which had existed at Witham since 1178,[27] had suffered very severely in the Great Pestilence of 1358–1360, and the material poverty of all succeeding foundations, with the possible exception of Mount Grace, was a very real fact of life.[28] In 1375, then, when the Charterhouse of Coventry was founded on the authority of John Luscote, then prior of the London "House of the Salutation," it was extremely poorly endowed. Nonetheless, three monks from Beauvale soon joined the three members of the London house who acted as the founders; and it was not until 1385, when Richard II took it under his personal protection and laid the foundation stone of the church, that it had any real security of tenure. It had previously been built cell by cell as money became available.[29]

The tenuous line of argument followed here is simply that one of the three monks from Beauvale in Nottinghamshire, a man from those parts who wrote in the dialect of "the north part of the central East Midlands,"[30] was the author of *The Cloud*. Beauvale had also suffered very severely in the pestilence, and it would seem that the means for their continuance came to them providentially in 1362.[31] We are saying

---

24. Chap. 23, infra, pp. 168, 167.
25. Cf. E. M. Thompson, *The Carthusian Order in England* (London, 1930), p. 129.
26. Ibid., p. 141.
27. Cf. *Maisons de l'Ordre des Chartreux* (Parkminster, 1919), Tome IV, p. 19.
28. Cf. Thompson, pp. 142ff.
29. Ibid., pp. 209–12.
30. H., *The Cloud*, p. 1.
31. Cf. Thompson, p. 160.

nothing more than that, granted the wealth of internal evidence for the hypothesis that the author of *The Cloud*, and the other treatises attributed to him, was a Carthusian, all the objections against such identification can be answered, and that whatever external straws there are favour it.

THE ADDRESSEE

Phyllis Hodgson has remarked that "the young disciple for whom these treatises[32] were written was not a scholar."[33] Others have queried the assertion that *The Cloud* at least was not addressed to a single individual; and it must be taken for granted that the "translations"—the *Mystical Theology* of the Pseudo-Denis, the paraphrase of the *Benjamin Minor* of Richard of St. Victor, and the *Discretion of Spirits*—were not written with any particular individual in mind.[34] The letter on prayer, as well as on privy counsel, was certainly addressed to the same individual, since the author says so himself.[35] *The Cloud*, it would appear, was not originally written to this same addressee, but the proemium, the repetition of a crucial part of the prologue, a highly individual context and a touchingly personal epilogue all point to the conclusion that the author was not having recourse to literary convention, but simply addressing, to an individual whom he knew and wished to help, a treatise previously written for beginners in the Dionysian contemplative method of prayer, and offering specific advice as to whether the neophyte was being called to this form of contemplation and the rule of life demanded for its practice.

---

32. I.e., those published in her *Deonise hid Divinite*, plus *The Cloud* itself and *Privy Counsel*.

33. H., *The Cloud*, p. lvii.

34. This matter will be taken up in the subsequent volume.

35. H.'s researches have established this beyond doubt; if indeed any argumentation were necessary, in view of the author's own words in *Privy Counsel* (H. 154/13–18), and the subject matter and language in *Impulses*.

INTRODUCTION

Dr. Hodgson bases her contention that the disciple was not a scholar on two passages, the first of which introduces five chapters (35–39) summarizing the traditional monastic contemplative process:

> ... there are certain preparatory exercises which should occupy the attention of the contemplative apprentice: the lesson, the meditation and the petition.

The second explains why the author has not annotated his book with reference to his sources:[36]

> ... at one time men believed that it was humility to say nothing out of their own heads, unless they corroborated it by scripture and the sayings of the fathers. But now this practice indicates nothing except cleverness and a display of erudition. You do not need it, and so I am not going to do it. (Chap. 70)

Neither passage, in fact, tells us anything of the theological erudition of the disciple. Guigo II wrote his short treatise, *The Ladder*, to one Gervase, whom he speaks of as his "master";[37] and our author is quite simply adapting the way to the *culmen contemplationis* to suit the Dionysian purpose and method, in which this and other previous and future readers are beginners. Indeed, this disciple, it would seem, is capable enough of reading the works of Denis for himself, which would certainly demand a considerable proficiency, both in the Latin language and in apophatic theology. Neither does the second reference tell us anything about the disciple's learning or lack of it; it merely emphasizes that the method and

---

36. The author is not quite consistent here. Besides his immediate reference to Dionysius, he will quote Augustine and Gregory the Great in his final chapter.
37. Op. cit., p. 81.

its purpose have nothing to do with intellectual erudition. There is, however, one very noticeable aspect of *The Cloud*, as opposed to the letters *Prayer* and *Privy Counsel*. It is that there are no scriptural citations in Latin: a fact that may indicate a lack of theological proficiency on the neophyte's part. He is a young man, only twenty-four when he begins to read *The Cloud;* and his learning may equally be that of a beginner. It could also be argued that, in the later treatises, the author is exercising a prudence in citing his scripture from the Latin Vulgate, since vernacular translations are by this time suspect. We notice that he always translates his quotations into English, doubtless in view of the increasing opposition during the closing decades of the fourteenth century to the use of Wyckliffite or Lollard translations.[38] It is much more likely, however, that between his reception of *The Cloud* and the letter *Privy Counsel*, the disciple's knowledge of the great monastic fathers—Cassian, Augustine, Gregory and Bernard, as well as of Denis and Hugo de Balma, had developed rapidly. If Richard Methley is right,[39] and our neophyte was already a Carthusian when he received his personal copy of *The Cloud*, then he must at least have finished his novitiate when he received *Privy Counsel*,[40] since our author insists on being his personal director: "I make no secret, as you see, of the fact that I want to be your spiritual father; indeed I do, and intend to be so."[41]

---

38. Cf. M. Deanesly, *The Lollard Bible* (Cambridge, 1920), esp. chap. 12, pp. 298ff.

39. Cf. infra, chap. 1, note 14, p. 116.

40. "After his (the novice's) introduction into his cell, one of the elders *(seniorum aliquis)* is deputed to instruct him in all necessary matters ... he is often visited by the prior" *(Consuetudines*, loc. cit., pp. 121–22).

41. From *The Letter of Private Direction*.

INFLUENCE, SOURCES AND DOCTRINE

It has been noticed that the prayer with which the treatise begins not only sets it firmly against a liturgical background,[42] but indicates that the Deity whom the author is addressing is the God, one and three, of Christian revelation. The title of the prayer in the Sacramentaries of the time would certainly have been "Petition for the grace of the Holy Ghost"; it is the Father who is the object of the petition, and "Jesus Christ our Lord" through whom it is made. When, therefore, in chapter 4, the author answers the prayer, real or imagined, of the reader, "Help me now for the love of Jesus," he says:

> This "for the love of Jesus" is very well said ...
> love Jesus and everything that he has is yours. By
> his Godhead he is the maker and giver of time.

As is implied very clearly in *Privy Counsel*,[43] unless the author for a particular reason is treating of the manhood of Christ in special, or of the work of the Holy Spirit in the order of salvation and perfection, he is never in doubt that the God who is the object of the contemplative effort is the Triune God of revelation. The addressee is directed to "knit yourself to him by love and faith" (chap. 4), and no distinction is made between the Persons. The author has neither Arian, Sabellian nor docetic leanings. What is more, his choice of the prayer is very deliberate. He leaves us in no doubt from first to last that the "work of this book" demands the ultimate in passive purification, and that its end is that for which every human being is created, the perfect praise and love of God.

As we have already indicated, it seems that the author has adapted a copy of his highly individual introduction to

---

42. Cf. infra, Prologue, note 2, p. 100.
43. Cf. the spiritual exegesis of *Ego sum ostium* (John 10:9), in *A Letter of Private Direction.*

and commentary on the *Mystical Theology* of the Pseudo-Denys for a particular addressee: one who has just undertaken the life of a solitary, or who has entered the Carthusian Order after spending some years as a Benedictine or a Cistercian. The very form of address used indicates that he has made profession in the form of the *propositum*. As Germain Lesage has written recently:

> The Latin word *propositum* . . . describes the constant spirit of the faithful Christian who determines to follow Christ in practising the evangelical counsels and in dedicating his or her whole life to this self-offering . . . [expressing] a desire of the religious consciousness to draw near to God, or to attain to actual union with him.[44]

The general prologue uses the same terminology: ". . . resolved with steadfast determination . . . in the contemplative life . . . whilst it (the soul) still dwells in this mortal body."[45] Centuries before, the Abbot Pachomius had written of his professed monks:

> You have chosen God as your fulcrum; you have become his beloved; you have decided to walk according to his commands . . . it cannot be that the one who has dedicated himself can turn back to worldly activity.[46]

Here our author makes the point that the neophyte to the contemplative life must have previously practised himself in the virtues and exercises of the active life. By the latter term

---

44. "Sacred bonds in the consecrated life," in *Supplement to the Way* 37 (Spring 1980), p. 79.

45. Infra, p. 101.

46. *Oeuvres de S. Pachôme et de ses disciples*, tom. 24 (Louvain, 1956), pp. 23–24, 29.

he primarily means the meditative prayer mentioned in chapter 7 and elsewhere. He speaks hardly at all of the corporal works of mercy. This is the force of the distinction as made by the "Abbot of Saint Victor," Thomas Gallus;[47] though our author's prologue adds:

> We must make an exception for those whose exterior state belongs to the active life; and yet, because they are inwardly moved through the hidden spirit of God ... are enabled by an abundance of grace to share in the work of contemplation at the highest level ... every now and then.[48]

It is hardly likely that he is speaking of those whose vocation is *tradere aliis contemplata,* the "ex professo" prelates and preachers, who are called to religious action as well as to contemplation, as Saint Thomas points out.[49] Rather he seems to have in mind the kind of Christian for whom Walter Hilton wrote his *Mixed Life.*[50] We cannot, however, presume that Hilton is his mentor here, since the devout laity of either sex, who were both literate and leisured enough, were enabled and encouraged, as a host of vernacular minor treatises bears witness, to attempt the practice of contemplative prayer.[51]

RICHARD METHLEY

A careful, accurate and idiomatic Latin translation of *The Cloud* is fortunately still extant.[52] What is more, the translator

---

47. Cf. infra, pp. 43ff.
48. Infra, p. 103.
49. Cf. *Summa Theologiae* 2-2ae, q. 188, a. 6.
50. Cf. C. Horstman, *Richard Rolle of Hampole and his followers,* vol. I (London, 1895), pp. 264ff.
51. Cf. Pantin, op. cit., p. 253.
52. In the library of Pembroke College (221) Cambridge. This MS was prepared for publication in 1967 by Father Edmund Colledge, O.S.A., and the present writer,

tells us that he finished it on the feast of Saint Lawrence in 1491.[53] It is the work of Richard Firth of Methley, a Carthusian of the Charterhouse of Mount Grace in Yorkshire. It was copied by another Carthusian, William Darker of Sheen (London) Charterhouse, with cross-references and some annotations.[54] The principal annotator is, however, another Carthusian, also at the time a monk at Sheen. He it was who annotated MS Harleian 2373, and is responsible for the conjecture that Walter Hilton was a Carthusian and the author of *The Cloud*.[55]

From the careful collation made by Father Colledge and the present writer of the MSS used by Dr. Hodgson in her critical edition, it has emerged that Richard Methley must have had access to a MS or MSS of *The Cloud* soon after he entered Mount Grace (1476/1477), or perhaps even before, since he was already a priest when he entered Mount Grace. Moreover, many of Methley's readings in the Latin obviously derive from an original(s) superior to any recorded by H. At the same time, there is no indication in his translation that he has knowledge of the other treatises attributed to the *Cloud* author, in spite of the fact that he is the only person who has described the use of the contemplative method advocated in *The Cloud*.

It is Richard Methley who makes the point, in his annotations to chapter 1 (cf. note 14 infra), that the "singular (degree is) of solitaries: that is, hermits, anchorites and especially Carthusians. Hence we may conclude that this book was written for a Carthusian, since in our day it is not customary, as it was in days gone by, to leave an approved religious order for a hermitage, but only for the Carthusians."

---

but it is still in proof-stage at the time of writing; all the information on Richard Methley here recorded is taken from this edition.

53. Cf. infra, chap. 75, note 475, p. 268.

54. The MS also contains Methley's translation of an English version of *The Mirror of Simple Souls*, which Darker attributes to "Russhbroke who was a prior of the Carthusian Order."

55. Cf. H., *The Cloud*, pp. xi, lxxxii.

INTRODUCTION

We recall that Methley's only extant English writing is the *Epistle to Hugh Hermit*,[56] whose spiritual director he clearly is, and that Miss Clay, in her list of English hermits, has identified a hundred *bona fide* recluses in Yorkshire,[57] the county of Methley's Charterhouse, more than in any other county,[58] and doubtless due to the influence, at least in part, of Richard Rolle, of whom our author seems to be objectively critical.[59] It follows, then, that Methley's firm statement here must be taken seriously. Miss Clay, in her chapter "Order and Rule," has much to say about ecclesiastical strictures against self-constituted solitaries, and she speaks of monks and friars obtaining special permission to become solitaries.[60] From the time of Saint Edmund, Archbishop of Canterbury (d. 1240), to become an anchorite required episcopal licence; an abbot's authority was not sufficient. It was necessary, before the end of the fourteenth century, for some members of religious orders to apply to the Holy See for permission to leave their order to become an approved solitary.[61]

Methley, for his own part, though he makes no mention of the circumstances of his ordination, stresses the apostolic importance of the priesthood in the life of a Carthusian solitary:

> It is burdensome to me to have to look at any other person; indeed, apart from the members of my order and of my fellow-priests, and the limitations of this mortal life, I would prefer never to look upon any other creature, before I looked upon Christ.[62]

---

56. Cf. MS Public Record Office 1/239.

57. Cf. Rotha Mary Clay, *The Hermits and Anchorites of England* (London, 1913), Appendix C, pp. 254–61.

58. Ibid., pp. 201–63.

59. Cf. infra, chaps. 48–49, and notes.

60. Clay, pp. 90ff.

61. Ibid., p. 93.

62. Cf. MS Trinity College Cambridge (TCC) 1160 f. 60r.

His autobiographical writings, which are still extant, give a rare instance both of the performance of the contemplative exercise that is the "work" of *The Cloud*, and his unselfconscious assumption that the exercise in no way clashes with the *opus Dei* of the community or of those times when the community takes its meals in common. The *Cloud* author, as we have noticed, whilst taking it for granted that the prayer of the Church obviously takes precedence over the private contemplative exercise, refuses to enter into any autobiographical detail, except to say how much he desires the perfection of the exercise, and how far he feels he is from achieving it (cf. infra, chaps. 26, 73). Methley, however, is convinced that his own particular brand of enthusiasm, of which the *Cloud* author is so rightly suspicious and which he castigates so severely (though he may well have been accused of it), is a special charism granted to very few. This "sensory mysticism," as it has been called,[63] popularized, apparently, by Richard Rolle, is clearly distinguished from the actual exercise of *The Cloud*, in Methley's description of his own practice of it. It is the prayer proper to the contemplative state, in the strict sense; and the contemplative is rightly disposed to enter upon it when he experiences such love that he is tormented because he cannot see God, when he is overwhelmed by the desire to look on the face of the beloved. Such a feeling of longing love, "the humble impulse of love," as the *Cloud* author calls it, is a sign that the exercise must be undertaken regularly. Methley advises his Carthusian brethren to retire to their accustomed place of prayer, concentrate the whole attention on God, hide from every creature, close their eyes, and begin with a simple affective preparatory prayer. His own practice is to make the exercise at dawn, midday and midnight for a quarter of an hour, and after Vespers or supper

---

63. Cf. A. G. Dickens, *Clifford Letters of the Sixteenth Century* (*Surtees Society* 172, 1957), p. 34. The Clifford family were great patrons of Mount Grace, until the Dissolution, as Dickens's collection shows.

for half an hour. He calls it "the way of non-intellectual ascension in purest contemplation" *(forma ascensionis ignote in purissima contemplatione)*, and describes it as follows:

> That alone for which I long is fixed in the mind ... and yet, through the power of love all the things you long for, whether in yourself or anyone else, are to be forgotten. And though you may have a vague remembrance of painful things, you will not feel any dismay for abundance of joy; rather you will rise above them in this lack of knowing, and forget them altogether. Notice that I say "altogether." Then—and this is the most astounding thing—you will find that you are even forgetting heavenly glory altogether. I say again, "altogether"; otherwise you could not reach that point of self-forgetfulness *(excessum mentis)* or overreaching of the mind where the glory of contemplation is experienced.... In order to be lifted up out of yourself *(consurgas ignote)*, you must forget everything which is either in the Creator or the creature.[64]

He adds that the exercise does not belong to the faculty of the reason—"for if it were, then perhaps non-Christians *(pagani)* could undertake it"; yet it is not against reason *(contra rationem)*, but "it overreaches it *(supra rationem est)*, because, just as we can never say what God is, neither can he be seen by the exercise of prayer."[65]

This emphasis on "forgetting" would seem to indicate that Methley's most immediate contact with medieval Dionysian spirituality is through *The Cloud* itself. His glosses on *The Cloud* reveal no acquaintance with his author's other works, not even with *Prayer* or *Privy Counsel*. Equally, on the evidence of his own works, as well as of his *Cloud* glosses, his knowledge

---

64. MS TCC 1160, ff. 16r–17r.
65. Cf. infra, chap. 71, note 455, p. 258.

of the Dionysian corpus appears strictly limited. His only citation from the *Divine Names* (cf. chap. 70) is a recasting, by Hugo de Balma, of a phrase from the translation of Sarracenus: *Et est rursus divinissima Dei cognitio quae est per ignorantiam cognita*, which Methley does not gloss at all. His dependence on De Balma is particularly noticeable in his citations from the *Mystical Theology*, which are almost entirely restricted to the short pericope from the first chapter, *Tu autem, o amice Timothee*, describing the anagogical exercise. This passage, equally, could be De Balma's version of Sarracenus. He invariably uses De Balma's term for *The Cloud's* contemplative exercise, *consurrectio anagogica*. In fact, it has not been possible to discover any Dionysian references in Methley's *Cloud* glosses that could not have been taken from De Balma. Nor do there seem to be any traces of the commentaries on the works of the Pseudo-Denis by the most prominent of the Dionysians, Thomas Gallus, known and referred to by name as the *Cloud* author's principal source in his translation of the *Mystical Theology*.[66] However, as we shall notice presently, Methley seems to have been acquainted with the *De Contemplatione* of another Carthusian of the Dionysian school, Guigues du Pont.

HUGO DE BALMA

Hugo de Balma, prior of the Charterhouse of Meyriat in Bresse from 1298–1340, is known as the author of one work, which traditionally takes its title from its opening phrase, *Viae Syon Lugent.* It was early attributed to Saint Bonaventure, whose authorship was firmly rejected and attributed to Hugo by the editors of what is accepted to be the definitive edition of the *Opera Omnia* of Saint Bonaventure, the Franciscans of Quarrachi, in 1895. The alternative titles of the treatise, *Mystica Theologia* and *De Triplici Via,* are clues to

---

66. Cf. the prologue to *Deonise hid Divinite* (H., p. 2).

its nature and content: It is a comprehensive treatment, for practical purposes, of the *Mystical Theology* of the Pseudo-Denis. Hugo's aim is to bring back to the reality of the contemplative vocation those religious, and especially his own, who have allowed themselves to be seduced from the true wisdom, the mystical theology, by the attractions of human (theological) learning and speculation. His treatise, as the third title indicates, is divided into the three parts or ways, based on the analogy of the Pseudo-Denis with the triads of the nine choirs of angels, the purgative, the illuminative and the unitive; and the first two parts are merely preparatory for Hugo's main purpose, his extended commentary on the Dionysian *Mystical Theology*.

As we have shown in our annotations to the various chapters of *The Cloud*, there are many similarities of idea and expression between our author and De Balma. A good many of them recur in his extended citation from Thomas Gallus's *Explanation on the Mystical Theology* of Denis,[67] to a point at which we must accept it as feasible that our author was acquainted with the *Viae Syon Lugent*; whilst it is equally feasible that, in other points of similarity, they are using a common source. An example of this may very well be the case in the first chapter, where both are saying much the same as the author of *The Ladder of Monks*, Guigo II. At the same time, the purposes of *The Cloud* and of de Balma run very close: the one writing for the "apprentice," the other to call those who have strayed, back to the true way that leads men to life. It is therefore as much in the purgative preparation for the unitive exercise, and in the description of the passing over from the "illuminative" graces and responses, as in the consideration of the key text in the first chapter of *Deonise*

---

67. The treatise entitled *Exposicio super Quedam Verba Libri Beati Dionisij De Mistica Theologia*, in the Bodleian Library MS Douce 262. The MS also contains, besides copies of *The Cloud* and *Privy Counsel*, the *De Septem Gradibus Contemplationis* of Thomas Gallus. H. (*Cloud* xv) accepts the attribution, and does not identify the *Exposicio* (English version, "The Ascent to Contemplative Wisdom," in *The Way*, 1969).

hid Divinite, that we notice the similarities. On balance, then, it would seem that our author was acquainted with the *Mystical Theology* of Hugo de Balma, particularly when we recall the influence at the end of the fourteenth century of Saint Bonaventure on the affective aspects of the contemplative life. And it would certainly seem relevant that by 1410, the translation of the *De Vita Christi,* also attributed to Bonaventure, and translated by Nicholas Love, then prior of the Mount Grace Charterhouse, was in circulation.[68]

Yet the differences remain obvious. Hugo is writing a formal treatise, and moves with precise logic from the consideration of the needs of those who are still moving towards the fulness of the experience of "the overpassing of yourself,"[69] and those who have arrived, along with the problems they still have to face. This is why Hugo bases his treatment of the third part of his book, the Unitive Way, which is the equivalent of Denis's *Mystical Theology,* on a careful exegesis of the key passage in chapter 1; and then proceeds, in the manner of the scholastics, to answer the objections of those who wish to assert the superiority of the symbolic theology of Hugh and Richard of St. Victor, or the "infused theology" expounded by Augustine in his *De Vera Religione,* or finally the recently developed scholastic theology. The *Cloud* author is at once more practical, more eclectic, and rather more at ease with his subject. He feels no compulsion to contrast "schools," or name names: rather the reverse (cf. chap. 70). He will write in the way that suits him, and take up the various themes he considers important in a modern treatment of the traditional Dionysian method of contemplative prayer, as they occur to him. This is why in so much of his book he appears to digress from his main purpose.[70] But he is

---

68. Cf. Thompson, op. cit., p. 339. After the title is written the comment, "to the confusion of all fals Lollards and heretickes."
69. From the first chapter of *Deonise hid Divinite.* (H., p. 3).
70. Such digressions account for about a third of his chapters.

free, wise and experienced enough at the end of his work
to stress the point already made in the beginning:

> ... take the time necessary to examine it right
> through. For it may happen that some question occurs
> at the beginning or in the middle which depends
> on what follows, and is not fully explained in that
> place. If it is not explained here, it will be so a little
> later on, or else at the end. (chap. 74)

Again, instead of wasting his time writing something fresh
for the "contemplative apprentice," he sends him what he
has already written with the minimum of adaptation, simply
adding:

> If you think that there is any point here that you
> would wish to have clarified in greater detail ... let
> me know what it is, and what you think about it,
> and I shall amend it to the best of my simple ability.
> (ibid.)

As a result we have from his pen the letters *Prayer* and *Privy
Counsel,* and (perhaps to another disciple) the letter *Discernment
of Impulses*—each a masterpiece in the art of spiritual direction
by letter; and, in the case of *Privy Counsel,* one of the best
short treatises ever written in the Christian West on dark
contemplation. It is equally characteristic of the man that,
having refused to bow to current convention and name his
authorities except for the Areopagite, he immediately cites
from Gregory and Augustine in the last sentences of his book
(chap. 75); whilst previously he has used Richard of St. Victor's
symbolic exegesis concerning the Ark of the Covenant, knowing well enough that his contemporaries would immediately
recognize his source (chap. 74). More than fifty years ago,
the late Dom David Knowles was so impressed by the author's
comprehensive knowledge of the teaching on grace of the
greatest scholastic of them all, Thomas Aquinas, that Knowles

gave it as his opinion that our author must certainly have been well versed in Thomism.[71] We shall have more to say on this matter when we come to examine the contents of the book. Meantime, there is one other Carthusian source with which our author may have been familiar, Guigues du Pont's *De Contemplatione.*

GUIGUES DU PONT

Guigues du Pont wrote his treatise *De Contemplatione* as a monk of the Grande Chartreuse, where he was professed in 1271, and died in 1297.[72] What he has to say concerning the imaginative contemplation of the mysteries of the Gospel Christ is reproduced verbatim in the work of another Carthusian, Ludolph of Saxony's *De Vita Christi*, which played so prominent a part in the conversion of Saint Ignatius Loyola. The most notable Carthusian writer of them all, Denis de Ryckel, calls Ludolph "that devoted man who writes so much that is profitable on contemplation." His work assumes the form of three more or less distinct treatises, connected one to another but in no strict sense progressive. He first writes of three degrees by which the sinful creature is gradually led towards mystical union: purification by means of contrition

---

71. Cf. "The Excellence of *The Cloud*," in the *Downside Review* 52 (January 1934): 74. There appears to be no specific scholastic approach to the *Mystical Theology* until Gerson's *Elucidatio scholastica mysticae theologiae*, dated June 1424, after which, according to André Combes, the Dionysian school began to lose its interest for the professional theologian. Cf. *La Théologie mystique de Gerson* (Rome, 1963–1964) tom. 2, p. 671. Combes asserts that from October 1425 the commentators on Denys are set aside, and mystical theology is no longer the work of an affective faculty, but an experimental perception of God at the apex of the soul's essence, sanctified by grace, in a mutual embrace which is none other than Denis's "super-intellectual union."

72. For much of the information on Guiges du Pont and his De Contemplatione we are indebted to Father J. P. Grausem's article "Le 'De Contemplatione' de Guigues du Pont," *RAM* X (July 1929): 259–89. To the three MSS listed by Grausem we have been able to add another, which is not only complete, but appears to give the best readings.

INTRODUCTION

and confession, union with Christ by means of meditation
on his life and passion, and contemplation of the Divine Majesty. In the first two degrees, Christ is at the heart of the
spiritual effort, and we are to cling to him with a familiarity
that increases daily. The persevering contemplation of Christ
in his mysteries, as Denis had said long ago,[73] is the unique
way in the ascent to the Godhead. So the soul is prepared
for contemplation in a fuller sense; and Guigues selects three
aspects of it, stressing first that a more than normal abundance
of grace is a requisite for humble and persevering prayer.
It proceeds largely from the "spiritual intelligence" *(est spiritualiter mentalis)*. Such contemplation is the expression of a
real intimacy and familiarity, one that helps us grow rapidly
in the knowledge and love of God. The second and third
aspects Guiges calls the "spiritual material" of this prayer,
and the manner of its exercise: intellectual and affirmative
contemplation, or affective and negative contemplation. According to the first mode, given the necessary conditions of
purity of heart, continual desire and filial love *(pietas)*, the
soul is lifted up to the heights of mystical union, so that
it catches every now and then a glimpse of that ineffable
light which is God himself. Here Guigues stresses the importance of those short prayers, "ejaculations," which spring
from our hearts unbidden.[74] The other mode leaves on one
side reflection or intellectual investigation; it consists entirely
in the affection of filial love *(pia affectione)* and that devoted-
ness which goes straight to God. This method, too, has three
degrees or attachments *(adhaesiones)*. The first is the loving
attachment to the Lord in his sacred humanity, given to us
in our daily contemplation of the mysteries of his life and
death; so that we pass over from his humanity to his divinity,
and thus "in a manner take hold of our God by devoutly
clasping his feet," which is the attachment of discretion. By

73. Cf. infra, chap. 7, note 72, p. 132.
74. Cf. infra, chap. 6, note 71, p. 131.

24

long and arduous exercise in these two attachments, the soul at length finds itself lifted straight to God in the attachment of "union of desire," without the mediation of either imagination or intellect. Both these modes of contemplation are equally ways to the heights of mystical union. He concludes this first treatise thus:

> My belief is that when the good Lord gives you both kinds of contemplating, you will exercise yourself oftener and more preferably in the anagogical way, which neither sees nor understands but keeps its eyes closed and its face veiled before the face of the Lord. It sees, with certain efforts and reachings out *(intensionibus et extensionibus)* of its humble desires, the presence of the Creator: and it strives with an increasing confidence in him to embrace him by clinging, as it were, to his feet. You prefer this to the other kind, which cannot see what it sees.[75]

Good Carthusian that he is, he cannot hide his preference for the affective-negative way: but not to the detriment of the affirmative, the graced spiritual intelligence. As the *Cloud* author will say himself:

> If you think that this way of working is not according to your bodily or spiritual disposition, you can leave it and take another safely and without reproach, as long as it is with good spiritual counsel. (chap. 74)

The second treatise deals with progressive consolations or supernatural favours leading the soul to the heights of contemplation. If our author had read it, its influence nowhere appears in *The Cloud*. The same can be said of the third, in which Guigues treats both of the two lives and the stages

---

75. Grausem, p. 276.

of the *lectio divina,* in neither of which is there any point of special comparison with the approach of *The Cloud.* They are at one in stressing the necessity, in normal circumstances, of a long apprenticeship in purification and meditation on the mysteries of Christ.[76] And Guigues finds himself under attack from carping critics, whom he flagellates much more sharply than does the author of *The Cloud.* Finally, it is worth noticing that of the four extant MSS (Grausem knew only three), the provenance of the MS Charleville 56 is the Charterhouse of Mont-Dieu, the recipient of the famous "Golden Letter" of William of St. Thierry, whilst the provenance of the fourth (MS Stonyhurst LXVIII) is the Charterhouse of Ruremonde; and one of the remaining two is from the Abbey of St. Victor.

GRACE AND THE VIRTUES IN THE CLOUD

It has been the tendency of editorial commentary on *The Cloud* to begin with the apologies of the author close to the end of the treatise:

> And now whoever cares to examine the works of Denis, he will find that his words corroborate all that I have said or am going to say, from the beginning of this treatise to the end. (chap. 70)

This statement is indeed a crucial one; but, at the same time, over-preoccupation with it, or with the works of the Pseudo-Denis, has not infrequently obscured the purpose, the context and the structure of the book. First of all, as the prologue to *Deonise hid Divinite* informs us, by "the works of Denis" the *Cloud* author is referring to his single paraphrase of the five short chapters of the *Mystical Theology,* four of which—

---

76. Ibid., p. 287.

apart from one or two insertions—are no more than a boringly
repetitious list of the various operations of the senses, attributes of intellect and affections of will that cannot be pred-
icated of God in himself. The author writes:

> The treatise that follows is the English translation
> of a book written by Saint Denis to Timothy, the
> title of which, in the Latin, is *Mistica Theologia*. It
> was mentioned in a previous book, called *The Cloud
> of Unknowing*, that what Denis writes will clearly
> confirm all that is written in that same book.[77]

Second, besides giving no indication here that he was acquainted with the rest of the Dionysian corpus, he shows
no awareness that Greek is the original language of the *Mystical
Theology*; even though, as our annotations to many of the chapters of *The Cloud* suggest, in some cases with a high degree
of probability, he was acquainted with the Latin text of the
other works of the Dionysian corpus. The *Mystical Theology*,
short as it is, presents a host of difficulties of interpretation
and obscurities of style: hence his constant recourse to "the
explanations of the Abbot of St. Victor." And it is highly
significant that, in what is probably his last and most mature
work, *Privy Counsel*, where he sets himself to elucidate the
several difficulties *The Cloud* has raised for his disciple, he
makes no mention either of Denis or of his works. The most
obvious reason is that the book is written, as the Prologue
insists, for those who aspire to the strictly contemplative life
in response to what they believe to be an authentic call. And
its author is convinced that the highest form of prayer proper
to this life is that revealed to Saint Denis the Areopagite
by Saint Paul himself. The fictional ascription that the early
sixth-century Eastern author of *Mystical Theology* arrogated
to himself was long-lasting; he purported to be the recipient

---

77. *Deonise hid Divinite* (H., p. 1).

of the mystery concerning the ascent of the human spirit to God revealed to Paul in ecstasy—the *excessus mentis*—and passed on by him to like-minded mature Christians.[78]

The modern editor of *The Cloud* will, on the one hand, be tempted "to get behind" the many medieval Latin commentators, and try to discover what the "original Denys" is saying. Equally, he or she will search for analogues among the later medieval "Dionysians," the vast majority of whom address themselves, like the *Cloud* author, to the *ex professo* contemplatives, whether monks or nuns, cenobites or solitaries. The dangers of the latter method are clearly signalled, for example, in the inordinate attention paid by Dr. Hodgson to the *De Adhaerendo Deo* ("On clinging to God"), long attributed to Saint Albert the Great, but now clearly demonstrated to be the work of John of Kastl, and which certainly postdates *The Cloud*.[79] Far more important is the spirituality expressed in the author's own work, the theological platform on which he is building, and the harmony he achieves between the two. It is here that *The Cloud's* strength and vigour lie, and indeed the clarity and brilliance of his exposition.

The *Cloud* author's span of life covers an extraordinarily turbulent period in England—social, economic, political, but not least intellectual. Though the fruits of the golden age of scholasticism were already withering on the tree, monastic theology and the theology of the schools were still flourishing side by side.[80] Our author not only shows himself a master in both, but makes it clear that knowledge for its own sake has no appeal for him. All that he knows or has acquired

---

78. As will be discussed at length in a subsequent volume, the *Cloud* author's "translation" is a conflation of the Latin translation of John Sarracenus, a twelfth-century Benedictine, the paraphrase of this translation by Thomas Gallus, and some glosses on Sarracenus that are still unidentified with any certainty. Cf. 2 Corinthians 5:13; Philippians 3:7–15; 1 Corinthians 2:13–16; 2 Corinthians 12:2–4. On the date and identity of the Pseudo-Denys, see the article "Denis L'Aréopagite (Pseudo)" in *DSp*. fasc. xviii, 245ff.

79. Cf. H., pp. lxiv–lxix; and Josef Sudbrach, "Jean de Kastl," in *DSp*, fasc. liv (1973), 592–94.

80. Cf. Pantin, op. cit., esp. pp. 105–84.

through his love of learning flows into the one simple channel—the desire for God, and the achievement of union with him insofar as is possible in this life. In fact, his learning has convinced him that this "perfection of man's soul," as he calls it in his *Letter of Private Direction*, "is nothing but the union made in perfect love between God and itself"; and that this is the wisdom of Christians, "in comparison with which all profound theological learning is plain foolishness."[81] Hence, it is a wisdom to which every Christian is called by virtue of his baptism, though for one reason or another, whether culpably or through ignorance, few achieve it, or are simply "not chosen" in this life, according to the mysterious designs of God. The author, then, is attempting to describe the "ecstasy of contemplation," or rather the way to it, for those who are chosen, and to refute both theoretical and practical errors about it. Saint Bernard had written that "there are two kinds of contemplative ecstasy, one in the intellect, the other in ardent love *(fervore)*; the one in comprehension *(agnitione)*, the other in devotion *(devotione)*."[82] It is the *Cloud* author's learning in monastic theology and of the scholastic theology taught by Aquinas, as well as his thorough acquaintance with current controversies, especially concerning grace and the virtues with their relationship to reason and will, that gives his book the anti-intellectual appearance on which so many have seized with eagerness, and applied to it Augustine's phrase *docta ignorantia*, "learned ignorance."

Anyone given a serious training in monastic theology in fourteenth-century Europe would have had impressed on him the crucial importance of Augustine's treatise on grace and free will—*De Gratia et libero arbitrio*. But he would be equally exposed to the teaching of Saint Thomas Aquinas, who was canonized in 1323, just less than fifty years after his death. *The Cloud* illustrates, from the proemium to the final blessing, the development of Augustine's theology through the thought

---

81. Again the allusion to Saint Paul in 1 Corinthians (1:25) is unmistakable.
82. *Sermo in Cantica*, XLIX, 4.

of Aquinas; and this may well be the substance of its genius. Again we must remind ourselves that the author has no cause to concern himself, as does his contemporary, the author of *Piers Plowman*, with the salvation, "the crown of life," of the heathen,[83] since he is writing for *ex professo* contemplatives. In the proemium itself, the reader is asked to turn his attention to the first grace of vocation and its circumstances, the grace of perseverance, which calls for his cooperation and the grace of final charity. The *Cloud* author, then, is already speaking of the operation and cooperation in the realm of grace, which changes the individual; and, as Bernard Lonergan in his study of the theology of grace in Saint Thomas asserts:

> ... produces in us a number of effects which follow one upon the other. First it gives a participation of divine reality; second, it causes the meritoriousness of our acts; third, there is the reward of merit, eternal life, which is the final effect of grace.[84]

Lonergan goes on to quote Augustine in the same context on prevenient and subsequent grace: "Grace goes before us *(praevenit)* that we might live a holy life, and it follows us *(subsequitur)* that we might live with him for ever; now it goes before us to call us, then it follows us to glorify us."[85] In his description of the stages of the Christian life in chapter 1, the *Cloud* author speaks of the grace that justifies the impious—"when you were lost in Adam"—and of that which "kindled your desire" and "fastened to it a leash of longing"; and finally "called you" with love and grace "to the third manner of life." Here we have the refinements of Aquinas

---

83. Cf. "Piers Plowman," in *Pre-Reformation English Spirituality*, ed. James Walsh (London and New York, 1964), pp. 128–31.

84. Cf. B. Lonergan, *Grace and Freedom: Operative Grace in the Thought of St. Thomas Aquinas* (London and New York, 1971), p. 30.

85. Ibid.

on the previous doctrine of grace stemming from Augustine—operative and cooperative grace:

> Operative and cooperative grace can be distinguished from the point of view of the gratuitous will of God himself and of the gift given to us. Grace is called operative in regard of the effects it alone achieves: cooperative with regard to the effect it achieves only when the free will cooperates. So from the point of view of God's gratuitous will, the justification of the wicked may be called operative grace, for it is achieved by the infusion of this free gift itself; this gift is achieved in us only by God's gratuitous will. With regard to the grace itself, it may be called co-operative grace because it works in the free will by causing it to spring into action, by expediting the carrying out of the external act, and by achieving perseverance; and in all these, the free will has some part to play. Hence the difference between operative and cooperative grace.[86]

We must also note the extraordinary "spiritual unction" that the *Cloud* author gives to Thomas's dry and abstract analysis. The same is to be said of the language of chapter 2, which is based on the Thomistic distinction between the two effects—operative and cooperative—of habitual grace, as curing or justifying the soul (operative) and as the principle of meritorious acts (cooperative). "Interiorly, God is the One who moves us, especially when the will begins to wish for the good, when before it willed what was evil. Then with regard to the external action ... God helps us by interiorly strengthening our will so that it springs into action."[87] The

---

86. From the De Veritate, q. 27, a. 5, 1, ad lum. The Latin is given in Lonergan, op. cit., p. 36.

87. Cf. *Summa Theologiae* 1–2ae, q. 111, a. 2.

Cloud author embellishes the doctrine when he adds: "He [God] asks no help but only you yourself. His will is that you should simply gaze at him and leave him to act alone. Your part is to keep the windows and doors against the inroads of flies and enemies." So he is ready to say that the contemplative exercise "is the easiest exercise of all and most readily accomplished, when a soul is helped by grace in this felt desire" (chap. 3). Thus with Aquinas he interprets the words of Augustine in terms of operative and cooperative actual grace; "God works, that we might desire: and when we desire, he cooperates with us that we might bring the desire to perfection."[88]

In chapter 4, the author strives to take this human impulse out of the context of time altogether. But he must insist with Saint Thomas that man is essentially a creature of time; and thus at birth his higher powers are indeterminate in their potentiality. They point at once in all directions. But Aquinas, like Augustine, is a wholehearted pessimist when it comes to human nature; so that, since God—the unique good—is alone outside time, and evil is essentially timebound and manifold, man is inevitably weighted towards evil.[89] It is only in the beatific vision, when God alone is the source and principle of his entire activity, that man becomes impeccable.[90] So our author points out that

> if you were reformed by grace according to the primal state of man's soul as it was before sin, you would always, by the help of that grace, be in control of that impulse or those impulses. None of them would go unheeded, but all would reach out to the preeminent and supreme object of your will and desire, which is God himself.

---

88. Ibid. Latin in Lonergan, op. cit., pp. 128–29.
89. Cf. Lonergan, op. cit., pp. 41–42.
90. Cf. *De Veritate*, q. 24, a. 7.

INTRODUCTION

Aquinas does argue that "to love God above all things is natural to man," and that the gifts of the Holy Spirit do "bring us into the region of pure supernaturality."[91] Furthermore, "he fits himself exactly to our souls by adapting his Godhead to them," and "our souls are fitted exactly to him by the worthiness of our creation," says our author in chapter 4, setting alight the dry wood of the language of Thomas:

> God changes the will in two ways: one, by a simple movement; second, by impressing a form on the will itself. For just as of its own nature, given it by God, the will is moved to desire something; so by the addition of something else, like a grace or a virtue, it now tends to desire something else, which it was not predisposed to do naturally.[92]

Hence the *Cloud* author confidently asserts that the exercise of contemplative love restores him, reforms him in grace; and by perseverance in this restoration, he rises ever nearer to God and further from sin. As Aquinas says, "when a person ... does not fulfil the law voluntarily, sin rules in him, so that his will is inclined to desire what is contrary to the law ... but grace makes men fulfil the law freely"[93]—charity, the law of the love of God. For this reason, then, it is logical that "if any thought should rise and continue to press (chap. 7) ... and say 'What do you seek and what would have have?' ... you must answer that it is the God who made you and ransomed you and with his grace has called you to his love." For the only permanent liberation from self-love, says Thomas, is the infusion of divine charity.[94]

At first sight, the distinction made in chapter 10,

91. Cf. Lonergan, op. cit., pp. 43–44.
92. *De Veritate*, q. 22, a. 8. Latin in Lonergan, pp. 54–55.
93. From Thomas's *Commentary on Romans*. Latin in Lonergan, p. 57.
94. *De Veritate*, q. 24, a. 12. Cf. Lonergan, p. 52.

... a sinful affection can be grave in worldly men
and women who have been living in serious sin. But
the same affection, which causes pleasure or resentment in the fleshly heart, is no more than venial
sin in you and in all others who have, with a sincere
will, forsaken the world ...

appears oddly conceived. It is again, however, a Thomistic
refinement on a passage from Augustine's *De Gratia et libero
arbitrio*, refuting the Pelagian error that, while grace is necessary for the forgiveness of past sins, it is not so for the
avoidance of future sins. Our author's distinction is based
on Thomas's assertion that, as opposed to the irrevocable obstinacy of diabolical evil, there is a relative obstinacy in this
mortal life which is acquired by sinful habits. Explicit deliberation is not necessary for an act to be free, or for the
sinner to avoid further sins. Equally, it is not possible for
man to deliberate explicitly before every act. Hence, anyone
with a vicious habit will freely and almost automatically sin
when the appropriate occasion arises. And if it be objected
that mortal sin requires full advertence and consent, Thomas
answers that the sinner can have these, and yet lack the measure of deliberation required to break down his spontaneous
orientation to execute the sinful habit. On the other hand,
the man without such a habit and, indeed, with a special
determination to avoid sinning, will succeed for a time in
avoiding sin;[95] precisely the doctrine of our author here:

Carelessness in venial sin should always be avoided
by all true disciples of perfection. Otherwise I would
not be surprised if they soon commit grievous sin.
(chap. 11)

"He who is drawn to the divine receives by divine communication a right judgment about divine things." So writes

---

95. Cf. Lonergan, op. cit., on *De Veritate*, q. 24, a. 11, pp. 48–51.

INTRODUCTION

Thomas in his Commentary on *The Divine Names* of the Pseu-do-Denis.[96] By the gifts of the Holy Spirit, understanding and wisdom, the Spirit himself effects a purification of the human spirit. It is an impregnation of love. This wisdom then belongs to the infused virtue of charity, and is thus incompatible with serious sin. Thomas makes the further point that "some receive a higher degree of this gift of wisdom ... which is not common to all who have sanctifying grace, but belongs rather to the gratuitous graces, which the Holy Spirit imparts to us when he wishes."[97] Furthermore, and this is the point made by our author in chapter 12, Aquinas states that the gift of wisdom corresponds to charity, "effecting that union with God towards which all things pertaining to the life of the spirit are ordained as to their last end.... For all the virtues about whose acts the precepts [the first of which is charity] are given are directed to freeing the heart from the onslaught of the passions."[98] Our author, however, shows his independence from the Thomistic Aristotelian categorization of the virtues in his treatment of the virtue of humility, as well as in his elaboration of the "two lives" (chaps. 13–23). Here, as with his treatment of charity, he firmly departs from Aquinas, who argues for a clear distinction between love of God and love of the neighbour, "because of those who are less intelligent and do not clearly understand that one of these precepts is included in the other."[99] Rather, says our author,

> In this exercise, God is perfectly loved for himself
> ... the perfect worker will not permit the awareness
> of the holiest creature God ever made to have any
> share ... in this exercise, the second, the lower branch
> of charity, that for your fellow Christian, is truly

---

96. *Qui afficitur ad divina accipit divinitus rectum iudicium de rebus divinis. In div. nom.*, 2, lect. 4.

97. *Summa Theologiae* 2–2ae, q. 45, a. 4 and 5.

98. Ibid., q. 44, a. 1.

99. Ibid., q. 44, a. 2.

and perfectly fulfilled. . . . For he considers all men his friends and none his foes. (chap. 24)

As far as the *Summa* is concerned, Aquinas treats of Christ's passion, and of his being the head of the Church, separately. He insists, however, that the preeminence of grace which Christ received in his human nature is bestowed on others—the same grace whereby he is justified, and also head of the Church. One would not wish to conjecture that such common doctrine affected the *Cloud* author (chap. 25) through Aquinas, especially as Thomas begins by citing the appropriate Johannine (1:16) and Pauline texts (Colossians 2:9).[100]

It is, however, likely that when the author resumes his consideration of the contemplative exercise in chapter 26, and speaks of habitual cooperation with ordinary graces, he relies on the Thomistic development of habitual operative and co-operative grace. "The work consists in treading down the awareness of all the creatures God ever made. . . . Here is all the labour; for this, *with the help of grace,* is man's work. And the other, beyond this, the impulse of love, *this is the work of God alone.*"[101] Lonergan, summarizing the development of Aquinas's thought from the *Commentary on the Sentences* through the *De Veritate* and the *Contra Gentiles* to the *Summa,* makes the point that man endowed with the virtues becomes an *agens perfectum* (a perfect operator), for the most part doing what is right. He adds:

> However, there does remain the objection from experience that the infused virtues [in our case, humility and the fortitude and patience of self-renunciation] do not appear always to make right action prompt, easy and agreeable. . . . the pleasure proper to virtuous action may be at times no more than the absence of the virtues . . . readiness, ease and pleasure [in our

---

100. Ibid., 3, q. 8, a. 5 and 6.
101. Italics mine.

INTRODUCTION

case, devotion] are the signs, the external consequences of the virtues; such secondary effects may
be covered over by other factors.[102]

And Aquinas agrees here with a gloss on Augustine's "Grace
and free will" that God operates in the hearts of men, inclining
their wills as he pleases.[103] It is worth noting that our author
also ends chapter 26 on a firm Thomistic note: "Some receive
a higher degree of the gift of wisdom in the contemplation
of Divine things by knowing more exalted mysteries, and
being able to pass on this knowledge to others."[104]

When the *Cloud* author begins to consider who are called
to this exercise, and when and how they should begin (chaps.
28–31), he has in mind particularly those who may tend to
think that they are barred from undertaking it because they
have in the past led sinful lives. And he is particularly insistent,
as he is also in his little treatise *Discernment of Spirits*, on
the need and power of the sacrament of penance. In fact,
it would seem from his language, here as well as elsewhere,
that those who practise this exercise regularly will feel the
need of frequent confession:

> Whoever, then, wishes to undertake this exercise let
> him first purify his conscience; and then when he
> has done all that he can in fulfilment of the Church's
> law, let him dispose himself boldly for this exercise.
> (chap. 28)

Aquinas insists that through the sacrament the penitent recovers his primary dignity as a child of God; and, quoting
a homily of Gregory, that sometimes he recovers something

---

102. Lonergan, op. cit., p. 46. See the whole chapter, "Habitual grace as *operans* and *co-operans*," pp. 41–61.
103. Cf. *De Veritate*, q. 22, a. 8; and *Summa Theologiae*, 1–2ae, q. 79, a. 1 ad lum.
104. *Summa Theologiae*, 2–2ae, q. 45, a. 5. (Cf. the final paragraph of chap. 26, infra, pp. 174–75.)

greater, making up for past losses.[105] But Saint Thomas insists on the distinction, as does our author, between the strictly sacramental grace, which causes the removal of sin, and that of the liberating effect of habitual healing grace *(gratia sanans)*: a point the *Cloud* author stresses in writing of the penitent Magdalen in chapter 22. When answering the objection that, through the sacrament, the penitent recovers all the virtue he had lost, Aquinas goes on to add:

> Grace is more abundant by its very nature, because to those who sin more, a more *gratuitous* favour is granted by the pardon ... so that they receive a more abundant habit of grace and virtue, as was the case with Magdalen.[106]

It is thus the quality of the contrition—"the heart's affection," as Thomas calls it, that affects "the whole root and ground of sin." Further, the act of love of God for his own sake, which is the object of the exercise of *The Cloud*, is not only feasible finally, formally and efficiently,[107] "but also preeminently or by unknowing, as Dionysius states (*Div. Nom* I)." And, therefore,

> aversion from God, which is brought about by sin, is removed by charity, not by knowledge alone. For charity, insofar as it is the act of loving God, unites the soul immediately to him in the bond of spiritual union.[108]

---

105. Ibid., 3 a, q. 89. a. 3.
106. Ibid., a. 2, *ad* 3.
107. Ibid. 2–2ae, q. 27, a. 3.
108. Ibid. q. 27, a. 4. The citation is the answer to the third objection. It is possible that the reference to the *Commentary on the Divine Names* is the immediate source of the quotation in chap. 70 (cf. infra p. 258), since, as we have seen, the reference to "the works of Denis" is not to the whole corpus, but simply to his *Mystical Theology*.

INTRODUCTION

It follows then, that since charity is the most excellent of
all the virtues, it is the most gratuitous; so that, as our author
says, though habitual past sinners find the exercise more laborious than most,

> yet it often happens that some who have been wicked
> and habitual sinners come more quickly to the per-
> fection of this exercise than those who have not. This
> is a miracle of mercy from our Lord, who gives his
> grace in this special way, to the wonder of all the
> world. (chap. 29)

The subsequent discussion on judging others (chaps. 30–
31), which *prima facie* appears to be a digression on the part
of our author, follows on the relation of charity with the
infused gift of wisdom, which corresponds, says Thomas, to
charity. There are those who receive a higher measure of
the gift of wisdom, which pertains to the active as well as
to the contemplative realm, and enables them to direct themselves, as well as others, according to the divine ordinances.[109]
But, as our author says (chap. 30), we need to exercise great
care here. For the rest, the judges of the deeds of others
are those who have the "power of the Keys."[110]

"The spiritual devices" that our author recommends to
beginners (chaps. 31–32), with their judicious mixture of hu-
mour and sobriety, are hardly likely to find any analogue
in a Thomistic treatise. But Thomas comments at length on
Augustine's gloss on the famous Pauline phrase *non volentis
neque currentis sed miserentis est Dei,*[111] which is the substance
of chapter 34 of *The Cloud.* Actual grace that is cooperative
means that the "gratuitous will of God works in the free

---

109. Ibid., 2–2ae, q. 45, a. 5.
110. Ibid., 3, qq. 19–20.
111. "It is not of him that willeth, nor of him that runneth, but of God
that sheweth mercy," (Romans 9:16 [Douai]).

will by causing its movement, expediting the execution of the exterior act and providing perseverance. In some way, the free will is at work in all this."[112] But habitual grace is both prevenient and subsequent. God goes ahead of man by aiding his good will, and follows up its action so that it might achieve its purpose. Thus the principal agent is always God, and the free will is secondary. Just as man is moved by God to the good (Rom. 8:14), so man's interior operation is to be attributed principally to God (Phil. 2:13).[113] As our author says:

> This is the work of God alone, brought about in a special way in whatever soul that pleases him, without any merit on its part. For without this divine work, neither saint nor angel can ever hope to desire it. . . . The grace is not given because of innocence, nor withheld because of sin. . . . Let it be the one that works; you must simply consent to it . . . it is God alone who moves your will and desire: he alone, entirely of himself, without any intermediary. (chap. 34)

It is hardly likely that the *Cloud* author would turn to Saint Thomas for information on the *lectio divina* (chaps. 35–40). Since he is writing for contemplatives merely, he would appear to take *The Ladder of Monks,* and perhaps the "Abbot of St. Victor," Thomas Gallus, as his masters here. And when Aquinas deals with the "two lives," he constantly cites the Victorines, Hugh and Richard; whilst Augustine and Gregory are his standard sources when he treats of the contemplative life.[114] And though he accepts that the contemplative life is superior to the active life *simpliciter,* he is more interested, as a mendicant friar, in maintaining that in certain cases one

112. The Latin is in Lonergan, op. cit., p. 118.
113. Cf. Lonergan, pp. 118–20.
114. Cf. 2–2ae, q. 180.

should prefer the active or the "mixed" life.[115] This is hardly to our author's purpose in chapters 35–40. Nor has Aquinas, in all probability, anything to teach him about discretion as applied to the contemplative exercise, or his attempts to describe it (chaps. 41–44). For Saint Thomas, inspired by Aristotle, discretion is no more than the application of the cardinal virtue of prudence, permeated by the infusion of the Holy Spirit, who breathes where he will.

Here also we begin to enter the precise area of the non-intellectual aspect of preparation for the "work of this book" according to the principles of the medieval Dionysians: chapters followed by a lengthy excursus (chaps. 45–61) on the illusions normally to be encountered by the beginner in the contemplative exercise proper. At the same time, as indicated in the notes, we may find many analogues with Saint Thomas's teaching in these chapters also.

Chapters 62–67 are so different in tone and temper from the *Cloud* author's normal style and approach that they have been transcribed separately in the important Cambridge University Library's MS Kk. vi. 26, which contains all the works attributed to him.[116] However, there is nothing here to interest him in Aquinas's manifestly Aristotelian approach: the equiparation of intellect with "mind"; the relegation of *memoria* to the "recall of past events"; and especially the apparent lack of interest in the faculty of imagination, and the preoccupation with the way in which the separated soul deals with its past dependence on the body.[117] Further, when Thomas comes to discuss the powers of the soul in Adam innocent, he is not inclined to decide whether they act under grace; so that if grace were removed, the flesh would no longer be subject to reason.[118] This is not a dilemma for the *Cloud*

115. Ibid., q. 182, a. 1.
116. Cf. H., *Cloud*, p. xiv.
117. Saint Thomas treats these matters, with immense insistence on the role of the Aristotelian *intellectus agens*, in his *Summa Theologiae* 1, qq. 77–89.
118. Ibid., q. 95, a. 1.

author. He is content to rest with the assurance that man's image and likeness to God comes to him through grace, a doctrine central to the teaching of monastic theology in its golden age:

> It is only by his mercy, and without any merit of yours, that you are made a God in grace, united with him in spirit without any division between you, both here and in the happiness of heaven without end. (chap. 69)

"Deification" is not a word that is a constant in scholastic language, even before Thomas's death in 1274, and much less afterwards. The irruption of the Dionysian school into a theological world of transition from monasteries to "universities" appears to be one of those unaccountable accidents of history. It would seem to have first raised its head in opposition to the excessive rationalism of Abelard, and was assured of a reverential hearing, especially in Paris with its devotion to the Areopagite, "Saint Denis of France." But it virtually disappeared with the dissolution of the monasteries. It is true enough that it played a considerable part in the origins of the *Devotio Moderna*; but it failed to withstand, through its later excessive anti-intellectualism and its relationship with Quietism, the attacks of scholastic theology. The result was that, once the Counter-Reformation was launched, with its emphasis on devotion to and imitation of Christ in his sacred humanity, it lay dormant until modern times.[119]

---

119. Cf. Pierre Debongnie, "Dévotion moderne," in *DSp*. fasc. xx, 727–47.

INTRODUCTION

THE ABBOT OF ST. VICTOR

We have already noticed that, towards the end of his book, the author quotes a sentence of "Saint Denis" from the *Divine Names,* and adds:

> Now whoever cares to examine the works of Denis, he will find that his words clearly corroborate all that I have said or am going to say, from the beginning of this treatise to the end. (chap. 70)

Furthermore, we have remarked that this statement itself presents its difficulties, in that the *Cloud* author's prologue to his "translation" of Denis's *Mystical Theology* equiparates these "works of Denis" to this single short treatise.[120] Though our notes to many of its chapters indicate that analogues abound between the teaching of *The Cloud* and the voluminous commentaries of the Abbot of St. Victor on the whole corpus of the extant Pseudo-Dionysian writings, it does not seem possible to say for certain precisely what the *Cloud* author had read of these commentaries. We know, of course, that he presumed the *Mystical Theology* to have been written by Denis the Areopagite, Saint Paul's Athenian convert mentioned by Luke in Acts (17:34), for the legend was never seriously questioned until Renaissance times.[121] Our author, then, takes it for granted that Denis's "Hid Divinity" was substantially the teaching divinely given to Paul, revealed by Christ to the Apostles when they had reached the maturity that was the gift of the Holy Spirit, and through them handed on to those whose "faculties were sufficiently developed" to take "the strong meat of the perfect."[122] With the "Mystical

---

120. Cf. supra, p. 27, and note 77. The "paraphrase" will be subjected to a detailed analysis in a subsequent volume.

121. Cf. Réne Roques, "Denys L'Aréopagite (Le Pseudo-)," in *DSp.* fasc. xviii, 245–46.

122. Cf. e.g., 1 Corinthians 2:10–16; Ephesians 3:9ff; Hebrews 5:11–14.

Theology" he is thus on the surest possible ground: "Saint Denis" is passing on to Timothy the apostolic teaching intended only for the spiritually mature. Such interior development is ordinarily acquired by the purity of heart that is the aim of the long contemplative apprenticeship—the reading, reflecting and praying described in chapters 35–39; and the immediate source of this doctrine, again as our notes indicate, is, in all probability, the *Scala Claustralium* [The ladder of monks]: the letter on the contemplative life by the Carthusian Guigo the Angelic, attributed in the *Cloud* author's time to Saint Bernard himself.[123] Yet he prefaces these chapters by pointing out that as one draws near to the "perfection of this exercise,"

> ... trust steadfastly that it is God alone who moves your will and desire ... [so that] in this exercise men must use no intermediaries, nor can they come to it through intermediaries. *All good intermediaries depend on it, but it depends on none of them.* (chap. 34; italics mine)

This, as we have seen above, [124] is the Thomistic development of Augustine's teaching on grace. And it is thus that the *Cloud* author inserts the words "by the impulse of grace" into his rendering of the first statement in the *Mystical Theology.*[125] The phrase occurs neither in the Latin version he uses, nor in the "explanations" of the "Abbot of St. Victor," whose life, times, antecedents and works we must now briefly examine.

Again, we are dealing with one of those thirteenth-century spiritual authors, the biographical details of whose life have been diligently pieced together from a mass of often con-

---

123. Cf. note 18, supra, p. 6.
124. P. 40. and note 113.
125. "My friend Timothy, whenever you apply yourself, by the impulse (ME 'steryng') of grace ..." Cf. H., *Deonise Hid Divinite*, p. 2.

tradictory assertions, and who, like the *Cloud* author, tells us next to nothing about himself. The Benedictine Bernardus Pez, one of the great librarians of the eighteenth century, says of him:

> There is scarcely another author in the whole of our collection the details of whose life are so perplexing and so obscure as Thomas, Abbot of Vercelli.[126]

However, due to the laborious researches of many scholars, principally G. Théry O.P., between the two world wars, we know now that he was a member of the canons regular of the Abbey of St. Victor in Paris,[127] that he studied at the feet of Richard of St. Victor in the same abbey, and was a mature theologian who concentrated the whole of his theological learning and erudition on the Dionysian corpus in the translation of John Sarracenus. His first extant work, a Dionysian commentary on the first four verses of chapter 6 of Isaiah, was written before he left Paris in A.D. 1219, as was his complete set of Concordances between the books of the Bible and the works of the Pseudo-Denis; and that the writings of one of his earlier venerable brethren, Hugh of St. Victor (d. 1141), were his constant inspiration.[128]

However, in 1219, his life took a completely different turn. He was taken to Vercelli in Northern Italy, to found

---

126. In *Thesaurus Anecdotorum Novissimus* (Augustae Vindelicorum, 1721), tom. II, p. xxii. Bernardus Pez was librarian at the Benedictine Abbey of Melk, in Lower Austria.

127. The Abbey of St. Victor was founded by William of Champeaux in 1113 (the most famous scholar of his day and teacher of Abelard). The Victorines were Canons Regular—followers of the "mixed life." Their rule *(Consuetudines)*, based on that of Saint Augustine, was allegedly drawn up under the influence of Saint Bernard. The abbey and its several dependencies were suppressed during the French Revolution, never to be restored. Cf. H. C. Van Elswijk, "Victorine Spirituality," in NCE, vol. 14.

128. It is from Hugh's *Homily on Ecclesiastes* that the "Abbot of St. Victor" begins to elaborate his "degrees of contemplation." In the book of Ecclesiastes, the disciple ascends to the first grade of contemplation. In the Canticle of Canticles, he is lifted up to the highest grade.

a Victorine Abbey there. As a result, he is generally known as *Vercellensis*. He later became embroiled in the Guelf-Gibelline disputes, was excommunicated, exiled to the neighbouring Ivrea, and appears to have died there in 1246.[129] Pertinent to our own enquiries is the fact that his patron was the Vercellensian Guala Bicchieri, cardinal and papal legate in England when Henry III was crowned king. The result was that the Church of Chesterton near Cambridge, in the Diocese of Ely, became a benefice of the Abbey of St. Andrew, Vercelli, of which *Vercellensis* (or Thomas Gallus, to give him his proper name) had become abbot. We also know that he wrote (or completed) his second commentary on the Canticle of Canticles in England, in 1238.[130] The extraordinary thing is that the *Cloud* author apparently knew nothing of all this; or if he did, he makes no mention of it. All that can be said for certain is that he knew the *Mystical Theology* in translation of Sarracenus, of which Thomas Gallus wrote a paraphrase, used by our author. What he knew or borrowed from the last work of Gallus, the "Explanation on the *Mystical Theology*," has yet to be discussed, in the forthcoming introduction to his other treatises.

What remains true is that, by the time *The Cloud* came to be written, the doctrine of the Pseudo-Dionysius, as we possess it in the Greek MSS still extant—and this is especially true of both *Divine Names* and *Mystical Theology*—was so diluted and reinterpreted over and again as to be scarcely recognizable. To take one example of moment: *The Cloud's* long disquisition on imperfect and perfect humility. In chapter 7 on humility in the Rule of St. Benedict, written, it would appear, at Monte Cassino during the last years of his life (d. c.477), we are

---

129. Cf. G. Théry, O.P., "Thomas Gallus, Aperçu Biographique," in *Archives d'Histoire doctrinale et littéraire du moyen âge* (AHDLMA) XII (1939): 141–208.

130. A certain amount of this information can be found in J. Walsh, S. J., "The Expositions of Thomas Gallus on the Pseudo-Dionysian Letters," in AHDLMA 38 (1964): 199ff. The relevant points will be discussed in detail in a subsequent volume in this series.

offered twelve degrees of humility. The twelfth step is quite clearly *The Cloud*'s imperfect humility:

> He [the monk] should constantly be repeating in his heart what the Publican said in the Gospel: "Lord, I am a sinner, I am not worthy to raise my eyes to heaven."

And then Benedict adds—in perfect humility—

> And when he has climbed up all these steps of humility, the monk will presently arrive at that perfect love of God which drives away all fear ... The Lord, working through his Spirit, will show this in his labourer, thus purified from vice and sin.[131]

Though the *Cloud* author has nothing to say of Benedict's degrees, clearly the distinction is a Western monastic commonplace: "It is impossible" he says, "for a sinner to obtain the perfect virtue of humility ... without imperfect humility" (chap. 14).

WESTERN SPIRITUALITY AND THE PSEUDO-DENYS

It is only after the arrival of the Irishman John Scotus Erigena at the court of Charles the Bald about 850 that the name and influence of Denis the Areopagite enter the Western World.[132] Though Erigena's immediate prominence there was due to the position he adopted in the theological controversy on the subject of predestination, his success in the West was not as an original thinker, but as the translator of the Di-

---

131. A handy and recent translation, with helpful notes "for monks and lay-people today," is Dom David Parry's *Households of God* (London, 1980).

132. Cf. Jean-Marie Déchanet, O.S.B., "John Scotus Erigena," in *Spirituality through the Centuries*, ed. J. Walsh, S.J. (London and New York, 1964), pp. 83ff.

INTRODUCTION

onysian corpus. We know now that his most important works are the *De Divisione Naturae,* and what remains to us of his commentary on Saint John's Gospel.[133] However, as far as *The Cloud* is concerned, we may well ask whether anything written in the reasonably literal Latin translation of Denis's *Mystical Theology* catches the mood of our author as do these words from Erigena's *De Predestinatione Liber,* condemned almost as soon as it saw the light at the instance of practically all contemporary theologians; whilst Hincmar, Archbishop of Rheims, who had commissioned it, kept a discreet silence:

> Nothing can be said worthily about God. Hardly a single noun, verb or any other part of speech can be used appropriately of God, in the strict sense. How indeed could visible signs, intimately dependent as they are on the material, manage to express exactly the Invisible Nature which has nothing to do with any bodily sense? Indeed, it so far surpasses all understanding that the purest spirit can scarcely attain to it. And yet, ever since the Fall, poverty-stricken human reason has been labouring with these words, these visible signs, to suggest and give some sort of hint of the sublime richness of the Creator.[134]

As is amply indicated in *Julian of Norwich: Showings,*[135] one of the paramount influences on the spiritual teaching of this Englishwoman contemporary of *The Cloud* is William of St. Thierry, companion of Saint Bernard. As J. M. Déchanet and several scholars after him have shown, William's teacher was Erigena, who in turn was inspired by Origen and Saint Gregory of Nyssa; and the Irishman's *chef-d'oeuvre* in all this was his spiritual anthropology, the *De Divisione Naturae.* Yet

---

133. Ibid., p. 84. And see R. Roques, "Jean Scot (Érigène)," in *DSp.* fasc. liv., 735ff.

134. P.L. 122, 390.

135. Eds. E. Colledge, O.S.A., and J. Walsh, S.J. (New York, 1978; the first volume in the Paulist Press series Classics of Western Spirituality).

this was the work that was condemned in 1225 by Honorius II. All extant copies had to be sent to Rome to be solemnly burned.[136] One can only surmise what would have happened to his version of the works of the Pseudo-Denis during the same years of controversy were it not for the impeccable name—Saint Denis of France, "the Areopagite," the disciple of Saint Paul.

The years immediately following the condemnation of Erigena's work saw the emergence of the great scholastics Saint Albert the Great and his disciple, Aquinas. Before 1250, Albert was devoting a considerable number of his university lectures in Paris to the exposition of the Dionysian corpus;[137] and a decade later, Aquinas was lecturing on *The Divine Names*.[138]

During this century, in particular, there flourished what has come to be called the Dionysian school of spiritual writers, which found its roots in the Victorines—first, and indirectly, in Hugh of St. Victor—and flourished more explicitly with Richard of St. Victor, and most of all with Thomas Gallus. Others followed them; but they have tended to be dismissed by modern scholars, as is Gallus himself, because of semi-agnosticism or because of belonging to that rather narrow-minded Victorine section represented by Walter of St. Victor (d. c.1200), a violent opponent of Abelard and the early school-men. These were the critics of the growing influence of Aristotle in the theology of the schools, summed up in the epigram "the spirit of Christ withers where the spirit of Aristotle flourishes."[139] But in fact, such opinions do scant justice to fourteenth-century English spirituality, which accepts the

---

136. Cf. J. Déchanet, *Guillaume de Saint-Thierry* (Paris, 1978), pp. 24–27.

137. Cf. P. Glorieux, *Répertoire des Maîtres en théologie de Paris au XIIIe siècle* (Paris, 1933) tom. 1, pp. 66 and 90.

138. Cf. P. G. Meerseman, *Introductio in opera omnia B. Alberti Magni* (Bruges, 1931), p. 104.

139. Cf. Daniel Callus, O.P., "The date of Grosseteste's translations and commentaries on the Pseudo-Dionysius," in *Recherches de Théologie Ancienne et Médiévale* XIV (1947): 100.

doctrine of "the Areopagite" at its face value. The "Dionysian world" or his "Cosmic Theology" is one that the *Cloud* author takes for granted.[140] In fact, it is his own milieu. It makes little difference whether he inherits it from the "two cities" of Augustine, or the harmony between the heavenly and ecclesiastical hierarchies of the Pseudo-Denis. He is writing in *The Cloud*, as is Thomas Gallus in his commentaries on Denis, or on the Canticle of Canticles, *more Dionysiaca* (in the style of Denys), for *ex professo* contemplatives. As we have noticed, the *Cloud* author shows no concern for the world around him, except for the theologians who tend to rely on their own speculative and rational abilities, rather than on that "impulse of grace" which manifests the active presence of the Holy Spirit. In fact, his starting point is a fourteenth-century equivalent of the "Dionysian universe." His ambience is that of the contemplative Richard of St. Victor as he inveighs against the theological climate of the schools. It is this that disturbs the other-worldly atmosphere, for which the Parisian Abbey of St. Victor was founded:[141]

> The problem of our times is the loud-mouthed, so-called philosophers who are trying to make a name for themselves by thinking up fictional speculations and searching for novelties.[142]

It may indeed turn out to be important to examine the immediate impact of the *Mystical Theology* of Denis on *The Cloud of Unknowing,* and of the Dionysian *Divine Names* on the development of thought in the *Letter on Private Direction.* But as we come to examine the structure of *The Cloud* itself, we shall find ourselves hard put to it to indicate any *direct* in-

---

140. Cf. R. Roques, *L'Univers Dionysien* (Paris, 1954); and Dom Denys Rutledge, *Cosmic Theology: The Ecclesiastical Hierarchy of Pseudo-Denys* (London, 1964).
141. Cf. H. C. Van Elswijk, "Victorine Spirituality," in NCE, vol. 14, pp. 650–51.
142. Richard of St. Victor, *Benjamin Maior*, P.L. 196, 80–81.

fluence of the authentic teaching of the *Mystica Theologia* of the Pseudo-Denis in *The Cloud*. It is true that Western mysticism is profoundly influenced by certain facets of Dionysian teaching; but most of these are anticipated by the influence of the Alexandrine Fathers, beginning with Origen and centring on Gregory of Nyssa, which develops the Augustinian approach to monastic theology, and is even anticipated in the all-pervasive influence of the Abbot Cassian, both directly and through the Benedictine tradition.[143] In other words, it is largely because the author surmises that, in the context of the last decades of the fourteenth century, the decline of authentic Thomism, coupled with the threat of the enthusiasm inherent in the first phases of Lollardy, might be detrimental to his contemplative teaching that he has recourse to what was still accepted as an impeccable source, the *Mystical Theology* of the Areopagite. He is under no illusion, either, about the difficult task with which he faces himself: so he repeats the *caveat* of his prologue in his final chapters (74–75), which are a kind of extended epilogue, containing the conventional warning, but also the personal invitation, of a competent, erudite and experienced spiritual director.

The Structure and Traditional Content of The Cloud

There has been a tendency to dismiss the prologue of *The Cloud* as conventionally imitative of the introduction to the *Mystica Theologia*. In fact there is little or no indication that the book contains arcane doctrine meant only for initiates. It is true that its first section indicates the rarity of the vocation to the solitary life. This of itself will, as the author stresses in his last paragraph, rule out those seekers after novelties, those with "itching ears" and the babblers who stray from the "charity which comes from a pure heart, a good conscience

---

143. Cf. infra, pp. 55, 56, 58, 60, 65, 66, 70, 72, 74, 77, 81, 87 etc.

and true faith," against whom Paul warns Timothy.[144] St. Bruno had similarly cautioned the brethren against the *gyro-vagi*, "who speak of things they do not understand, for which they have no liking and contradict by their words and actions ... who think themselves worthy of acclamation by defaming the very people they ought to praise."[145] Our author is highly aware of his own emphatic style, with its propensity to draw out his matter through sheer relish for his own vigorous and highly-wrought rhetoric, as he revels in his ability to express the traditional figures of the accomplished Latinist in his native tongue, in which synonym and antonym are pressed into alliterative service not simply for the sake of emphasis, but lest any point should be lost or overlooked. His digressions, though multifarious, are all purposeful; and he expects his reader to stay with him, so convinced is he of the crucial importance of all that he writes for anyone who has made it his avocation to be a perfect follower of Christ. And though, like many another before and after him, he must write as if addressing himself to one individual "whether in game or in earnest," he is aware that the true word is never bound, and may take root in ground unprotected by the walls of the religious cloister or solitary's cell.

He is writing, then, for those who are called to "the perfect forgetting of those things that are behind and the perfect reaching out to those things that lie ahead."[146] In fact, if one were to search through the outstanding monastic literature of the high middle ages, of which the *Cloud* is possibly the youngest heir, one would find nothing nearer to it, in intent, singleness of purpose and assured confidence of direction than the twelfth-century Letter to the Carthusians of Mont-Dieu of William of St. Thierry, the Benedictine turned Cistercian, bosom friend of St. Bernard, in whose shad-

---

144. Cf. 2 Tim 4, 3–4; 1 Tim 1, 5–7.
145. *Letter to the brethren at Chartreuse*, PL 152, 419.
146. William of St. Thierry, adapting Philippians 3, 13–14, in his *Epistola ad Fratres de Monte Dei*, 9.

ow he languished for so long.[147] He, too, is writing for the beginners, "to the younger brethren and to the novices who come to you, whose teacher is God alone, that they may have and read therein whatsoever they find profitable to the comforting of their solitude and a spur to their holy intent."[148] We are not claiming for *The Cloud* either William's wide learning or theological originality, any more than William's Latin can stand out against the power and freshness of *The Cloud's* English. What is true is that in comparably turbulent times, they share the same limited world of the *ex professo* contemplative solitary. And what William says at the end of his letter is at the forefront of our author's mind from the beginning to the end of *The Cloud:*

> And though to conceive this unspeakable [that is, "the sovereign Essence from which all being proceedeth"] we be all unable, yet doth our Beloved pardon us; for though we confess that of him we may not worthily speak or think, yet to that speaking and that thinking we are stirred and drawn by love of him or love of the love of him. Wherefore it is the part of him that thinketh to humble himself in all things, to glorify in himself the Lord his God, to become as nought to himself in the contemplation of his God.[149]

With a brief mention of this humility, and an exhortation to shake off the "slothful leisure" which is the curse of the

---

147. The rehabilitation of William in recent years is attested to by the bibliography given in NCE Vol 14, p. 938. His influence on the *Cloud* author's contemporary, Julian of Norwich, is dealt with at length by Edmund Colledge, O.S.A. and the present writer in *Showings,* and especially in the critical edition of Julian.

148. From Walter Shewring's translation. His is still the most satisfactory English version of the 'Golden Epistle,' in spite of the contrived archaic style; and it is competently edited by the late Dom Justin McCann (London, 1930), to whom all students of the *Cloud* in the last half-century are indebted, directly or indirectly.

149. Ibid., p. 120; and cf. p. 119.

solitary life,[150] the author immediately (ch ii) issues the challenge to his disciple to enter on the way of the perfect following of Christ. By a weaving together of scriptural allusions from the prophetical literature, the psalms, the Canticle of Canticles and the Christological hymn in Philippians, he stresses the divine condescension in both its incarnational aspect and God's personal relationship with the individual soul who seeks his solitude in order "to stand in desire" of this union of wills "all your life long." Loneliness, and the dangers which attend it, in no way turn him from his immediate purpose. He is not concerned to describe the "busy leisure" of the contemplative's day.[151] He will mention these in passing later on. The solitary is committed to respond to the divine proffer of God himself: ". . . to woo him humbly in prayer (who) is always most willing and is only waiting for you." We may note that this is one of the rare occasions that he permits himself to use the "spiritual" erotic language in which Cistercian and Dionysian literature indulged so freely in the thirteenth and fourteenth centuries: the theme of God as the jealous lover.

This is the context in which he introduces the "work" of his book with its double cloud of "forgetting" and unknowing. A truly adequate response will be as permanent and continuous as the divine proffer itself; so that the human effort must always be the positive cessation of any mental activity interposing itself between God himself and the creature. He is content here to describe it briefly in terms of conversion—the turning to God which gives joy to the angels, the act of *pietas* proper to the prodigal Son,[152] the act of love which is the fulfilment of the great commandment, bring-

---

150. Ibid., p. 41 (ch. 8, 21).
151. This is what William of St. Thierry does when he poses the same question as the *Cloud* author at the end of ch. ii: 'Askest thou what thou shalt do?' ibid., p. 42 (ch. 8, 22).
152. Cf. Luke 15, 10ff.

ing life to the whole body of the Church and overthrowing the devil's envy which brought death into the world:[153] the work which is burdensome until the soul begins to feel drawn by the Lord, when it becomes a task that is easy and delightful.[154] Again the scriptural allusions abound, with that medieval familiarity with the moral or "tropological" sense of the sacred word, which tends always towards the building up of charity, permeating the mind and heart with God's supreme love.[155] He is also beginning to introduce, along with the stock Dionysian vocabulary revealed in words such as "extended" and "the simple reaching out (nakid entente) to God," the traditional monastic teaching on compunction both as a special contemplative grace and a movement of the heart, which Cassian describes as "a nakedness and contempt of all the faculties, which leads to the perfection of apostolic love,"[156] yet which will always in this life contain that element of painful longing to see God's face and experience the sweetness of his love, expressed perhaps most poignantly by the Counter-Reformation poet Richard Crashaw (1649), in his version of the last verse of the *Adoro te*:

When this dry soul those eyes shall see
And drink the unsealéd source of Thee,
When glory's sun faith's shade shall chase
Then for Thy veil give me Thy face![157]

Though from many points of view chapter iv may be said to be the heart of the *Cloud's* Dionysian teaching, his

---

153. Cf. Luke 10, 27ff and parallels; Ephesians 4, 12; Wisdom 2, 24.
154. Cf. John 6, 44; Matthew 11, 28–30.
155. Cf. H. De Lubac, *Exégèse Médiévale* (Paris, 1959) Tome II, p. 569, where the author is discussing the mystical aspect of the tropological sense, and citing St. Gregory's Homilies on Ezechiel.
156. Cf. *Institut. IV*, 43; P.L. 49, 202.
157. On the attribution of the *Adoro Te* to St. Thomas Aquinas, cf. Joseph Connelly, *Hymns of the Roman Liturgy* (London, 1955), pp. 118–19.

introduction of the question of time owes nothing to its treatment by the Pseudo-Denis in *The Divine Names* (ch. 10), which
is concerned with the various scriptural ascriptions of time
to God—"the Ancient of days" or "reaching from end to
end," or "the source of all time, whilst being before and above
time." His seems to be the severely practical question that
since, according to Paul, God is to judge man's secret thoughts
(Romans 2:4), then we may be held responsible for giving
all our impulses their God-intended direction. However, as
the chapter unfolds, we see that, like Augustine, he is thinking
of time not so much in terms of duration, but of number.[158]
The number of our impulses are to all practical purposes
infinite, and their "quantity" infinitesimal. It follows, then,
that in man's fallen state he cannot hope to handle this indefinite number of impulses, even though perfect self-control
which primal grace imparted might enable us to direct all
such impulses to their proper object. The answer to the difficulty (which indeed indicates that the author expects the
reader to follow a fairly subtle argumentation) is that God
does not expect us to measure or to comprehend, much less
to account for, an indefinite number of impulses, minimal
in size, which will, in man's finite condition, naturally go
astray. Instead God both adapts himself to our condition and
lifts us up by grace to his own. It is within his power and
according to his good pleasure "to fulfil the will and desire
of our souls." Such is the author's introduction to the crucial
distinction between the "knowing power" and the "loving
power," which has been so often castigated as a radical anti-
intellectualism due in no large measure to the interpretation
by Thomas Gallus of John Sarracen's rendering of the Dionysian corpus.[159] For the *Cloud* author, however, the grace
of the divine compassion, manifested in the mystery of redemption, which not only restores man to his state of in-

---

158. Cf. *De Civitate Dei XII*, 18: P.L. 41, 368.
159. Cf. chapter iv, infra, notes 41–43, pp. 122–23.

nocence, but makes him co-heir with Christ and a fellow-worker of God,[160] can only be described as "the everlastingly wonderful miracle of love which shall never have an end." Man can participate in the divine charity, even though he will never cease to be finite; through charity then he will come to share God's nature, life and endless happiness. And through the same grace he is destined for the same end. Meantime, this gift of love and faith which unites us to him in this life and is imparted in this stream of sudden impulses—the spark of divine life, can never be the product of our own reasoning or imaginative faculties; nor can its nature be discovered, determined or fashioned by them. We comprehend him by love, but the how of it is enshrouded in darkness.

Chapter iv, then, briefly describes the unique nature of what the author considers to be the ultimate contemplative exercise, its supreme worth, the basic implications of its practice—the demands it makes and the dangers attendant on it. It is the initial statement of his thesis, of which the rest of the book is an elaboration. Of the exercise in itself there is little to be said, or indeed that can be said, as the author himself several times asseverates;[161] so that his book is largely concerned with the accidentals (using the word in its Aristotelian sense): when, with what dispositions, and by what means. So in chapter v he begins to speak of the need to put a "cloud of forgetting between you and all the creatures that have ever been made," for anyone who comes to live and work in this cloud of unknowing. Since, in all probability, the author's earliest work is his paraphrase of Richard of St. Victor's *Benjamin Minor*, and it is Richard who seems to have coined the term in this same allusive context to Moses in the book of Exodus, one would expect him to be using the phrase in the same sense as Richard in his *Benjamin Maior*,

---

160. Cf. Romans 8, 17; 1 Peter 3, 17; 1 Cor. 3, 9.
161. Cf. chapters vi, xxxiii–iv, lxxiii.

which treats of the last steps in the ascent to contemplation. The latter, however, writes:

> Moses enters the cloud when the human spirit, overtaken by the immensity of the divine light, becomes wholly passive in a profound forgetfulness of self ... One and the same cloud has overshadowed it by its brightness and enlightened it by its darkness: that is, filled it with light to see divine things and brought the human into the shade.[162]

The *Cloud* author, on the other hand, is using the term to interpret the initial description of the exercise from the active point of view, which, at the beginning of the *Mystica Theologia*, he paraphrases thus:

> ... whenever, under the impulse of grace, you come to apply yourself to the practical exercise of your dark contemplation, take care that you abandon with an intense, adroit and loving contrition, your bodily senses ... and also your spiritual faculties—your intellectual operations, as they are called, and all those things outside yourself which can be known by any of your five bodily senses; all those things within you which can be known by your spiritual faculties; all the things that now exist, or have existed in the past and now exist no longer ... [163]

He returns, as he will over and again, to the fact that the contemplative exercise with which he is dealing concerns only those who are called to be *perfect* followers of Christ: those, that is, who are passing out of the illuminative way to the unitive, in which meditation, or even contemplation as it is defined, say by St. Bernard in his *De Consideratione*, is "the

162. *Benjamin Maior* 4, 22; 5, 2: P.L. 196, 165 bc and 171 bc.
163. *Denis' Hidden Theology*, ch. I. Cf. H., *Deonise hid Divinite*, pp. 2–3.

true and certain intuition of any object by the intellect, or the certain apprehension of the truth."[164] The author does, however, make this psychological concession to those who are beginners in this way of the "perfect": that when not actually engaged on the exercise itself, it is taken for granted that the disciple will live in that spiritual environment in which the objects of one's unfocussed attention will be "the things of heaven," God's goodness, heaven, our Lady and so on. Nor does he deny, in his simple "I don't know" to the argument, "How might I think of him in himself?" that the knowledge of these other creatures, and indeed of God's works of salvation—which, says Bernard, are the proper object of Christian consideration, since they are concerned with the soul's salvation[165]—is the work of grace, "a light and a part of contemplation" (ch. vi). It is simply that they do not belong to what the author considers to be the consummate contemplative exercise. He would seem to have in mind Paul's elucidation of his statement that "the -Spirit himself gives testimony to our spirit that we are God's children": that since we are hoping for and striving after what we do not see, "the Spirit helps our weakness ... and makes petition for us with ineffable sighs."[166] It is love which, as the more excellent way than that of the gifts of prophecy, miracle or vision, "never falls away," but remains as God's greatest gift.[167]

The author proceeds in chapter vii to examine in detail what tends to happen in the mind and heart of the one who applies himself to this contemplative exercise. Using the device of personification, he develops the imaginary dialogue between the soul and this thought which is always trying to interpose itself between the self and the darkness which is God's hiding-place. He employs his considerable psychological as well as

164. Cf. *St. Bernard's Treatise on Consideration*, trans. 'A priest of Mount Melleray' (Dublin, 1922), p. 39.
165. 'Let nothing occupy thy mind except what conduces to thy salvation.' Ibid., p. 41.
166. Cf. Romans 8, 14ff.
167. Cf. 1 Corinthians 12, 30–31; 13, 8. 13.

INTRODUCTION

rhetorical skill in the argumentation, to show how, if the self actually plays thought's game, he finds himself involved in a process which scatters the concentration and dissipates the contemplative effort. Without making explicit mention of the fact, he is giving a lesson in the practice of discernment of spirits, showing how the bad spirit—under the guise of "thought," "transforms himself into an angel of light," offering "many sweet meditations" which in themselves are "both good and holy." But again, the allusion to the Pauline "forgetting what lies behind and reaching out to what lies ahead . . . the upward call of God," in the manner of the medieval exegete, is what dictates our author's single-minded intent. Yet mindful too of the arduous nature of the exercise, he is prepared to make a further concession, which accords with the traditional nature of ejaculatory prayer, but which he patterns to suit the immediate contemplative purpose. There is, of course, no intention of advocating some rhythmic technique to help in "stilling" the faculties; and it seems probable, as we have noted above, that he has learnt something from the Carthusian, Guigues du Pont, on the subject of contemplative aspirations. What is perhaps of greatest moment is that he is offering a *media via* between the voluntarist position of Bonaventure, and perhaps of Hugh of St. Victor, that petitionary prayer is an affective movement of the heart, and St. Thomas, who insists that such prayer is the expression and interpretation of that desire and is thus an intellectual act.[168] It is here a symbol which signifies and is linked with the affective impulse, rather than a simple expression or reasoned interpretation of it, a view which he will clarify when explaining what he means by the "short prayer which pierces the heavens" in the immediate preparation for the contemplative exercise as taught in Denis's *Mystical Theology*; it becomes itself the lifting up of the spirit. Here, however, it

---

168. For Bonaventure, see *In III Sententiis*, 17, 1, 1; For Hugh, *De Sacramentis*, II, 9: P.L. 176, 474; for St. Thomas, *Summa Theologiae* 2–2ae, q. 83, a.l, ad 1.

is to be an instinctive though God-given device, to protect
the spirit against subtle attack.

The argument follows on logically in chapter viii—how
can this obviously good thought be evil "when it serves so
well to increase a person's devotion?" The author again has
recourse to the traditional teaching on discretion as his guide,
with the Dionysian capital text from the Epistle of James
(1:17) as background: "Every best gift and every perfect gift
is from above, coming down from the Father of lights, with
whom there is no change nor shadow of alteration." In itself
then, it is always good—"a ray of God's likeness." But any
reflection can be distorted and thus fail to meet the unitive
purpose of the divine gift, which so easily happens when
a man makes himself the source and origin of his likeness
to God, since he possesses, as did Adam, the intellectual power
of deciding what is good and what is evil, making himself
like to God. With a simplicity born of common sense, the
author paints no lurid picture of this clash of spiritual cosmic
forces, though he speaks of "proud scholars of the devil and
masters of vanity and falsehood." Instead, with a firm prac-
ticality, he introduces the disciple to the important distinction
between the "two kinds of lives in Holy Church," for what
is good for one state of life can be destructive for the other.

The traditional spiritual doctrine in the medieval West
on the two lives, and the superiority of the contemplative
over the active, is normally based on Augustine's several ex-
egetical references to the story of Martha and Mary in Luke,
though he also uses as types of the active and the contemplative, St. Peter and St. John, and in a more elaborate moral
exegesis, the two wives of the Patriarch Jacob, Leah and Ra-
chel. In the *City of God*, however, he distinguishes three
kinds—the leisurely or contemplative, the busy or active, and
the life which combines the two.[169] The primitive division

169. Cuthbert Butler in his *Western Mysticism* (2nd edition, London, 1951), has
gathered for us all the relevant texts, pp. 157–67. He has done the same for St.
Gregory the Great and St. Bernard (*ibid.* pp. 171–85, and 191–96).

is simply life in the world and the religious life of the cloistered monk; a further elaboration is the distinction between the corporal and spiritual works of mercy—charity in the temporal and spiritual or ministerial contexts; and finally the kinds of prayer and praise which distinguish them. As the tradition develops amongst the Dionysians, the emphasis is almost entirely on the latter. Thomas Gallus, for example, constantly uses the figures of Martha and Mary to distinguish two ways of knowing God—the *duplex Dei cognitio.* The contemplative life in its strict sense is the way to the perfection of living faith: that inseparable attachment to the love of Christ which is the unitive Christian knowledge of the true God. This faith, truth, life and wisdom can be achieved only by those who have reached "that maturity which is proportioned to the completed growth of Christ."[170] It is this perfection and God-given prerogative—union with him as far as is possible in this mortal life—which is the objective of the contemplative work of the *Cloud.* He is at pains here to explain precisely why, in terms of the rich tradition of the Church, these meditative reflections, and the consolations of devotion attaching to them, are inappropriate in "the higher part of the contemplative life," where human activity must be totally dependent on God's special gift, in the sense that the "loving power" must strive to match the divine condescension, according to the thesis stated in chapter iv. Any interference then, on the part of the "knowing faculty" or the untutored imaginative faculty, must inevitably lead to disaster for the contemplative solitary. How this happens, he will go on to explain in chapter ix.

In chapters ix–xii, the author continues his examination of the intellectual and affective movements which belong to the lower part of the contemplative life. He first explains why, in the case of those who are experiencing "the upward call of God in Christ Jesus," such movements have to be

---

170. Cf. Ephesians 4:15. The allusions here to Thomas Gallus are taken from his glosses on *The Divine Names,* ch. 7.

repulsed in favour of those described as "a blind impulse of love towards God for Himself alone, this secret beating of love on this cloud of unknowing." In the first place, the sharp stirrings of the understanding, these clear beholdings of holy things which often bring feelings of consolation in their train, are not the mind's responses to God's active presence, but its occupation with one or other object beneath him. They are, therefore, less profitable than the blind affective impulses, both for the contemplative's personal growth in union with God and for the unitive development of the whole body of Christ: the Church in glory, the Church suffering and the Church on earth. These movements of dark contemplation are thus preferable to any kind of preternatural sight or sound of saint or angel—the sensible or spiritual consolations of "mirth and melody." For there is no face-to-face vision in this life—again the allusion to I Corinthians 13 is transparent; but to those whom God endowed with this ability "to forget all that lies behind" (cf. Phil. 3:13) in that stillness of a mind and heart which waits on God alone, he sometimes grants the experience of his felt presence.

If then the recollection of saints and angels is to be rejected during the time given to the higher contemplative exercise, how much more so the sudden thoughts which rise from the recesses of our minds and hearts concerning earthly relationships, with people or with material objects. The author states the doctrine clearly in traditional theological language, and from his experience that scrupulosity is a proximate danger for the beginner in the solitary life. He first distinguishes between the sinful impulse which impinges unbidden on the surface of the consciousness, emanating from the relics of original sin—the "pain" due to ignorance and the frail tendencies to self-love and self-aggrandizement—the roots of all our fleshly desires and hatreds. For those whose intentions are habitually oriented to the love and service of God, the momentary acceptance of such thoughts is not seriously sinful. This happens only when a person deliberately permits such a thought to take control, to draw the consciousness to itself.

Nor is the inexperienced solitary freed from the temptation to any kind of sinful thought or act: hence the author's categorization of the capital sins. No one, least of all the solitary, can afford to trifle with interior temptation.

However, perserverance in the exercise of contemplative love is the sovereign remedy against the peril of bad or idle thoughts. The hope which endurance engenders is never disappointed as long as we are responding to the divine love poured out in our hearts. Neither corporal penances nor the meditative reflections which occasion the appropriate sorrow or joy are of any avail without the practice of the love which comprehends all the contemplative virtues: again the allusion to Paul's eulogy on charity as the personification of ordered human attachment to God, seen in Christ's unitive love—and the obediential humility to the Father which is so clearly expressive of it[171]—is not lost on one grown accustomed to the monastic *lectio divina*.[172]

The quality of the contemplative effort which measures all progress in the interior life of the solitary is immediately related to the reflex conscious awareness of the self in its relationship to God, the supreme and single object of its desire. Thus, at the end of Chapter xii, he adapts Richard of St. Victor's definition of virtue as an ordered and controlled affection of the spirit,[173] by adding that such affection "has God for its single object, himself alone." In the preparation of mind and heart for unitive contemplation, this control is none other than discretion, traditionally the "mother of all virtues," on which the author has much to say, throughout the *Cloud* and elsewhere. But the virtues *par excellence* in the exercise of contemplation are humility and charity. It is with the first of these that the author concerns himself in chapters xiii to xv. And where later authors will coin the terms "ac-

---

171. Cf. 1 Corinthians 13:4–8; Philippians 2:3–11.
172. *Lectio Divina* for the contemplative solitary is treated specifically in chs. xxxv–ix.
173. Cf. *Benjamin Minor*, ch. 7.

quired" and "infused," he himself speaks of imperfect and perfect meekness. Good Thomist that he is, he offers a definition of *humilitas* which will embrace the distinction—"humility is nothing else but a man's true understanding and awareness of himself as he really is"; but he prefers the current English word "mekenes" to the imported *humilite*. This would also appear to point to a scriptural source as the basis of the distinction: the revelation of the divine wisdom in the eternal Son in the all-important chapter ten of Luke's gospel (21–24), alongside the identical passage in Matthew (11:25–30), with its different conclusion, "Come to me, all you who labour and are heavy-burdened, and I will refresh you. Take my yoke upon you and learn of me, for I am meek and humble of heart."[174]

St. Bernard's frequently-cited definition in this context—"humility is the virtue by which a man abases himself by reason of his perfect self-knowledge"[175]—is thus too pointed for the *Cloud* author, who here, as in his treatment of the monastic *lectio divina* (chs. xxxv–ix), avoids the ladder image, and thinks in Aristotelian terms of genus and species. At the same time the substance of his teaching is to be found in Gregory the Great's commentary on a verse in the first book of Kings (6:13): "the Bethsamites were reaping wheat in the valley ... the valley signifies the humble ... It is to those who have prepared themselves by humility that the Lord sends the floods of his grace," so that "it occasionally happens that by God's grace we are lifted up to divine contemplation without any thought whatever of his fearful judgments."[176]

---

174. The author, in speaking of "imperfect humility," would appear to be thinking of those who, accepting the burden of sin and learning from Christ in his humanity, will find refreshment from the God-man. *Venite ad me ... discite a me quia mitis sum et humilis corde.* There is no Latin noun which corresponds to the adjective *mitis*—meek. In the Vulgate Latin the nearest equivalent is *mansuetudo*, or 'mildness' in the author's English.

175. *Humilitas est virtus qua homo verissima sui cognitione sibi ipsi vilescit* (*De gradibus humilitatis*, cap. 1).

176. *In 1 Reg.*, III, 3, 4; ibid., II, 8.

And Bonaventure, in the prologue to his *Ascent of the Soul to God*, writes:

> In order to be disposed for the divine contemplation which leads to ecstasy ... I first invite the reader to pour forth prayers and groans to Jesus crucified ... It is to the humble, prepared by the divine grace, that I offer my considerations—to hearts devout and contrite, filled with the unction of heavenly joy and in love with the divine Wisdom.[177]

In other words, imperfect humility—"this true knowledge and experience of myself as the wretch that I am" (ch. xiv)—is the grace given to those exercising themselves in their immediate preparation for the "work of this book," but it is not its result. So the author is at pains to stress that this passive purification, for which a sacramental grace is a necessary first condition (ch. xv), will set us on the road to perfect humility only if conscience and counsel testify that we are being called to take the path of that contemplation which leads to the perfection of God's love, as far as this is possible here below.

The force of his argumentation, a commonplace since the time of Cassian,[178] is that compunction is not complete simply because we recognize with Bernard that we are "reduced to nothing" by our own sinfulness, or even that the chastisement of our sins is visited upon Christ the suffering Servant (cf. Isaiah 53:4ff). There is another step yet along the road to contemplation, which is equally an ingredient of the divine compassion, as we ought to be able to perceive in the humility of Christ himself or of Mary his mother. The author is, however, at pains to embellish his argument with what he considers

---

177. Cf. *Itinerarium mentis in Deum*. The translation is my own.
178. Cf. *Collationes*, I, 19; *Institutiones* 12, 16.

INTRODUCTION

to be the most forceful example of perfect humility preached
by Christ himself in the gospels: Mary Magdalen the great
sinner who becomes the great saint "because she loved much"
(ch. xvi).[179] Though her spiritual environment, as the ideal
penitent, was imperfect humility, in that "she knew well,
by her own experience in sober truth, that she was a viler
wretch than anyone else," the perfection of her humility was
in her total self-forgetfulness. In the author's memorable and
symbolic phraseology, "she hung up her love and her longing
desire in this cloud of unknowing."

The immediate consequence of these rare touches of perfect love and/or humility is the gift of contemplative patience,
identified for our author in the stillness of Mary of Bethany.[180]
"She had no leisure," he says, "to listen to her (Martha's)
complaints" (ch. xvii). This is the key-word which leads him
into his lengthy excursus on the two lives and the superiority
of contemplative quiet, and a deceptively simple grammatical
explanation of how one may conceive of the best life when
there are only two (chs. xvii–xxiii). He has already made the
assertion that the call to contemplative solitude is the perfect
following of Christ, and he will tell us later on why he refuses
"to cite any doctor" in support of his views.[181] He simply
recounts the history of the main text of Luke 10:38–43: that
is, "all these works, words and looks which passed between
our Lord and these two sisters"—Martha and Mary; adding
that "they are given as an example of all actives and all contemplatives that have lived in holy Church since that time,
and shall live ..." It would be difficult to find a briefer and

---

179. Julian of Norwich, in the long text of her thirteenth revelation on the
same topic of compassion and compunction, "sees" a whole procession of penitent
saints, beginning with David in the Old Testament, and with the Magdalen in
the New. Cf. *Showings*, ch. 38, pp. 242 ff.

180. As has been noted, Mary of Bethany, the woman who was a sinner (cf.
Luke 7:36) and the Magdalen were invariably taken as the same person in the Middle
Ages.

181. Cf. infra, ch. lxx, p. 256.

more complete medieval exegesis of the passage, according to the time-honoured distich:

Littera gesta docet; quid credas, allegoria;
Moralis, quid agas; quo tendas, anagogia.[182]

His immediate concern is the "moral" sense of the passage (chs. xviii–xix). The strictly contemplative life is under attack because of current laxity, real or imagined; but—and more to the point—because the solitary appears to be doing nothing. The first accusation he lets pass for the moment; there is much truth in it, which he will deal with later on. What he is immediately concerned about is that the authentic apprentices "who turn from the business of this world and dispose themselves to be God's special servants in holiness," should show Christ's own forgiving spirit—"Father forgive them, for they know not what they do"; and "forgive us our trespasses." In addition, they should act like Mary—leave it to the Lord to come to their defence (ch. xx). For they have chosen to do the one thing necessary: to love and praise God for himself, "above all other business, bodily and spiritual." For the part which Mary has chosen is indeed the best:[183] the higher part of the contemplative life; whilst Martha's is the lower part, though complementary to her sister's (ch. xxi), consisting as it does in the "good spiritual meditations" which must be joined to the "good and honest corporal works of mercy." Let each understand the other; but let the Marthas realize that Mary stands for those who are genuinely called

---

182. "The letter (of Scripture) instructs in what is said and done; the allegory, in what you are to believe; the moral sense, what you are to do; the anagogical, what your goal is to be." The verses are attributed to the Dominican, Augustine of Dacia (+1282). Cf. H. DeLubac, *Exégèse Médiévale* (Paris: 1959), tome I, pp. 25 ff.

183. The Latin Vulgate, cited by all the Dionysians after Gallus, reads *Maria optimam partem elegit.* Earlier writers on the "two lives" tend to cite, after Augustine, *meliorem partem,* 'the better part.' Cf. C. Butler, op. cit. pp. 160 ff. Where he treats of a third kind, it is the "mixed" life, ibid. pp. 164 ff.

to exemplify the true and perfect end of the Christian life—
quo tendas, anagogia: the life of God's love, which will never
be taken away. Meanwhile, with his accustomed dexterity,
the author reminds us that he is still making his point about
imperfect and perfect humility. The authentic contemplative
will be endowed with a lively faith in the word of the Lord:
"Be not solicitous ... seek first the kingdom of God," and
he will provide whatever else may be necessary (ch. xxiii).
"Choose rather to be humbled under the wonderful height
and worthiness of God, which is perfect, rather than under
your own fears and hesitations or those of others, which is
imperfect."

At the end of chapter xii, the author had declared his
intention of demonstrating how the contemplative exercise—
the work of his book—is the most direct way to the perfect
following of Christ not only as destroying sin and controlling
concupiscence but because, at its consummate point, it contains
all the virtues proper to perfect man. His thesis, he takes
it for granted, will be established by treating of humility and
charity, the twin pillars of contemplative life and prayer. His
way of proceeding with charity (chs. xxiv–xxx) is similar to
that of humility: to offer a definition; to examine its component
parts; to deal with objections, and to explain how these may
apply to other states of life, and of the methods of reflection
and prayer proper to them; so that, even whilst he is elucidating his own teaching, he is at the same time instructing
the beginner. Here (ch. xxiv) he starts from the definition
of charity in its fullest scriptural sense, and constructs upon
the definition—'charity means nothing else than the love of
God for himself above all creatures'—what the mediaeval rhet-
oricians call the 'most complete and perfect argument', consisting of five parts: a) the *proposition:* 'It is very obvious ...';
b) the immediate *reasoning* ('ratio') supporting the proposition:
'the essence of the exercise ...'; c) a *confirmation* of the reasoning ('confirmatio rationis'): '... a simple reaching out, because in this exercise ... he asks for nothing but God himself';
d) an *embellishment* of the argument ('exornatio'): 'so much

so ... that the will of him whom he loves be fulfilled'; e) the *complexio* or conclusion, which clinches the argument by repeating it in its context: 'It is evident, then, that in this exercise God is perfectly loved for himself above all creatures.'[184]

The author must then anticipate the commonplace objection that the *ex professo* contemplative fails to fulfil the second part of the great commandment 'which is equal to the first'.[185] Reminding us that he is firmly within the monastic tradition, which takes for granted the superiority of the contemplative life over that of the active, and that it is not ordinarily permitted for the monk to leave the exercises proper to his state except to succour his neighbour either in his temporal or spiritual need, he also argues positively, along with the theologians from Augustine to Aquinas. It would indeed be hard to find so succinct a statement of the current soteriology, the developing understanding of participation in the fulness of Christ's grace, and a defence of the authentic cenobitic and eremitical lives as truly apostolic:[186]

---

184. Cf. Harry Caplan's edition of the *Rhetorica ad Herennium*, (London: 1956), pp. 107 ff.

185. Cf. the Vulgate translation of Matthew 22:39.

186. He begins the passage by demonstrating his familiar grasp of the doctrine of Irenaeus on the recapitulation of all humankind in the Incarnation, Passion and Resurrection of Christ: the universality of salvation history in the whole Christ. "When God's Son took flesh and became human he gathered up into himself the entire history *(expositionem)* of humankind. He summed up salvation for us in such a way that what we lost in Adam—our being after the image and likeness of God—was restored to us in Jesus Christ." Cf. *Adversus Haereses* III, 19, 1 (Harvey, II, p. 95); V, 14, 2 (Harvey, II, pp. 361–62).

St. Thomas, whilst following the same line of argument, approaches the question with less assurance in treating of the transmission of original sin, in *Summa Theologiae*, 2, q. 81, a. 1.

The monk, as Jean LeClerq notes (*Études sur le vocabulaire monastique du Moyen Age*, p. 38), is the successor, heir and imitator of the apostles, citing the twelfth-century treatise *De vita vere apostolica;* he is also the follower of the true philosophy, in accepting to suffer indefinitely, like Job, for the love of God and of the neighbour (ibid., p. 54), citing a gloss by St. Odo in the tenth century, on Gregory the Great's commentary on the book of Job.

INTRODUCTION

For as all men were lost in Adam, and as all men who bear witness to their desire of salvation by good works, are saved and shall be by the power of Christ's passion alone, a soul whose affection is perfectly extended in this exercise and thus united to God in spirit, not exactly in the same way, but as it were in the same way, does all that in it lies, as the experience of this work bears witness, to make all men as perfect in this work as it is itself (ch. xxv).

Then he sews up his exposition by paraphrasing the capital Pauline texts on the Mystical Body. The flexibility, moderation and sound theological sense of the passage[187] underline his erudition and his experience in faith of the Christ who suffered by lifting up his body on the cross. "For all those who desire to forsake sin and ask for mercy are to be saved through the power of his passion."

In chapter xxvi, the author proceeds to particularize this compendious teaching on the great commandment by insisting that love's labour lies in the contemplative's effort to respond to his continual awareness of the divine loving and saving action: "he loved me and delivered himself for me" (Galatians 2:20). Such a habit of recollection is ordinarily achieved only over a long period, "unless the person receive a very special grace." The divine power is always at work in us to fulfil his purpose in us;[188] or, as the author paraphrases his text contemplatively, "the hand of almighty God is always ready to perform this work in every soul that is disposed for it."

---

187. The allusions are to the reality of the interior poverty—the medieval exegesis of the story of the rich young man; the call to divinization in the saying, "Be perfect as your heavenly father is perfect," with its Lucan overtones that this is the perfection of compassionate love; and finally, the linking of the true imitation of Christ with the exaltation of Christ crucified and glorified—the drawing of all humankind to himself by the power of the Spirit released through his "obedience even to the death of the Cross"—in the Christological hymn of Philippians 2:6–12.

188. Again the response is to Paul's great trinitarian prayer of petition in Ephesians 3:14–20.

INTRODUCTION

Whether or not he is acquainted with Gallus's thrice-repeated categorization of the "hierarchies of the mind," where "mind" denotes the *principale mentis,* the spiritual intelligence which embraces the graced powers both of understanding and of loving,[189] or whether his source is Richard of St. Victor's distinction, in the contemplative ascent, of the operation of man's natural powers assisted by grace, and "the work of God alone," is perhaps irrelevant. The agonizing struggle for the contemplative apprentice is to focus his attention—"to reach out to God alone"—by that persevering contrition and ardent desire which are imaged in the action of "the treading down of the awareness of all the creatures that God ever made, and in keeping them under the cloud of forgetting." Again we have the allusion to the "Come to me" of Matthew (11:25 ff); the gift of rest and sweetness which results from constant response—conversion.

There is an ambiguity in the last paragraph of this chapter. "Then perhaps it will be his will to send out a ray of spiritual light . . . and he will show you some of his secrets." Thomas Gallus teaches that when the perfection of union is attained at the apex of the affection—*The Cloud* author's "sovereign point of the spirit"—the intellectual faculties are also specially graced in consequence. But Gregory the Great had written of the *culmen contemplationis* that "love itself is understanding" *(amor ipse intellectus est)*; and the author here speaks of being shown God's secrets as well as the feeling: "the affection all aflame with the fire of his love." Again one suspects a scriptural allusion: here to the capital text of Paul (Ephesians 3, 1–21), where the subject is the revelation of God's mysteries now unfolded, and the prayer that Christ may dwell in our hearts by faith; that our lives might be rooted in love and

---

189. In the *Explanation of the Angelic Hierarchy,* ch. x, in the *Prologue to the Third Commentary on the Canticle of Canticles,* and in the Prologue to the *Explanation of the Mystical Theology.* We recall that Gallus acknowledges Richard of St. Victor as his master. Cf. J. Walsh, "Thomas Gallus et l'effort contemplatif," in *Revue d'Histoire de Spiritualité,* tome 51 (1975), pp. 18–42.

founded on love; and that we might come to know with all
the saints the pre-eminent knowledge of Christ's love—*su-
pereminentem scientiae caritatem Christi*. The author is always
sufficiently independent of his immediate sources when it
comes to his scriptural recollections; not least, the Pauline
paradox.

He is equally Pauline in the short chapter which follows
(xxvii); all Christians are addressed in Paul's letter, though
not all have forsaken the world for the contemplative life
"with a sincere will." Those who have (ch. xxviii), begin to
manifest this good will "according to the ordinary direction
of holy Church." A little more than a century later, Ignatius
Loyola, couching his constitutions and also his directives for
the professed priests of his infant Order according to the
traditions of the high middle ages,[190] will recommend to them
daily confession of devotion,[191] in the search for that purity
of heart consonant with the celebration and the reception
of the Eucharist, which Guigo the Angelic, in one of his
meditations, will describe as the most efficacious means to
union; as indeed did the Pseudo-Denys in his Explanation
of the Ecclesiastical Hierarchy. Certainly it is in accord with
the Church's custom at the time of our author's writing, that
Communion should always be preceded, if possible, by Confession,[192] "even though (the person) may never have sinned
seriously." Loyola, too, will proffer in his direction a form
of dark contemplation, and recommend, in his "rules of modesty," that custody of the senses which will guard against
the tendency in fallen man to distraction and dissipation of
recollection,[193] though he does not state such practices as dis-

---

190. Ignatius gives, amongst his reasons for writing Constitutions at all, the
precedent of the Monastic and Mendicant Orders. Cf. *Constitutions of the Society
of Jesus* (ed. and trans. by George Ganss, St. Louis: 1970), "Proemium," pp. 119–
120.

191. Cf. "Regulae Sacerdotum," in *Regulae Societatis Jesu*, (Rome: 1932), pp.
29–35.

192. Cf. "Confession," in NCE, Vol. 4, pp. 131–2.

193. Cf. *Rules of the Society of Jesus*, (London: Roehampton 1929), p. 33–35.

posing his religious for the fulfilment of the commandment of God to love him for himself alone.

For our author, he who desires to advance to the perfection of contemplation (ch. xxix) will labour in the practice of the love of God by means of the love of the good for itself, moved neither by fear nor by hope of reward to achieve that communion with God "where all sorrow passes away"— the assimilation and divine communion described in the Apocalypse (21:4), when all mourning and pain shall have an end. The author makes the point, however, doubtless recalling Paul's frequent confession of his sinfulness, and his insistence that "God's grace is not void in him," that past sinfulness is no barrier to the call to the perfection of contemplation. Rather, the gratuitous nature of unitive love shines more clearly in the penitents who have become saints. One of the marks of the gift of this love is that we judge no one, except perhaps out of this love (ch. xxx). Ordinarily, it simply leads us to judge ourselves, with the help of counsel. Our author is not concerned with the details of the general distinction which he draws here concerning this aspect of the exercise of charity, though he indicates that he is well acquainted with the monastic tradition, especially as expressed in the rule of St. Benedict concerning the duties and obligations of the Abbot,[194] and doubtless of the local bishop in the case of approved solitaries. Richard Methley, in his century-old glosses on this chapter,[195] may indicate how times have changed within the context of the Charterhouse; whilst the author will show himself much more sensitive to criticism when he comes to write his letter of private direction to this same disciple to whom *The Cloud* is addressed.

In chapters xxvii and xxviii, the author had begun to ask who should undertake this special exercise of unitive love, and the proximate preparation demanded by it—the cleansing of the conscience which a thoroughly adequate confession of

---

194. Cf. Ch. IV of the *Rule*, on obedience to the Abbot.
195. Cf. the annotations to the chapter, infra, pp. 178–79.

his sins is designed to effect. Yet only the practice of the exercise itself can reach down to the roots of our sinful tendencies: a process of purification which is passive rather than active, involving special graces which do not necessarily correspond to our own efforts, our state of soul when we begin or the grievous nature of our past sins. One's inclination is to think that God's compassionate love will correspond to the comparative experience of a blameless life—as we read in the first song of the Psalter (Psalm 1). The parable of the labourers in the vineyard corrects such an over-literal interpretation—"is thine eye evil because I am good?" (Matt. 20:16)—and its conclusion, "the last shall be first and the first last." It is a reflection which leads the author to ponder the human proclivity to judge others, an attitude particularly detrimental to the perfection of charity which is the object of the contemplative exercise. Only those who have God-given authority or who have experience of the gift of this charity can presume to offer these spiritual alms to their neighbours: to instruct the ignorant and counsel the doubtful, with the interior assurance that in a particular instance they are the instruments of the Holy Spirit in converting the sinner. Let the beginner be content with judging himself.

The author now proceeds to instruct the apprentice in the practice of the exercise itself (chs. xxxi–iv). His main concern is with what sacred learning and his own experience have taught him: what is most inclined to dissipate the single-minded concentration of the solitary is the recollection of his past sins, their circumstances, and the temptations to fresh sins (ch. xxxi). This labour of treading down these thoughts and covering them "with a thick cloud of forgetting" is a particular mode of the traditional "spiritual combat" against the law of sin (cf. Rom. 7:21–25).[196] Though his immediate source for this image of self-forgetfulness may well be Richard of St. Victor, the "spiritual tactics" he recommends in chapter

---

196. Cf. P. Olphe-Galliard's magisterial article, "Cassien," in *DSp*, fasc. vii, pp. 239–40.

xxxii are his own special invention for lightening the load of the beginner and encouraging him to persevere. Here the vivid power of his creative imagination and the freshness of his literary style are allied to his mastery of the spiritual tradition and medieval exegesis:

> You are to do all that in you lies to act as though you did not know that they are pressing very hard upon you ... Try to look over their shoulders as though you were looking for something else: the something else that is God ... I believe that when this device is well and truly understood, it is nothing else but a longing desire for God, to experience him and see him ... This desire is charity, and it always wins easement. (cf. ch. xxxii)

"To him that does all that in him lies, God does not refuse his grace," is a commonplace Augustinian aphorism, summarizing the interplay between grace and free will.[197] What wearies the psyche is the constant battling against distraction: trying to handle—to still—the incontrollable operation of the imaginative and intellectual faculties by one's own efforts. Instead, "let us fix our eyes on Jesus, the author and finisher of our faith, who for the joy that was set before him, endured the cross ... and you will not falter, you will not find your souls unmanned ... Take your standard from him. Thus we will be rid of the sinful habit that clings so closely."[198] If one truly believes that one belongs to those to whom God will reveal himself, then to come to him, bearing the burden of self, and realizing one's own powerlessness, with such a longing desire, will win easement.[199]

---

197. *Homini facienti quod in se est, Deus non denegat gratiam.*
198. Hebrews 10:1–3.
199. Cf. Matthew 11:25–30.

The second device also employs the image of the spiritual combat, but leans on the paradox that to lose is to win: "he that loses his life for my sake will find it" (Matt. 16:25). It is the acceptance of one's spiritual poverty, powerlessness, an exercise in the reduction of oneself to nothing, so as to experience the power of God's love; an ingenious pastiche of scriptural allusions and of passing references to the traditional *ludus amoris,* the love-play between the parent and the child: the father's constant looking out for his little one, whether it is lost in the woods (wild boars) or among the crowds at the medieval fair (bear-baiting). However, the experienced spiritual father is not in love with his own powers of direction. The novice must discover for himself the costly nature of the exercise. Its consummation is heavenly bliss, and the only way to it is through that purification which is the necessary prelude to resurrection. The higher part of the contemplative life—no matter how far we advance in it— will never find its perfection here: "there is no absolute security nor any true rest in this life." Again he picks up the language of the spiritual combat, fastening it to his exegesis of Hebrews (4:11ff). We attain to God's rest, holding fast to the faith we profess by wielding the sword of discretion: God's word which separates the evil from the good in every thought and impulse of our hearts (ch. xxxiii). It is God alone, then, who is the teacher and director in this school of contemplation; which is why we cannot, with any certainty, answer the questions "who" and "when." The grace is measured according to the God-given capacity for its reception; and those who are given the capacity, no matter what their previous spiritual history, will never lack the gift (ch. xxxiv). There is, perhaps, no more difficult chapter in the whole of the *Cloud.* The author is obsessed with the mystery of God's love, revealed in the word of Scripture and in the hearts of those who welcome that word. Hence the importance of humility in "the right feeling for this divine work." At the same time, he expresses his own feeling for the mystery with a tranquillity and lucidity which invites us to the same serenity of reflection:

> The capacity for this exercise is inseparably united to the exercise itself ... as long as you have a will for it and a desire for it, in so much you possess it, neither more nor less. Yet it is not a will nor a desire, but something which you are at a loss to describe, which moves you to desire you know not what. You must not care if you understand no more of it; just press on ... To put it more clearly, let it do with you and lead you as it will (ch. xxxiv).

It is clear, then, how important to the author is a right understanding of the word "unknowing." It has nothing in common with mere human ignorance. Knowledge, sacred learning, can be useful in the approach to it; but these are not necessary to it, and they can even be a positive hindrance to it, because the desire for knowledge and understanding tends to provide its own answers, and these almost inevitably lead to the pride "which blasphemes God in his gifts," and blinds us to the truth that all is divine gift, most of all the gift that shows us that knowledge of God is hidden in love. This is rooted in the manifestation of the Incarnate Word according to the aphorism of Athanasius: "God became man that man might become God."

It is typical of our author's self-assuredness that, immediately after stressing the impossibility of discovering out of one's learning or past experience any appropriate point of entry into the practice of the contemplative exercise which is the "work of this book"—"it is enough for you to feel moved in love by something, though you do not know what it is" (ch. xxxiv)—he should turn his attention to "certain preparatory exercises which should occupy the attention of the contemplative apprentice" (ch. xxxv–x1).

We have argued consistently, here and elsewhere, that when the author says in chapter xxxv, "you will find in another man's book a much better treatment of these three (i.e. reading, reflecting and praying) than I can manage," he is in all probability referring to the *Scala Claustralium,* or as the ME translation entitles it, "A Ladder of four rungs by means of which men may truly climb up to heaven."[200] What we do notice, as well as his first reference to the monastic distinction between the beginners, the proficients and the perfect in the contemplative state of life and his equiparation of reading and hearing,[201] is the emphasis given to the relationship between these first three degrees of the contemplative process: that profitable reflection demands reading in the traditional sense of *lectio divina,* and that "beginners or proficients will not come to true prayer without previous reflection." God's word so pondered will enable us to discern whether our spiritual blindness is due to any particular sin; and here the remedy will be sacramental confession. Otherwise any impulsive movement towards sinning will find healing in devoted prayer to the Father of mercy and all consolation (cf. 2 Cor. 1:2).

However, for those aspiring to the perfect following of Christ, meditation or thinking will take on a different meaning (ch. xxxvi). It is at a deeper level of consciousness, and, to use a later terminology, it is infused, rather than acquired by intellectual labour. It will normally be an intuitional experience, either of one's own sinfulness or of God's goodness. It is thus more akin to the definition of the contemplative prayer of petition, which he gives in chapter xxxix, than to meditation; though the apprentice will need the help of his spiritual director to reassure himself that the movement which

---

200. Cf. *Deonise hid Divinite,* H., pp. 100 ff. (The only other candidate is Walter Hilton's Latin letter to a priest, "*Epistola ad quemdam solitarium.*") It remains possible that the *Cloud* author's reference is to the ME version, still extant in three fifteenth-century manuscripts, made from a later recension of the *Scala,* and antedating the *Cloud.* Cf. *The Ladder,* pp. 39 ff. But no detailed philological study of this version has yet been made. Until this is done, we can only surmise that the addressee knew enough Latin to read it in the original.

201. Cf. ch. xxxv, notes 244–45 infra, p. 187.

he experiences within himself is directly from God. This is why he is not concerned to use the analogies of digestion and the hammering out of the metal by the hammer on the anvil to illustrate the function of thinking.[202] Indeed, the word is already masticated, or, as he has already indicated, the coal is already ignited and enabled to give off its sparks.[203] The scholastics, following St. Thomas, will speak of it as the *scintilla synderesis*, the self-authenticating judgment of the moral consciousness. But the Dionysians applied it equally to the affective consciousness of the Divine Presence in the "sovereign point of the spirit." Our author's intent here is that the addressee keep the fire burning brightly; and this can no longer be achieved by intellectual considerations on the words of Scripture. It is more than enough to be aware of oneself as an undefined lump of sin, standing in the presence of the God who contains in himself all goodness. This is the final simple movement from imperfect to perfect humility.

What holds the author's attention is the quality of the personal prayer acquired in the proximate preparation for this exercise (ch. xxxvii), which can scarcely be distinguished from contemplation properly so-called: "for a spiritual worker in this exercise should always find himself at the supreme and sovereign point of the spirit." Here he uses a most vivid and telling "example" from everyday life, in the manner of the medieval preacher: how a person threatened by imminent danger can gather all his human powers, faculties and feelings, and express them in a single cry, like, "Fire!" It stops people short in their tracks, gets them out of their beds and calls up every shred of natural compassion in their hearts, whether they are friend or foe (ch. xxxviii). How much more, then, will the divine compassion incite and respond to the *sursum corda* in the contemplative context, when one cries from the

---

202. Cf. *The Ladder*, pp. 84–85, and pp. 27 ff.
203. Cf. ch. iv: infra, p. 126. The analogy is a commonplace, and used by Hugh of St. Victor at least twice. Cf. *Homilia in Ecclesiasten* I, and *De Arca Noë Morali*, III, 7.

length and breadth and height and depth of the spirit, now at one with God's Spirit: that supereminent love of Christ which surpasses all knowledge (cf. Ephesians 3:19). So it is that pure prayer, as Cassian had insisted a thousand years earlier, will be very short. Augustine had compared it to the arrow shot from the bow, the *oratio iaculata*. It is the prayer characterized by Guigues du Pont as the grace-given aspiration of the devout contemplative, which, for a brief moment, enables him to comprehend the eternity, the power, the love and the wisdom of God. It is thus that God responds to the soul "which is so nearly conformed by grace to the image and likeness of God his maker."

The author thus combines his rhetorical skill with the spiritual exegesis which St. Bernard had spelt out in his letter to Pope Eugenius IV, on Consideration. The result is the interpretation of the traditional definition of contemplative petition—"the devout reaching out of the soul in order to attain the good and to do away with evil"—literally in words of one syllable (ch. xxxix). For "every evil is comprehended in the word *sin*," and "in the word *God* is contained all good." The very brevity of the words will help the apprentice to rivet his loving attention on that which his intellect cannot comprehend. Similarly, to use the aphorism of Gregory the Great, "love itself is a comprehensive knowledge."[204] He is careful to observe, however, that these short prayers will be so frequent as to approximate to the "praying without ceasing" (cf. Lk. 18:1). Again it was Cassian who had taught that Paul's exhortation to the Ephesians to pray at all times in the Spirit (6:18) means a perpetual response to the Father's indissoluble love for us.[205] "It must never end," says our author, "until what we long for is fully achieved."

In chapters xl–xlii, he anticipates a psychological difficulty

---

204. *Amor ipse notitia est.* Or, as William of St. Thierry will phrase it, *Cogitatio amantis fit amor contemplantis*—"the thinking of the one who loves becomes the love of the one who contemplates."

205. Cf. "Cassien," *DSp.*, art. cit., col. 265.

which may occur in the practice of such prayer, and also the question "how often is frequent?" As to the first, he alludes briefly to the advice given earlier (ch. vii) on the notorious tendency of the young solitary to a neurotic obsession with his past sins, the desire to classify them and the evil spirits traditionally supposed to occasion them. His own observation is simple and acute: "What does it matter to a contemplative what sin it is, or how great a sin?" For "during the time of this exercise he will feel that the smallest sin separates him from God and is an obstacle to his inward peace" (ch. xl). Recalling his earlier exposition on the contemplative virtues of humility and charity, he expects the reader to take it for granted that all virtues are found and experienced in the gift of God's own self; so that both will and understanding have the same object, in what John of the Cross will later call the prayer of loving attention.

As to the frequency of these short prayers, there is in fact no limit other than the psycho-physical frailties of human nature. And in so far as these are within our control—for example, avoiding exposing ourselves to sickness and other disorders of body and soul—it belongs to the contemplative to exercise discretion. "For the love of God, govern yourself wisely in body and soul, and keep in good health as much as possible" (ch. xli). This apart, he is insistent that patience in sickness and in various other tribulations is the authentic response to God's proffer of himself. At the same time (ch. xlii), he maintains that such prudence and patience will be more readily taught by the same God in his loving readiness to adapt himself to the individual temperament of those he calls to exercise themselves constantly in the contemplative search to attain the good and to do away with evil.

In what follows (chs. xliii–iv), the author appears to come to the Dionysian heart of the matter—the strict anti-intellectualism of negative or dark contemplation, the prayer which corresponds to the *via negativa*, the apophatic or mystical theology taught by the Areopagite: "Try to destroy all understanding and awareness of anything under God and tread everything down deep under the cloud of forgetting." It must first be noticed, however, that this is the immediate answer to the hortatory prayer at the end of chapter xlii: "May the good God help you, for now you have need!" In his initial description of the vocation of the solitary, he had made it clear that it does not of itself make a person holier or better; it is simply that "now you have to stand in desire, all your life long, if you are to make progress in the way of perfection."[206] Here then he addresses himself in detail to the teaching of Gregory, the "doctor of desire," on the two faces of compunction: the longing for the love of God for himself alone, and the self-forgetfulness, the mortification involved in the contemplative effort. And the conclusion of his initial argumentation is the starting point of his description of the self-loathing which is so often the psychological reaction of the young solitary:

> For the perfect lover's way is not only to love the thing that he loves more than himself; he must also, in a sense, hate himself for the sake of the thing that he loves (ch. xliii).

His teaching here is at bottom no different from that of Julian of Norwich, when she tells us how she was shown the "naked word, sin . . . an ugly sight." She immediately refers principally to Christ's passion, but goes on to speak of the incorporation of all his followers into him, with the result that we share and shall continue to share his sorrow and trouble, even unto death (cf. Matt. 26:38), until we are completely purified of our mortal flesh and of all those inward tendencies towards sin.[207] But *The Cloud* author has already spoken at length of the common teaching on recapitulation in chapter xxv. Here

206. Ch. ii, Cf. infra, p. 118.
207. Cf. *Showings*, ch. 27, p. 224.

he is more concerned with the individual contemplative, as is Gregory when he says:

> The mind overwhelmed with the awareness of its sinfulness, strikes itself with the sword of sorrow, or pierces itself to the heart with the lance of compunction so that it can do nothing but weep . . .[208]

"Pour forth into our hearts tears of compunction, so that we may bewail our sins . . ." So reads the ancient liturgical prayer for the gift of tears, which played so strong a part in the devotions of the Franciscan spirituality which dominated the life of the late medieval Church, but which, as our author will stress later, lays itself open, especially in the contemplative environment, to semi-Pelagianism and the excesses of the flagellants. So he stresses how grace and nature must come together for the reception of this gift of compunction:

> Without a very special grace which God gives out of his absolute bounty, and along with it a corresponding capacity for receiving the grace, this simple awareness and experience of your being (i.e., the 'lump of sin') can in no way be destroyed. This capacity is nothing else but a strong and profound spiritual sorrow (ch. xliv).

It is a sorrow, however, which is sustained by holy desires—an observation so frequently made by Gregory: for example, in the passage cited above from his homilies on Ezekiel: "but also from time to time it is lifted up to the contemplation of heavenly things, and its desire is tormented with a sweet weeping . . . and its fervour finds rest in tears."[209] Ultimately when compunction is understood in this way, it will be seen

---

208. *Homilia in Ezech.*, II, 2, 1.
209. Cf. Butler, pp. 71–75.

to be the unique means to union with God in perfect charity, "in so far as this union can be possessed in this life": the anagogical exegesis of the beatitude, "Blessed are they that mourn; they shall be comforted."

After this description of the contemplative effort proper to solitaries, with its passing reference to the need for discretion under the pressures of this sorrow, it is natural that the author should turn his attention to the various kinds of illusion which will afflict the beginner, and how they might be positively discerned in order to avoid them (chs. xlv–xlviii). He is reflecting now, at a deeper level, on the need for discretion, "the mother of all virtues," in the spiritual combat proper to the contemplative solitary, where everything happens in the sanctuary of the heart, where knowledge or ignorance of the truth, the love of virtue or its opposites will indicate who has the mastery, Christ or the devil.[210] The failure to recognise the healing needed by beginners in their fleshly nature, so that God's spirit may rule in them, leads to tepidity, that "languid weakness in body and soul, which tempts them," in their first failures to lift up their hearts to God, "to go out of themselves and to seek some false and empty sensible and physical comfort" (ch. xlv). More serious is that *elatio cordis* (the phrase is again Cassian's) which deceives the young disciple into mistaking sensible reactions and unnatural fervours for the felt experience of God's love; whereas it is the typical reflection of the devil's pride, the lie *par excellence*.[211] This is how the devil comes to have "his contemplatives, even as God has his." Experience seems to have taught our author that a certain excess of zeal in the novice results in a psycho-physical reaction which needs to be countered by a first freedom: this is none other than a flexibility of body and spirit which is a response to Christ's "Come, you who labour and are overburdened ... learn gentleness and meekness" (ch. xlvi). Without this gentle approach, there

---

210. Cf. Cassian, *Collationes*, 1, 13.
211. Cf. "Cassien," *DSp.*, art. cit., 240.

INTRODUCTION

will follow an avidity, due to the over-reaction of psycho-physical movement which effectively prevents the action of grace; or to a kind of spiritual gluttony which hungers after sensible consolation. One remedy recommended by the author, it would seem, to his "special friends in God" is to reverse the roles of the traditional *ludus amoris*: that is, to hide from God one's desire for him. Such a concealed revelation of one-self can have the psychological effect of "bringing you out of the ignorant state of sensible feeling into the purity and depth of spiritual feeling" (ch. xlvii). Such a reverential attitude will prepare the soul for that union of wills in which God's children are led by his Spirit (cf. Romans 8: 2–17). It is a device which can counter the tendency to create a God out of our own sensible or conceptual experience, as though he were simply a human being. In fine, it is an allusion to the Pauline teaching on spiritual maturity (cf. 2 Corinthians 5: 15–17). This is not to say that we should cease to regard ourselves, or indeed Jesus, as bodily persons (ch. xlviii). This would be to deny his word: "What God has joined together, let no one put asunder" (Matt. 19:6), a text which, according to the spiritual exegete, applies to the mystery of Christ's union with his Church (Ephesians 5:13), and to the great prayer in John's Gospel (John 17:21 ff). God's call to loving service is an invitation to the *rationabile obsequium* of the liturgy,[212] which for the author would be the earthly anticipation of the bliss of heaven. But this "pledge of future glory," as St. Thomas Aquinas calls it,[213] comes from within, rising and springing up out of the abundance of spiritual gladness and of true devotion in the Spirit. Any consolations from outside sources need the most careful discernment, since "the devil can disguise himself as an angel of light."

---

212. Cf. the prayer which precedes the consecration in the roman canon (the first Eucharistic prayer) . . . *"benedictam, ratam, rationabilem, acceptabilemque facere dig-neris."* The scriptural source is the Latin Vulgate of 1 Peter 2:5.

213. Cf. the antiphon to the *Magnificat*, on the feast of *Corpus Christi*.

INTRODUCTION

Chapters l–lxi deal with the discernment of the spiritual impulse—the exercise with which he is concerned throughout his book at progressively deeper levels. He proceeds first by stating the dangers attendant on them at each level, and the remedies to be applied to them. He introduces the section by describing the initial grace from which the authentic stirring arises (ch. xlix): the goodly will which, in its fulness, is independent of "all sweetnesses and consolations, sensible and spiritual." Rather they are the accidentals attaching to the substance. The perfection of it, which is described at such length and with great theological precision by Julian of Norwich,[214] our author calls chaste love (ch. 1). The concern is its connection with authentic consolation of the rarer sort: visions or locutions. As long as the person is indifferent to their presence or absence, the purity of love is not affected. In fact, some solitaries are never without them, a commonplace observation taken up by Cassian from his Eastern masters, Origen and Evagrius Ponticus.[215] The author makes the additional point, however, that the spiritual or bodily temperament of some souls is not strong enough to persevere to the ultimate point of passive mortification without these "great graces in spirit, sweet consolations and tears." But he will not presume to judge which kind of spirit, the strong or the weak, is holier or more pleasing to God. What is important (ch. li) is first to distinguish between sensible consolation and the whims and fancies of one's own making if one is naive enough, as some beginners apparently are, to interpret the dimensions of the Spirit (cf. Ephesians 3:14) in a physical way. There is, he says, an instant presumption to plunge into this exercise, born of a hidden desire of the flesh for the pleasantness of sense experience coupled with natural curiosity for the knowledge of hidden things, which takes it for granted that the soul may turn from humble prayer and penance—the advice received in sacramental confession. Thus the

214. Cf. the note to this chapter, 321, p. 215.
215. Cf. 'Cassien,' *DSp*, art. cit., 261–63.

seeds of an unnatural activity are sown by the devil, even though the intention of the beginner is "to think of nothing except God."

We are then offered a host of examples of this lunatic behaviour (chs. lii–liii), which are in reality manifestations of temptations to active vices as opposed to the sloth which is traditionally the seduction of the noonday devil (ch. lii). He is not so much concerned with the contravention of the traditional "rules of modesty" which govern the outward behaviour of religious novices—listed for example, by Hugh of St. Victor in his *De Institutione Novitiorum*. The point is the very dangerous temptations, hidden under such behaviours, to the obduracy and particularly the hypocrisy so vehemently condemned by Richard of St. Victor, because it is so redolent of the heretical behaviour of theological unorthodoxy and the moral laxity of thirteenth-century gnosticism (ch. liii). In fact, decorous and "courtly" general behaviour is an authentic outward sign of the inward grace of the true contemplative: the bearing traditionally associated, by St. Jerome, for example, with that of Christ himself. The exercise itself provides its own rules for discernment with regard to "every kind of natural behaviour and disposition" (ch. liv). Though the author's vocabulary here is that of the courtly love tradition, and his observations are based on the assumption that the truly spiritual man is wont to attract even the most hardened sinner, the substance of his teaching is scriptural, as the annotations to this chapter indicate.[216] Contrariwise, the false contemplative, even though his first intentions may have been good, imperceptibly tends towards pharisaical behaviour. Chapter lv, with its bizarre reference to the devil's appearance in human form, with only one nostril and the fire of hell for a brain, is evidence that the author is well acquainted with the Lives of the Fathers of the Desert and their many tales of positive combat between the solitary and devils in human form. It also indicates that he is not unaffected by the current

---

216. Ch. liv, notes 342–45: infra, p. 224.

INTRODUCTION

obsession with diabolic temptation. He does, however, state firmly that these are "illusions" (ch. lvi). Perhaps the modern equivalent of the term would be "hallucinations"; especially when he goes on to speak of those who are not deceived in this way, yet because of their pride and worldly cleverness "desert the common teaching and counsel of holy Church." His point again is the asceticism which is a *sine qua non* in the life of the solitary. Without it, one is quickly tempted to set one's own standards of worldly living. Thinking with the Church, as Ignatius Loyola was later to teach,[217] is integral to any true process of discernment: a point of view which the author underlines with his allusion to Matthew (7:13–15), "that he who does not wish to go by the narrow way to heaven, shall go the soft way to hell."

The exercise, it has been said, demanded the *sursum corda* necessary for truly spiritual communion. From the simple observation that there are those who interpret this "lift up your heart" in a bodily sense, the author first indicates that his cosmology is Copernican, and that there are those who, perhaps, like Mechtild of Hackborn,[218] "fashion a God according to their own fancy, dress him in rich clothes and set him on a throne" (ch. lvii). The attribution of the various hysterical phenomena attaching to false mysticism and "enthusiasm"[219] to the activity of evil spirits was common to the scholastic theologians, St. Thomas in particular,[220] as well as to the monastic tradition.[221] However, his principles for discerning the false from the true are consistently drawn from the spiritual exegesis of Scripture, as he anticipates the possible objection that the disciples saw Jesus ascending bodily up

---

217. Cf. *Spiritual Exercises*, 353 ff.

218. The ME translation of Mechtild's *Liber Specialis Gratiae* is contemporary with the *Cloud.* One of Mechtild's main themes is Jesus on his throne in the midst of her heart.

219. Cf. R. A. Knox, *Enthusiasm* (Oxford, 1950), *passim;* and Herbert Thurston, *The Physical Phenomena of Mysticism* (London, 1953).

220. Cf. *Summa Theologiae*, I, 51.

221. Cf. *Chastising*, pp. 55–56.

to heaven (Acts 1:9–11), and that St. Stephen "saw our Lord standing in the heavens" (Acts 7:55). In fact he goes on to use the example of Stephen along with the traditional story of St. Martin of Tours[222] in the following chapter (ch. lxviii) to instruct his reader as to the spiritual purpose and meaning of "revelations in bodily likeness." In summary, "we need know nothing of his (Christ's) sitting or lying down, but only this, that he is there present as pleases him, and he is so disposed in body as is most seemly for him to be."

Christ's ascension is a particularly apt example, since, the objection runs, "it took place bodily and for a bodily purpose as well as a spiritual one" (ch. lix). It serves to instruct us that before our bodies are refashioned according to the image of his glorified body (Philippians 3:21), we can only ascend spiritually. And the conclusion is that though "the exercise described in this book is called a movement," it is not "a local movement" of any kind, but rather "a sudden change." This is not to say that the words "upwards" and "downwards" used of Christ's ascension and of the coming of the Holy Spirit are inappropriate (ch. lxi). At the same time, the way to heaven is measured not in yards but in desires (ch. lx), as Scripture and the Fathers witness; so that though the body of Christ went "upwards in visible appearance" (ch. lxi), this merely indicates, in the unity of the persons of the Trinity, the subjection of the physical to the spiritual. And as far as human nature is concerned, the seemliness of the vocabulary is attested by Scripture—"God made man upright" (Ecclesiastes 7:29), to distinguish him from the beasts, because his soul is made in God's image and likeness.

The influence of Richard of St. Victor on *The Cloud* author is soundly established through the latter's paraphrased synopsis of *Benjamin Minor*, itself an introduction to the higher stages of contemplation treated by Richard in his *Benjamin Maior* and his *De Trinitate*. The synopsis, which the author entitles *A Study of Wisdom*, omits Richard's classification of

---

222. Ch. lxviii, note 368; infra, p. 232.

the soul's powers. He develops them here (chs. lxii–lxvi) to introduce the final section of his exposition of the contemplative exercise of the solitary, apparently because they help to explain the tension existing between the work of forgetting and the desire to find the point of rest in *The Cloud of Unknowing*. Though one extant MS, containing *The Cloud*, gives four of these five chapters separately, with the title "How the powers of man's soul are five in number,"[223] this is the only external evidence that it may have been written as a separate treatise, and then inserted at this point.[224] Though it is rather more didactic and more systematic in style than much of the rest of the book, such treatment suits the author's purpose at this particular juncture. He needs to explain more precisely these stages in the ascent to the sovereign point of the spirit for the contemplative solitary, and to indicate his preference for the form of Augustinian psychology stated simply by Richard: "bodily things are outside us, spiritual things within us, divine things above us."[225] For he has already stated the distinction in his first discussion of the two lives, in chapter viii, in an extremely terse and didactic fashion.[226] Now it is time for him to explain more fully what part the various powers of the soul play in the contemplative exercise, which must concern itself only with "the things that are above" (ch. lxvi). The implicit reference to Paul's teaching in Colossians (3:1–4) again provides him with the scriptural foundation: "seek the things that are above, where Christ is, seated at God's right hand. Set your minds on things that are above, not on things that are on the earth. For you have died, and your life is hid with Christ in God. When Christ

---

223. Cf. MS Cambridge University Library, MS Kk, vi. 26 (H., p. xiv).

224. Cf. *The Cloud*, H., p. xiv. In her introduction to *The Study of Wisdom*, in *Deonise hid Divinite*, pp. 43ff., she makes no reference to the chapters in her discussion either of style or content.

225. *Extra nos corporalia, intra nos spiritualia, supra nos divina. Benjamin Minor*, c. 55.

226. Infra, pp. 137–38. Justin McCann (ed. cit., p. 32) notes that Bonaventure in his *Itinerarium mentis in Deum*, ch. 5, employs the same distinction.

our life appears, you also will appear with him in glory."
An apt summary, for the medieval exegete, of the work of
this book, from start to finish: one according to which "the
nature and worthiness of your work is to be judged."

"Mind," the word used to translate Augustine's *memoria*,
is the *principale cordis*, "the head of the heart," which is so
specially graced in the pure prayer of Cassian,[227] and the
principale mentis of William of St. Thierry, the spiritual intelligence. This, for Thomas Gallus, as for our author, is the
apex affectus, the sovereign point of the spirit, which is intended
to govern, direct and comprehend the whole of man's spiritual
activity, "and all the objects on which these powers work"
(ch. lxiii). First is the reason, whose principal activity is discernment properly so-called: it separates out "the evil from
the good," positively, comparatively and superlatively (ch.
lxiv). Now it is ever engaged in the spiritual combat, because
after the fall man became blinded in his reason, so that he
can no longer appreciate everything at its true heavenly worth
without being strengthened by grace. Thus it affects the will's
power of choosing rightly. The reason is intrinsically linked
to the imaginative faculty (ch. lxv); and since the fall it has
greatly troubled the spirit by presenting the reason with inappropriate, distracting and even sinful fantasies and images.
It can be controlled only by the light of grace, "as it is in
continual meditation on spiritual things" in those recently
converted from the world to a "life of devotion." Most important to our author's purpose is his description of the secondary power called sensuality, in its relationship to the will
or affection (ch. lxvi). Here the author manifests that pessimism so noticeable in most followers of Augustine, though
it will be described with a refreshing optimism in the *Showings*
of Julian of Norwich, as she explains how the Incarnation
was, in fact, the Son's taking of our sensuality.[228] The author
continues to dwell on the "wretched state into which we

---

227. 'Cassien,' *DSp.*, art. cit., pp. 247, 262–63.
228. *Julian of Norwich: Showings*, Introduction, pp. 248ff.

are fallen because of original sin" in chapter lxvii. But it is very profitable for the solitary contemplative to know "the way in which these powers operate" if he is to strive by grace to reach the point whence he cannot come by nature: that is, "to be made one with God in spirit and in love and in oneness of wills." Though in his later letter on prayer to the same disciple, he will speak of "the marriage which is made between God and the soul," the full force of the Dionysian doctrine of deification was losing its impact in the nominalistic and classical theology of the later scholastics. It would be taken up later, for a brief spell in the sixteenth century, by John of the Cross; but the Christian soul's desire for that transforming union will always remain hidden like the child's secret, usually under the dry dust aroused by theological controversy, which is always striving unsuccessfully and often arrogantly to penetrate the union of the divine and human in the mystery of the Incarnate Word. This is perhaps why the author does not feel too happy with the emphasis given by so many to the immanentist teaching on introversion, with its tendency to symbolic overstatement (ch. lxviii). If there is a connection between the charge of anti-intellectualism and the desire to be rid of time-worn imagery, then it would seem that the author would be happy with the indictment, since nothing and nowhere bodily is to be preferred to "this everywhere and everything"—a spatial and therefore doubly deceptive image for the divine immensity. The wonder of it is that this experience of nothingness paradoxically and gradually effects a radical change in the spiritual character; and this is the reason why it is so difficult to persevere in the exercise: the pain experienced in the gradual movement to total detachment causes many beginners to relinquish the effort (ch. lxix). That Christ-like patience signalized from the beginning in the mystery of Gethsemane is truly the gift of the Holy Spirit, "the angel of the agony" (cf. Luke 22:43). And even when he becomes the angel of the resurrection—"he is risen, he is not here," the search in faith must continue. It is in the moment of his disappearance

INTRODUCTION

that we recognize him and "stand in desire for him" (cf. Luke 24:31–32).

So at length, in his last chapters (lxx–lxxv), the author takes up the Dionysian torch openly. It is better to turn one's back on the bodily senses and their physical objects, "since neither God nor spiritual things have any of their qualities and quantities" (ch. lxx); and the same is true of the spiritual powers when they strive to have God for their object. Even to imagine the effort involved in "trying to think of nothing at all," as Teresa of Avila somewhat disparagingly described it, is daunting enough. Yet there are some few souls who persevere in this toil until they experience him by that rarest of graces, "which," says the author, "is what is meant by rapture" (ch. lxxi). It is at this point that he borrows heavily from Richard of St. Victor's spiritual exegesis concerning the Ark of the Covenant (Exodus 24:15 ff.). And it has been his principle from the beginning that the marvellous miracle of God's love is in the way he adapts himself to individual needs and temperaments; so that it would be foolish to judge the experience of another in the light of one's own (ch. lxxii). Moses, Beseleel and Aaron, "the three men who were chiefly concerned with this Ark," are examples of how "we make progress in this grace of contemplation" (ch. lxxiii). The author expresses his willingness to take up the office of Beseleel, the maker of the Ark; whilst the addressee may take on the role of Aaron, and exercise himself continually in this grace for them both.

Finally, the author shows the spiritual freedom and flexibility which attaches to discretion by accepting the possibility that the exercise may not suit the temperament or the bodily health of every solitary. But he does expect his book to be studied diligently by those for whom he has written it (ch. lxxiv). Thus he repeats the *caveat* of his prologue word for word. And he concludes the book with brief remarks on the authentic signs that a person is being called to this way of dark contemplation, and the possibility that it can also be a temporary call, since the grace can be withdrawn for the traditional reasons.[229]

CONCLUSION

The purpose of this introductory essay has been to set the *Cloud*, its author, and its highly selective audience—those who were convinced that the God of the Christians was calling them to the extraordinary life of solitude—in the context of the late fourteenth-century Church. Some of the more important aspects of the religious life-style, and the various strands of the twelve hundred years or so of Christian tradition, in theory and in practice, began to disappear in the Europe of the early sixteenth century, especially in England, and lay dormant like the Sleeping Beauty for more than three hundred years. The time and environment of its rude (and sometimes crude) awakening was the second half of the nineteenth century: the age of Darwin, Freud and Marx, of Mendel and Marconi and Pasteur; the time of the Roman Catholic Church's "second spring" in England, with its bitter controversies in the ecclesiastical politics surrounding the first Vatican Council;[230] a time when new criteria of linguistic, literary and historical criticism were being formulated by European scholars of Protestant or wholly non-Christian persuasions, with a few Catholic voices crying in the wilderness. The views of these latter were effectively silenced for three decades by the Modernist crisis, in which the newly-discovered "mysticism" of the fourteenth century religion in England fell into official disrepute. By the time it began to creep back into favour in the early twenties, works like *The Cloud* still remained closed to all except a handful of Patristic and medieval scholars, whose first theological formation was the

---

229. Cf. ch. lxxv, notes 468 and 470; infra, p. 266.
230. Cf. J. D. Holmes, *More Roman than Rome*, (London, 1978), *passim*.

climate of what was fondly, or foolishly, called neo-Thomism. And most of these were inclined to categorize it as "anti-intellectual" at best, and at worst positively dangerous as propagating an argument for God's existence from religious experience: one which had been condemned, or was thought to have been so, at the Vatican Council in 1870.

Today we are living through a new wave of anti-intellectualism,[231] and, at the same time, a search for common ground, not only among Christians of all persuasions, but among all the great world religions. If there is one touchstone in this great quest, it is the common and substantial element which transcends all human varieties, religious experience itself.[232] Our consistent thesis in offering this new edition of *The Cloud* to a general public is that it could never have been written outside the Christian tradition of the Western Church, and that the author's erudition, common sense, love of Sacred Scripture and deep familiarity with the Christian contemplative process, familiarly known as *lectio divina*, reflect some of the best elements in that tradition.

Finally, if we are content to leave the word "mysticism" in the linguistic and a-cultural limbo into which modern usage has finally driven it, we may find ourselves, as we read *The Cloud*, in substantial agreement with what Dom Cuthbert Butler wrote of the "old authentic Western tradition" some sixty years ago:

> There are four elements in religion: the institutional element of Church, sacraments, and public worship;

---

231. For a useful general survey of the underlying problem, cf. Simon Tugwell, O. P., 'Intellectualism and Anti-Intellectualism,' in *The Way*, vol. 20 (October, 1980), pp. 253 ff.

232. It is doubtful whether, in William James' classic *Varieties of Religious Experience*, the word 'religious' can any longer be considered univocal. The valiant effort of the late Dom David Knowles to rescue the meaning of the word 'mysticism' by drastically restricting its use to the ultimate contemplative point by John of the Cross in *The Living Flame of Love* was the defence of a lost cause. Cf. his *What is Mysticism?* (London: 1967). Perhaps Rudolf Otto's *Idea of the Holy* may still provide a new approach acceptable to the majority.

the intellectual element of doctrine and dogma and theology; the mystical (sic!) element of will and emotion and personal religious experience; and the element of service of others. A fully developed, properly balanced, personal religious life must be the result of an harmonious blending of these four elements, not one of which may be neglected except at the cost of a one-sided, distorted, enfeebled type of religion.[233]

---

233. *Western Mysticism*, ed. cit., p. 22.

The Cloud Of Unknowing[1]

1. R. M. says that he has added the word "divine" *(divina)* to the title in his translation (f.1 c). He was therefore unaware, as was James Grenehalgh and William Darker of the Sheen scriptorium, or anyone else who annotated MS Pembroke 221, of the title of the MS Royal 17C xxvi, if the accepted dating of this MS is exact (H., p. xi).

PRAYER

*To you, O God, every heart stands open
and every will speaks; no secret is
hidden from you. I implore you so to
purify the intention of my heart with
the gift of your grace that I may love
you perfectly and praise you worthily.
Amen.*[2]

---

2. Of the MSS collated by H., only one indicates that this prayer is the *Oratio ad postulandam gratiam Spiritus Sancti.* Har[2] reads, instead of "your grace," "the holy Ghost" (H., p. 1). One would surmise that it was so well known in Carthusian Houses that adaptations like Methley's, for instance, would hardly be considered worth a comment.

PROLOGUE

*In the name of the Father and of the Son
and of the Holy Spirit. Amen.*

To you, whoever you are, who may have this book in
your possession, whether as owner or custodian, conveyor
or borrower: I lay this charge upon you and implore you
with all the power and force that the bond of charity can
command. You are not to read it yourself or to others, or
to copy it; nor are you to allow it so to be read in private
or in public or copied willingly and deliberately, insofar as
this is possible, except by someone or to someone who, as
far as you know, has resolved with steadfast determination,
truly and sincerely to be a perfect follower of Christ;[3] and
this not only in the active life,[4] but in the contemplative
life, at the highest point which a perfect soul in this present
life can possibly reach, with the help of grace,[5] whilst it still
dwells in this mortal body.[6] He will be one who is doing

---

3. It is clear that the author is speaking of one who has already made monastic
profession: the terminology is wholly redolent of the monastic *propositum*. Cf. G.
Lesage, "Sacred Bonds in the consecrated life," in *Supplement to The Way* 37 (Spring
1980): pp. 79. It follows too, at least by implication, that the author had made similar
profession (cf. Introduction, supra, p. 13).

4. He uses the term "active life" in the sense in which he is going to
define it in chapter 8: not simply of the corporal works of mercy, but of the virtues
described in his version of Richard of St. Victor's *Benjamin Minor*, and particularly
of the prayer proper to the lower stage of the contemplative life, which is also
the higher stage of the active life.

5. R. M., in his translation, writes in *supremo affectivo apice vitae contemplativae*,
Dionysian terminology used by Hugo de Balma and his immediate source, Thomas
Gallus.

6. As the *Regula Solitarium* of Grimlaic (c. 900) stresses, the distinction between the active and the contemplative is that between those leading the cenobitical
and the eremitical lives. The normal candidate for the latter will be the monk,
since the monastic life as such is the ascesis, the purification necessary for the
contemplative life. Hence it was recognized that the Carthusian was an order never

all that he can, and has been, presumably, for a long time past, to fit himself for the contemplative life by the virtues and exercises of the active life. Otherwise this book is not for him.[7]

I lay a further charge on you, and ask it of you with the authority of charity. If any such people do read it to themselves or to others, or copy it, or else hear it read in private or in public, you must bid them as I do you, to take time to read it in private or out loud, to copy it or listen to it, right through. For it may happen that there is something there, in the beginning or in the middle, which depends on what follows and is not fully explained in that place.[8] If so, it will be explained a little later on, or else by the end. Thus if a man looks at one part and not another, he could quite easily be led into error. It is to avoid such errors, both for yourself and for anyone else, that I beg you of your charity to do as I say.

As for the worldly chatterboxes, who brazenly flatter or censure themselves or others, the rumour-mongers, the gossips, the tittle-tattlers and the fault-finders of every sort, I would not want them ever to see this book. It was never my intention to write on these matters for them. I would refuse to have them interfering with it, those clever clerics, or layfolk either. For no matter how excellent they may be in matters pertaining to the active life, my subject is not for them. We must make

---

in need of reform. The further from the world, the nearer to God: the eye of the hermit is on the future realities—*quo pervenire desiderat*. The text of his rule is printed in P.L. 103, 575–663. Cf. also P. Doyère, "Erémitisme," in *DSp*. fascs. xxxiii-ix.

7. Confer the similar warning in the author's version of Denis's *Mystical Theology*, chap. 1: "Take care that none of those who are unwise, who still dwell in their natural minds, hear of these things." His translation of this work may have been intended as an apologia. He certainly emphasizes the point in both his *Letter on Prayer* and *Private Direction* ("Privy Counsel").

8. The author appears to be aware of his diffuse style, and his readiness to digress. In fact, twenty-five out of seventy-five chapters may be considered as *prima facie* digressions—hints on how to cope with the difficulties and dangers arising from undertaking this contemplative exercise: sc., chaps. 10, 11, 15, 18–20, 22, 23, 30, 45, 52–66.

an exception for those whose exterior state belongs to the active life; and yet, because they are inwardly moved through the hidden Spirit of God, whose decisions none can read, they are enabled by an abundance of grace to share in the work of contemplation at the highest level; not of course continually, as is proper to true contemplatives, but every now and then.[9] If men like these read this book, it should by God's grace be a great source of strength for them.

The book is divided into seventy-five chapters; and the very last sets out particular indications by which a person can find out by experience whether or not he is called by God to exercise himself in this work of contemplation.

9. The translator of MS Bodleian 856 adds here: "... unless the working of the Holy Spirit produces in them such a firm and sound purpose of amendment that they determine to live contemplatively, to be converted and entirely changed in soul and body. When this happens, everyone ought to recognize that man's deepest malice cannot stand against the goodness and grace of the Holy Spirit" (f. 14a).

TABLE OF CONTENTS

LV. To condemn sin without discrimination through excessive fervour is erroneous. [226]

LVI. To pay more attention to intellectual acumen or to speculative theologians than to the ordinary teaching and counsel of holy Church is erroneous. [228]

LVII. Young disciples in their presumption misunderstand this other word "up," and the illusions which follow from this. [230]

LVIII. Saint Martin and Saint Stephen are not to be taken as examples of straining upwards in our sensible imagination during the time of prayer. [232]

LIX. The bodily ascension of Christ is not to be taken as an example of straining upwards in our sensible imagination in time of prayer. Time, place and the body are all three to be forgotten during this spiritual exercise. [236]

LX. The high road and the nearest way to heaven is measured not by yards but by desires. [238]

LXI. All bodily things are subject to spiritual things; it is in the order of nature that they follow the rule of the spiritual, and not vice versa. [239]

LXII. How a man can know when his spiritual activity concerns what is beneath him or outside himself, when it is within him and on a par with himself, and when it is above him and under his God. [241]

LXXI.   Some may experience the perfection of this exercise only during rapture, but some can experience it whenever they will, in their normal conscious state. [*257*]

LXXII. He who habitually practises this exercise must not take it for granted that other workers have his precise experience. [*259*]

LXXIII. This grace of contemplation is prefigured in the Ark of the Covenant: in the sense that Moses, Beseleel and Aaron, in their dealings with the Ark, are three types of how we exercise ourselves in this grace. [*260*]

LXXIV. A man is rightly disposed to the contemplation which is the subject matter of this book when he cannot read or speak about it, or hear it read or spoken about, without feeling that he is really suited to this work and its effects. A repetition of the directions given in the prologue. [*262*]

LXXV.   Of definite signs whereby a man may test whether or not one is called by God to take up this exercise. [*263*]

CHAPTER I

*The four degrees of the Christian life; and how he
for whom this book was written advanced in his vocation.*[10]

Proemium

My spiritual friend in God:[11] I pray and beseech you
to pay very close attention to the progress of your vocation
and the way in which you have been called; thank God from
your heart, so that through the help of his grace you may
stand steadfast in the state, degree and manner of life that
you have undertaken with full deliberation in spite of all
the subtle attacks of your bodily and ghostly enemies,[12] and
so win through to the crown of life[13] that lasts forever, Amen.

My spiritual friend in God, you are to understand that
according to our rather crude reckoning, there are four degrees
and forms of the Christian life. They are: ordinary, special,

---

10. In repeating the chapter headings, we are following R. M., who says:
"Though the author of the book does not set out the various titles at the head
of each chapter throughout the book, but only at the beginning, it seems better
to me, all things considered, not only to put them all together at the beginning,
but one by one at the head of each chapter."

11. Like three other works which can be attributed with certainty to our
author, the *Cloud* itself is couched in the form of a letter to a young beginner
from an older monk or spiritual father. (We have referred to the Carthusian practice
in this regard in the Introduction, p. 40). However, it must also be noticed that
many writers in this genre, with varying degrees of awareness, were simply per-
petuating the tradition and adopting the style of the first apostolic writers, beginning
with SS. Luke and Paul, on the understanding that their writings would be passed
from hand to hand, and read aloud in quasi-ecclesiastical gatherings: in this case,
monastic refectories or chapter halls. An outstanding example is the letter on the
contemplative life by the Carthusian Guigo the Angelic, whose epistolary introduction
is omitted in literally scores of extant MSS. Cf. *The Ladder of Monks*, p. 81; Introduction,
supra, p. 78.

12. Cf. Ephesians 6:10ff.

13. The reference to James 1:12 is taken up at length by the author in his
letter on *Discernment of Spiritual Impulses*.

singular and perfect. Three of these can be begun and ended in this life; and one may begin the fourth by grace here below, which is to last without end in the happiness of heaven. These degrees are set out here in order, successively, first ordinary then special, after that singular and finally perfect.[14] It is in this same way, I think, according to this very order and progress, that our Lord has, in his great mercy, called you and led you to him by the desire of your heart.

First, then, you are well aware that once you lived in the ordinary degree of the Christian life in the world with your friends. And I believe that the everlasting love of the Godhead through which he made you and fashioned you when you were nothing, and then bought you at the price of his precious blood when, in Adam, you were lost, would not allow you to be so far away from him in the manner and state of your living.[15] And so with his great grace he kindled your desire, and fastened to it a leash of longing,[16] and with this led you into a more special state and degree of life, to be a servant of the special servants of his;[17] where you could

14. "The ordinary degree is of laypeople, the special of clerics or religious, and the singular of solitaries: that is, hermits, anchorites and especially Carthusians. Hence we may conclude that this book was written for a Carthusian, since in our day it is not customary, as it was in days gone by, to leave an approved religious order for a hermitage, but only for the Carthusians" (R.M.). Cf. Introduction, p. 15. The commentator on MS. Harleian 674 gives the example of Christ himself, who "whilst he was subject to his parents, was in the ordinary degree; whilst he was about his business, in the special; whilst fasting in the desert and praying on the mountain, in the singular; and in the transfiguration, resurrection and ascension, in the perfect".

15. Cf. *The Ladder:* "When you were nothing I created you, and after you had sinned and made yourself a slave who once were free, then I redeemed you out of slavery with the price of myself. Then afterwards you hunted with the sinners of this world, and I caught you back from them, and I gave more of my grace to you than to others, because I wanted you to be my own" (ME version).

16. "A leash of longing." This is one of the more outstanding examples of the author's ability to drive home an essential theological point: the reconciliation of "you have not chosen me, but I have chosen you," and human freedom, with a vivid and self-clarifying metaphor.

17. Hugo de Balma, in speaking of the steps to union, stresses the importance of reflecting on the benefits the disciple has received: first, of creation and of re-

learn to live in his service more particularly and more spiritually than you did before or could do in the ordinary way of life. What is more, it appeared that he was not going to leave you alone so easily, because of the love in his heart which he has always had for you since you first existed. What is it that he did? Do you not see with what love and with what grace he has called you up to the third degree and manner of life, which is called singular? And in this state and manner of life of the solitary you are to learn to lift up the foot of your love,[18] and step outwards towards that state and degree of life that is perfect, the last state of all.

CHAPTER II

A short exhortation to humility and to the exercise described in this book.

Look up now, feeble creature, and see what you are. What are you, and how have you deserved to be called by our Lord? A weary and wretched heart, indeed, is one fast asleep in sloth,[19] which is not awakened by the drawing power of his love[20] and the voice of his calling! It is time, too, wretched

---

demption by the Incarnation and the Passion; and secondly of the grace of the Carthusian vocation, which is not merely a call out of the world, "because he has called him (the disciple) not to the rule of the holy Benedict or Augustine ... but has chosen him for that most blessed life which he himself chose when he was led into the desert. He was our forerunner, showing what it means to be a servant, by serving us".

18. The source of this image is Augustine's commentary on Psalm 9: "Rightly understood, the foot of the soul is love; for it moves by means of love to the place it is going" (PL 36, 124). De Balma speaks of the "plateau of unitive love towards which the mind hastens, supported by the feet of the affections".

19. On Sloth, cf. Siegfried Wenzel, *The Sin of Sloth: Acedia in Medieval Thought and Literature* (Chapel Hill: University of North Carolina Press, 1967).

20. One of staple themes of medieval contemplative exegesis, especially as inspired by Bernard of Clairvaux. Cf. P. Dumontier, *S. Bernard et la Bible, passim,* esp. pp. 39ff.

man,[21] to have a care of your enemy. Do not consider yourself holier or better simply because of the value of this vocation, and because of the singular state of life in which you find yourself. You are to consider yourself even more wretched and accursed, unless by grace and by direction you do all that in you lies, to live according to your calling. You are to be as meek and as loving to your spiritual spouse, that is, to almighty God, the King of Kings and Lord of Lords, as he is himself. For it was his desire to humble himself, so as to be on a level with you, and out of the whole flock of his sheep, it was his will graciously to choose you to be one of his special disciples. And then he brought you into this place of pasture, where you may be fed with the sweetness of his love; all this is a pledge of your heritage, the kingdom of heaven.[22]

Press on then with speed, I pray you. Look ahead now and never mind what is behind;[23] see what you still need, and not what you have; for this is how meekness is most quickly won and defended. Now you have to stand in desire, all your lifelong,[24] if you are to make progress in the way of perfection. This desire must always be at work in your will, by the power of almighty God and by your own consent. One point I must emphasize: He is a jealous lover and allows no other partnership, and he has no wish to work in your

---

21. It is worth recalling that the repetition of words like "wretched" is in no way an indication of a limited vocabulary. This sentence, for instance, is rhythmic alliterative prose. Literally: "Beware now wretch, in this while/with thine enemy."

22. For the medieval exegete this paragraph is a pastiche of scriptural allusions, all stressing the following of Christ: here, for example, we have references to the Canticle of Canticles 1:6, 2:16; Philippians 2:6–8; Ezechiel 34; I Timothy 6:15; Psalm 22; Romans 13:11, etc. Cf. Introduction, pp. 54-55.

23. The allusion is to Philippians 3:13: "Forgetting what lies behind and reaching out for what lies ahead, I press on towards the goal."

24. The phrase is an example of the rhetorical figure *inclusio* with the last sentence of the book, 'the whole life of good Christian men is nothing else but holy desires': a citation from Augustine. Cf. infra, p. 266.

will unless he is there alone with you, by himself.[25] He asks
no help, but only you yourself. His will is that you should
simply gaze at him, and leave him to act alone. Your part
is to keep the windows and the door against the inroads of
flies and enemies.[26] And if you are willing to do this, all
that is required of you is to woo him humbly in prayer,
and at once he will help you. Call upon him then, and let
us see how you get on. He is always most willing, and is
only waiting for you.[27] So what are you going to do? How
will you move him?

CHAPTER III

*How this exercise is to be made; how it is worth
more than all other exercises.*

Lift up your heart to God[28] with a humble impulse of
love; and have himself as your aim, not any of his goods.
Take care that you avoid thinking of anything but himself,
so that there is nothing for your reason or your will to work

---

25. The idea of God as the jealous lover may derive in the West from the
Pseudo-Denis: "Those strong in divine things [i.e., the contemplatives] call him the
jealous one." Cf. *Divine Names*, chap. 4. Cf. also *The Ladder:* "This is a jealous spouse.
He will leave you at once ... if you play him false with anyone ... he will at
once turn away from you" (pp. 91–92). R. M. comments: "No-one can love God
unless he is mentally alone, and also, when possible, a solitary *(corpore solitarius)*
as well." This is certainly to be the attitude of the professed contemplative. Cf.
Introduction, p. 53.

26. A traditional metaphor for the five senses, by means of which idle reverie
or noxious sensations lead to evil thoughts and desires. So Augustine and Gregory
comment on Jeremiah 9:21 (Vulgate): "Death is come up through our windows"—
the 'moral' sense. Cf. Introduction, p. 68.

27. Cf. Matthew 11:28.

28. This is clearly a reminiscence of the *Sursum corda*, at the beginning of
the preface to the Eucharistic prayer: "Lift up your hearts/we lift them to the
Lord." The author deals at length with the contemplative implications of "Lift up"
in chaps. 58ff.

on, except himself. Do all that in you lies to forget all the creatures that God ever made, and their works, so that neither your thought nor your desire be directed or extended[29] to any of them, neither in general nor in particular. Let them alone and pay no attention to them. This is the work of the soul that pleases God most.[30] All saints and angels take joy in this exercise, and are anxious to help it on with all their might.[31] All the devils are furious when you undertake it, and make it their business, insofar as they can, to destroy it. We cannot know how wonderfully all people dwelling on earth are helped by this exercise. Yes, and the souls in purgatory are eased of their pain, and you yourself are purified and made virtuous, much more by this work than by any other.[32] Yet it is the easiest exercise of all and most readily accomplished when a soul is helped by grace in this felt desire; otherwise, it would be extraordinarily difficult for you to make this exercise. Do not hang back then, but labour in it until you experience the desire. For when you first begin to undertake it, all that you find is a darkness, a sort of cloud of unknowing; you cannot tell what it is, except that you experience in your will a simple reaching out to God.[33] This darkness and cloud is always between you and your

---

29. "Extended" (ME "streche") is perhaps the most typical word used by the Dionysian school to describe the contemplative effort.

30. This first part of the exercise is illustrated, for the medieval exegete, in Psalm 44:11–12: "... forget thy people and thy father's house. And the king shall greatly desire thy beauty: for he is the Lord thy God."

31. Hilton also teaches that contemplative progress is achieved through the "great fellowship" of the angels: "They are full tender and full busy about such a soul to help it" (Scale II, 46: Underhill, pp. 460ff).

32. De Balma, in a similar passage, says that through the work of this contemplative wisdom the soul is graciously disposed to those rejoicing in glory, that prayers are multiplied for the rescuing of lost souls so that those who are dead in sin may be raised up by the life of divine grace. It is this wisdom that disposes the soul to govern its body with respect to worldly things, and the virtues achieve sovereignty.

33. The ME for this often repeated phrase is "a nakid entent unto God" (H., 17/2).

God, no matter what you do, and it prevents you from seeing him clearly by the light of understanding in your reason, and from experiencing him in sweetness of love in your affection. So set yourself to rest in this darkness as long as you can, always crying out after him whom you love.[34] For if you are to experience him or to see him at all, insofar as it is possible here, it must always be in this cloud and in this darkness. So if you labour at it with all your attention as I bid you, I trust, in his mercy, that you will reach this point.

CHAPTER IV

The brief nature of this exercise; it cannot be attained by intellectual study or through the imaginative faculty.

To prevent you from making mistakes in this exercise, and from thinking that it is other than it actually is, I am going to tell you a little more about it, as I believe it to be. It is an exercise that does not need a long time before it can be truly done, as some men seem to think; for it is the shortest possible of all exercises that men can imagine.[35] It is neither longer nor shorter than an atom. The atom, if we follow the definition of good philosophers in the science of astronomy, is the smallest particle of time.[36] It is so little

---

34. "So the soul, seeing that it cannot attain by itself to that sweetness of knowing and feeling for which it longs . . . betakes itself to prayer" (*Ladder* p. 86).

35. This exercise can be made "as often as the soul wishes, day or night, a hundred or a thousand times, as long as the body can stand it" (De Balma). In a more modern context, the late Father Willie Doyle, S.J., kept careful note of his daily aspirations, which reached astronomical proportions. Cf. Alfred O'Rahilly, *Fr William Doyle S.J.* (London, 1931), pp. 114ff.

36. According to medieval reckoning there are 22,560 atoms in an hour. Cf. C. Du Cange, *Glossarium mediae et infimae Latinitatis*, tom 1, p. 462.

that, because of its littleness, it is indivisible and almost un-perceivable.[37] It is the time of which it is written: "All time is given to you, it shall be asked of you how you have spent it."[38] And it is right that you should give account of it, for it is neither longer nor shorter but exactly equal to each single stirring that is in the chief working power of your soul, that is, your will. For as many choices and desires, no more and no less, as there can be and are in your will in one hour, so are there atoms in an hour. If you were reformed by grace according to the primal state of man's soul as it was before sin,[39] you would always, by the help of that grace, be in control of that impulse or of those impulses. None of them would go unheeded, but all would reach out to the preeminent and supreme object of your will and your desire, which is God himself.[40]

He fits himself exactly to our souls by adapting his God-head to them; and our souls are fitted exactly to him by the worthiness of our creation after his image and his like-ness.[41] He, by himself alone, and no one but he, is fully sufficient, and much more so, to fulfil the will and the desire of our souls. And our soul, because of his reforming grace,

---

37. Julian of Norwich speaks in similar vein of the "littleness" of all creation (*Showings*, p. 183).

38. "What shall your answer be on that day when there shall be asked of you an account of all the time of your living, how you have spent it, even to the twinkling of an eye" (S. Anselm, Meditations, 2 [PL 158, 723]). Richard Rolle in *The Form of Perfect Living* makes the same point. Cf. H., 17/20.

39. The burden of Hilton's *Scale of Perfection, II*, is the reformation of the soul to its pristine likeness to God, in faith and in "feeling." The latter refers to the highest state to which the contemplative is called in this life.

40. The underlying scriptural reference here is Ephesians 3:19–20. The author is making the point that through the divine condescension, of which the mystery of the Incarnation is the proof, it is possible for the individual to direct all his impulses to him who is preeminently desirable.

41. "So great is the power of the true love of the good and the beautiful that not only does it lead men and angels to outstrip their natural powers so that they can ascend to God, but it causes God to leave behind as it were his own nature, and to descend below it to the creature" (Gallus, Explanation on the *Divine Names*, chap. 7).

is wholly enabled to comprehend by love the whole of him who is incomprehensible to every created knowing power: that is, to the souls of angels and of men. I speak of their knowing and not of their loving; that is why I call their souls in this case knowing powers.

Now all rational creatures, angels and men alike, have in them, each one individually, one chief working power, which is called a knowing power, and another chief working power called a loving power; and of these two powers, God, who is the maker of them, is always incomprehensible to the first, the knowing power.[42] But to the second, which is the loving power, he is entirely comprehensible in each one individually; in so much that one loving soul of itself, because of love, would be able to comprehend him who is entirely sufficient, and much more so, without limit, to fill all the souls of men and angels that could ever exist.[43] This is the everlastingly wonderful miracle of love, which shall never have an end. For he shall ever work it and shall never cease to do so. Let him understand it who can do so by grace; for the experience of this is endless happiness, and its contrary is endless suffering.[44]

If a man were so reformed by grace as to have constant control of the impulses of the will, he would never be without some taste of that everlasting sweetness in this life,[45] or with-

---

42. "There is a double kind of apprehension according to the twofold natural power of reaching out to God: every soul has the power of understanding and the power of loving which is called the affection" (De Balma).

43. "We are convinced that the affection is ineffably more profoundly and more sublimely drawn to God by God himself than is the intellect, because men and angels love more than they have the power to reason or understand. For it seems a little thing to the faithful soul—even of a mortal man—to enclose in his affection all men and angels, even were they as numerous as the grains of sand on the sea-shore. And what is there in God that is not loved by the affection? It is as if the whole of him is clasped by the affection and rejected by the understanding" (Gallus, *Commentary on Isaiah 6:1-4*, loc. cit., f.107d).

44. That is, the comprehension of God in love is everlasting bliss; its absence is the "pain of loss," which is everlasting suffering.

45. "Taste" is the image used in medieval Western spirituality to convey this loving comprehension of God in contemplation. Cf. Psalm 33:9 and 1 Peter

out the full food in the happiness of heaven:[46] It is his nature never to be without these impulses. So do not be surprised if I am urging you to this work. This is the exercise, as you shall hear later on, in which man would have persevered if he had never sinned. Man was made for this working, and all other things for his sake, to help him and speed him on to it.[47] By this exercise he is to be restored; and for want of it, he falls deeper and deeper into sin and further and further from God. By perseverance and continual working in this exercise alone, without anything else, a man continues to rise higher and higher away from sin, and nearer and nearer to God.

So take good care of time, therefore, and how you spend it. Nothing is more precious than time. In one small particle of time, little as it is, heaven can be won and lost. This is a sign that time is precious: God, who is the giver of time, never gives two particles of time together, but one after the other. This is because he refuses to reverse the order and the regular chain of causes in his creation. Time is made for man, not man for time.[48] Therefore God, who is the ruler of nature, in giving time refuses to anticipate the natural impulse in a man's soul, which is exactly equal to one particle of time. So it is that man will have no excuse before God at the judgement and at the giving of the account of spending of time; he will not be able to say: "you gave two times at once and I have only one impulse at once."

Now I hear you say sorrowfully: "How shall I fare? Since what you say is true, how shall I give an account of each particle of time separately: I who am now twenty-four years

---

2:3. For similar language, see *Showings*, p. 255. On the spiritual senses in general, see Walsh, J., "Guillaume de St-Thierry et lessens spirituels," in *RAM* 137 (1959), pp. 28-42.

46. The scriptural allusion is Wisdom 16:20 "... the food of angels ... bread from heaven ... having in it all that is delicious, and the sweetness of every taste."

47. Cf. Genesis 1:28–30.

48. Cf. Mark 2:27.

of age and never up to this day did I take heed of time?[49] If I am to make amends now, as you well know because of what you have just written, this cannot be in any natural way or through any ordinary grace, that I should be able to control, or make satisfaction for, any more particles of time than for those that are yet to come. Yes, and more than that. I am well aware, by experience, that of the times that are to come I shall no more be able to have control of one out of a hundred because of my great frailty and spiritual slowness. My reasoning is irrefutable. Help me now for the love of Jesus."

This, "for the love of Jesus," is very well said. For there in the love of Jesus is your help. Love is so powerful that it makes everything ordinary. So love Jesus, and everything that he has is yours.[50] By his Godhead he is the maker and giver of time. By his manhood he is truly the keeper of time. And by his Godhead and manhood together he is the truest judge and accountant of the spending of time. Knit yourself, then, to him by love and by faith. And in virtue of that knot you shall be a regular partner with him and with all who are so well fastened to him by love: that is, with our Lady, Saint Mary, who was full of all grace in the keeping of time,[51] and with all the angels of heaven that can never lose time,[52] and with all the saints in heaven and on earth, who by the grace of Jesus keep time in perfect justice because of love.[53]

---

49. R. M. was twenty-six when he entered the Carthusian Priory of Mount Grace.

50. Cf. Luke 15:31.

51. Cf. Luke 1:28.

52. According to scholastic teaching, there is no time without motion and magnitude. Thus, though only God dwells in eternity, pure spirits cannot be subjected to time. They do however have a beginning, though not an end. The term *aevum* was used to denote this "middle" between eternity and time.

53. By the love of Jesus, says our author, we enter the communion of saints; and Julian of Norwich writes: "For his precious love, he never allows us to lose time" (*Showings*, p. 302).

THE CLOUD OF UNKNOWING

Look and see what comfort there is here. Understand it as a theologian would,[54] and get profit from it. But one warning I give you above all others: I cannot see who may truly claim this fellowship with Jesus and his holy mother, his high angels and also with his saints, unless he be such a man that does all that in him lies with the help of grace to value time; so that he may be seen to be one who makes a profit on his part, little as this is, for the whole fellowship, as each of the others does on theirs.

Pay careful heed, then, to this exercise, and to the wonderful way in which it works within your soul. For when rightly understood, it is nothing else than a sudden impulse, one that comes without warning, speedily flying up to God as the spark flies up from the burning coal.[55] Marvellous also are the number of such impulses that can take place in one hour in a soul that is properly disposed for the exercise. Yet in one stirring out of all these, a man can suddenly and perfectly have forgotten every created thing. And equally quickly, after each impulse, because of the corruption of the flesh, the soul falls down again to some thought or some deed done or undone. But what matter? For straightaway it rises again as suddenly as it did before.

In this, then, one can quickly understand the way of this working, and realise clearly that it is far removed from any fancy or false imagination or subtle opinion;[56] for all these are brought about not by that devout and humble, simple, impulse of love, but by a proud, speculative and over-imaginative reasoning. These proud and elaborate speculations

---

54. The scholastic nature of this discussion on time makes the reading "klerk-ly"—like a theologian—much more likely than "clearly." Cf. H., 21/21 *(apparatus)*.

55. For the use of this simile of the spark by all the Dionysians, and particularly by those with whom our author seems to have been acquainted, cf. Introduction, supra, p. 80.

56. Cf. Walsh, J., *The Ascent to Contemplative Wisdom*, p. 245.

must always be pushed down and heavily trodden under foot,[57] if this exercise is to be truly understood in purity of spirit.

Whoever hears this exercise read or spoken of may think that he can or ought to achieve it by intellectual labour; and so he sits and racks his brains how it can be achieved, and with such ingenious reasonings he does violence to his imagination, perhaps beyond its natural ability, so as to fashion a false way of working which fits neither body nor soul. Truly such a man, whoever he be, is perilously deluded; and so much so that unless God in his great goodness show him his wondrous mercy, and quickly lead him away from his imaginings, to put himself meekly under direction of those experienced in the exercise, he shall be overcome by frenzies or else fall into other great mischief, spiritual sins and the devil's deceits;[58] and through these he may easily be robbed of body and soul for all eternity. So for the love of God, take care in this exercise and do not labour with your senses or with your imagination in any way at all. For I tell you truly, this exercise cannot be achieved by their labour; so leave them and do not work with them.

Now when I call this exercise a darkness or a cloud, do not think that it is a cloud formed out of the vapours which float in the air, or a darkness such as you have in your house at night, when your candle is out. For such a darkness or such a cloud you can certainly imagine by subtle fancies, as though it were before your eyes, even on the clearest day of summer; and likewise, on the darkest night of winter, you can imagine a clear shining light. But leave such falsehood

---

57. This is the *forti contricione* of the Latin version of *Denis's Hidden Theology*. Cf. Introduction, supra, p. 58.

58. Again the author's language is very reminiscent of de Balma, who writes a little more soberly: "This wisdom penetrates the mind only by means of the loving union—the mind of one overshadowed by the supremely inaccessible. . . . It is quite another thing with the human philosophers who, inflated by the arrogance of their pride, disdained to attribute to the fount of all knowledge whatever they could grasp with their own understanding."

alone. I mean nothing of that sort. When I say "darkness," I mean a privation of knowing, just as whatever you do not know or have forgotten is dark to you, because you do not see it with your spiritual eyes. For this reason, that which is between you and your God is termed, not a cloud of the air, but a cloud of unknowing.[59]

CHAPTER V

During this exercise, all creatures and all the works of creatures, past, present or future, must be hidden in the cloud of forgetting.

If ever you come to this cloud, and live and work in it as I bid you, just as this cloud of unknowing is above you, between you and your God, in the same way you must put beneath you a cloud of forgetting, between you and all the creatures that have ever been made.[60] It seems to you, perhaps, that you are very far from him, because this cloud of unknowing is between you and your God. However, if you give it proper thought, you are certainly much further away from him when you do not have the cloud of forgetting between you and all the creatures that have ever been made. Whenever I say "all the creatures that have ever been made," I mean not only the creatures themselves, but also all their works and circumstances. I make no exceptions, whether they are bodily creatures or spiritual, nor for the state or activity of any creature, whether these be good or evil. In short, I say that all should be hid under the cloud of forgetting.[61]

---

59. The teaching of this last paragraph is expanded below in chapters 51–61, infra, pp. 218ff.

60. "To enter the Cloud of Unknowing is to rise above mind, and by means of the cloud of forgetfulness, to hide from the mind the awareness of whatever lies at hand" (Richard of St. Victor, *Benjamin major*, V, 2).

61. Creatures reveal God to us indirectly, insofar as they are limited reflections of his goodness and love. But they cannot reveal him or lead us to him directly,

For though it is very profitable on some occasions to think of the state and activities of certain creatures in particular, nevertheless in this exercise it profits little or nothing.[62] Being mindful or thinking of any creature that God ever made, or of any of their works either, is a sort of spiritual light.[63] The eye of your soul is opened on it and fixed upon it, like the eye of the bowman upon the eye of the target that he is shooting at.[64] I have one thing to say to you: Everything that you think of is above you during this time, and between you and your God. Insofar as there is anything in your mind except God alone, in that far you are further from God.[65]

Yes, and if one may say it courteously and fittingly, in this exercise it is of little or no profit to think of the kindness or the worthiness of God, or of our Lady or the saints or angels in heaven, or even of the joys of heaven;[66] that is to say, with a special concentration upon them, as though you wished by that concentration to feed and /increase your purpose. I believe that it would in no wise be so in this case and in this exercise, for though it is good to think of

---

which is the object of this exercise. So, in the words of de Balma, "we are directed to banish not only the activities which proceed from the sensible and intellectual powers, but also the objects of sense and intellect." (Cf. *The Ascent* . . . , p. 246.)

62. Though the author avoids any reference to the *triplex via*, both the context here and what he says elsewhere indicate that he is referring to the purgative and illuminative ways.

63. As Thomas Gallus says, "in this exercise, the intellectual eye cannot see, since the object is union with the invisible God. We achieve union with the divine knowledge by a more efficacious power than the natural exercise of reason and intellect."

64. The immediate source of the simile would seem to be Guiges du Pont. Cf. infra, chap. 6, note 71, p. 131.

65. So Hugo de Balma: "One must think neither of creatures nor of angels, nor of the Trinity."

66. The author makes, at least by implication, an important psychological qualification about his dark contemplation. Special concentration is an essential element of meditation or meditative reflection: what Saint Bernard calls "Consideration." In dark contemplation this concentration is in love, in the will. But there will always be a vague, obscure, general "seeing" in the understanding, against which the effort of this exercise is directed.* Cf. Introduction, pp. 58-60.

the kindness of God and to love him and to praise him for that, yet it is far better to think upon his simple being and to love him and praise him for himself.

CHAPTER VI

A short appreciation of this exercise by means of question and answer.

But now you put me a question and say: "How might I think of him in himself, and what is he?" And to this I can only answer thus: "I have no idea." For with your question you have brought me into that same darkness, into that same cloud of unknowing where I would you were yourself. For a man may, by grace, have the fulness of knowledge of all other creatures and their works, yes, and of the works of God's own self, and he is well able to reflect on them.[67] But no man can think of God himself. Therefore, it is my wish to leave everything that I can think of and choose for my love the thing that I cannot think.[68] Because he can certainly be loved, but not thought.[69] He can be taken and held by love but not by thought. Therefore, though it is good at times to think of the kindness and worthiness of God in particular, and though this is a light and a part of contem-

67. Cf. *The Ascent to Contemplative Wisdom*, p. 249.

68. R. M.: "We read in the book of Wisdom, 'To know thee is perfect justice' (15:3). And what does it mean to know God, except to praise him and thank him in faith mentally, and vocally if it is opportune? What the author says, however, is that one cannot speak in true praise of God because of his surpassing excellence. Whatever you conceive or say of God is always less than true praise. So Ecclesiasticus: 'Praise him as much as you can, and he will still surpass your praise; for he is beyond all praise' " (43:32–35).

69. R. M.: "Man's thought or mental skill can never find God. So, according to Denis the Areopagite, it is by an incomprehensible ascent that we find union with him who is above every substance and all knowledge."

plation,[70] nevertheless, in this exercise, it must be cast down and covered over with a cloud of forgetting. You are to step above it stalwartly but lovingly, and with a devout, pleasing, impulsive love strive to pierce that darkness above you. You are to smite upon that thick cloud of unknowing with a sharp dart of longing love.[71] Do not leave that work for anything that may happen.

CHAPTER VII

How to deal with all thoughts during this exercise, particularly those which result from one's own investigation, knowledge and natural acumen.

If any thought should rise and continue to press in, above you and between you and that darkness, and should ask you and say: "What do you seek and what would you have?" you must say that it is God whom you would have. "Him I covet, him I seek, and nothing but him." And if the thought should ask you who that God is, you must answer that it is the God who made you and ransomed you, and with his grace

---

70. R. M.: "It is absolutely certain that the whole of sacred scripture is true, as it is written in the book of Wisdom, 'He has given me the true knowledge of the things that are' (7:17); but in Ecclesiastes it is said: 'Even if [the wise man] shall say that he knows, he shall not be able to find.' So we must distinguish and in our devout recollection realize that he who is enlightened has full knowledge of things that are, only insofar as he is enlightened; and insofar as he is not enlightened, he cannot discover the reason for all that God has made."

71. The source of this image is, as we have said, probably Guigues du Pont in his *De Contemplatione:* "It often happens that God, for the soul's sake, causes certain rents to occur in the cloud itself. Through these rents the divine goodness is reached by means of secret aspirations—sharp arrows of loving impulses *(acutas sagittas piarum affectionum)* which penetrate the Cloud. When this happens, the soul has a sweet and spiritual taste of divine things, which it savours but does not see" (Cf. J. P. Grausem, S.J., "*Le* de Contemplatione du Chartreuse Guigues du Pont," in R.A.M. X [1929]: 274).

has called you to his love.[72] And say: "You have no part to play." So say to the thought: "Go down again."[73] Tread it down quickly with an impulse of love, even though it seems to you to be very holy; even though it seems that it could help you to seek him.[74] Perhaps the thought will bring to your mind a variety of excellent and wonderful instances of his kindness; it will say that he is most sweet and most loving, gracious and merciful. The thought will want nothing better than that you should listen to it; for in the end it will increase its chattering more and more until it brings you lower down to the recollection of his passion.[75] There it will let you see the wonderful kindness of God; it looks for nothing better than that you should listen to it. For soon after that he will let you see your former wretched state of life;[76] and perhaps as you see and think upon it, the thought will bring to your mind some place in which you used to live.[77] And so at the end, before you are even aware of it, your concentration is gone, scattered about you know not where. The cause of this

---

72. Gallus, in quoting the verse I Peter 4:1, "Christ having suffered in the flesh, you must arm yourselves with a mind like his," makes the point that "the mysteries of the divine humanity are like a ladder which bring[s] us up to the contemplation of the divinity" (Explanation on the Ecclesiastical Hierarchy, chap. III).

73. The ME reads: "In him sei thou kanst no skile." The "thou" is ambiguous: Does it refer to the thought or the thinker? R. M.'s Latin can be definitely rendered: "I am unable to express what he is; and so, thought, go down again!"

74. Gregory the Great, speaking of the grades of contemplation, says that in the third, the mind is to rise above itself and turn to the contemplation of the invisible creature; but that it cannot begin to do this unless it learns to reject and tread under foot *(calcare)* whatever comes into its mind by way of the senses and imagination. Cf. *Homilies on Ezechiel* II, V, 9 (PL 76, 993–4).

75. The author continues his teaching that in this exercise, the purgative and illuminative ways, and the exercises proper to them, must be rejected. So de Balma on the purgative life makes the point that reflections on the Lord's passion are especially necessary for beginners.

76. Prior to such meditations on the passion, the novice must first bring to mind his sinfulness—and particularly the grave sins he has committed in the past (De Balma).

77. In the *Spiritual Exercises* of Ignatius Loyola, the author first deals with the purgative life; and in offering a meditation on the "tale of one's personal sins," directs the "worker" to think of the places where he used to live (Exx 36).

dissipation is that in the beginning you deliberately listened to the thought, answered it, took it to yourself and let it continue unheeded.[78]

Yet what it said was nonetheless both good and holy. Yes indeed, so holy that if any man or woman should think to come to contemplation without many sweet meditations of this sort, on their own wretched state, on the passion, the kindness and the great goodness and the worthiness of God, they will certainly be deceived and fail in their purpose.[79] At the same time, those men and women who are long practised in these meditations must leave them aside,[80] put them down and hold them far under the cloud of forgetting, if they are ever to pierce the cloud of unknowing between them and their God.

Therefore, when you set yourself to this exercise, and experience by grace that you are called by God to it, then lift up your heart to God by a humble impulse of love, and mean the God who made you and ransomed you, and has in his grace called you to this exercise. Have no other thought of God; and not even any of these thoughts unless it should please you. For a simple reaching out directly towards God is sufficient, without any other cause except himself.[81] If you like, you can have this reaching out, wrapped up and enfolded

---

78. "Those who are called to this exercise of dark contemplation cannot afford to relax in the ascent to God; they must never turn away their concentration deliberately, but only when necessity demands" (Gallus, on the *Divine Names*, chap. I).

79. "That most excellent of speculative contemplations [sc. of the trinitarian processions] must be relinquished, not because it is not good and noble, but because there is an apprehension by which alone the supreme Spirit can be grasped: and this alone is the best part of Mary" (Gallus, Explanation on *The Mystical Theology*).

80. The teaching of John of the Cross is exactly the same: e.g., in the *Ascent of Mount Carmel* II, 12:6: "Great, therefore, is the error of spiritual persons who have practised approaching God by means of images and forms and meditations, as befits beginners. God would now lead them on to further spiritual blessings, interior and invisible, by taking from them the pleasure and sweetness of discursive meditation."

81. "He is attained and perceived by the grasp of the affection which reaches out for him above mind and thought" (*The Ascent to Contemplative Wisdom*, p. 247).

in a single word. So as to have a better grasp of it, take just a little word, of one syllable rather than of two; for the shorter it is the better it is in agreement with this exercise of the spirit.[82] Such a one is the word "God" or the word "love." Choose which one you prefer, or any other according to your liking—the word of one syllable that you like best. Fasten this word to your heart, so that whatever happens it will never go away. This word is to be your shield and your spear,[83] whether you are riding in peace or in war. With this word you are to beat upon this cloud and this darkness above you. With this word you are to strike down every kind of thought under the cloud of forgetting; so that if any thought should press upon you and ask you what you would have, answer it with no other word but with this one. If the thought should offer you, out of its great learning, to analyse that word for you and to tell you its meanings, say to the thought that you want to keep it whole, and not taken apart or unfastened. If you will hold fast to this purpose, you may be sure that the thought will not stay for very long. And why? Because you will not allow it to feed itself on the sort of sweet meditations that we mentioned before.

---

82. This is the author's practical application of Denis's teaching in *The Mystical Theology*, chap. III: "We ascend from the lowest to the highest ... and when the ascent is complete, there will be no words at all."

83. Cassian (or Abbot Isaac) *Collationes* X, 10: "Take a short verse of a psalm and it shall be your shield and buckler." "This short verse," says Cassian, in his conferences of the Abbot Moses—he is speaking of the invocation "O God, come to my aid: O Lord, make haste to help me"—"shall be your impenetrable breastplate and stoutest shield" (*Collationes* X, 10, PL 49, 833). De Balma chooses to offer a spiritual exegesis of Exodus 17:11–12: "Moses merited to be Israel's victor by lifting up his hands in burning prayer to heaven—a shield and a spear of love and courage reaching out to God."

Chapter VIII

An accurate treatment, by question and answer, of certain doubts that may arise during this exercise; the suppression of rational investigation, knowledge and intellectual acumen; distinguishing the various levels and divisions of the active and contemplative lives.

But now you will ask, "What is this thought that presses upon me in this work, and is it a good or an evil thing?" "If it is an evil thing," you say, "then I am very much surprised, because it serves so well to increase a man's devotion; and at times I believe that it is a great comfort to listen to what it has to say. For I believe that sometimes it can make me weep very bitterly out of compassion for Christ in his passion, and sometimes for my own wretched state, and for many other reasons. All these, it seems to me, are very holy and do me much good. And therefore I believe that these thoughts can in no way be evil; and if it is good, and their sweet tales do me so much good, then I am very surprised why you bid me put them deep down under the cloud of forgetting!"

This strikes me as being a very good question. And so I must reflect in order to answer it as well as my feebleness permits. First, when you ask me what this thought is that presses so hard upon you in this exercise, offering to help you in this work, I answer that it is a well-defined and clear sight of your natural intelligence imprinted upon your reason within your soul. And when you ask me whether it is good or evil, I say that it must of necessity be always good in its nature, because it is a ray of God's likeness.[84] But the use of it can be both good and evil. It is good when it is

---

84. The author is speaking of the "divine immissions," the *theoriae* that in Dionysian language are the graces proper to the purgative and illuminative lives. As Julian of Norwich teaches, in her own clear and simple language, the Christian

illumined by grace, so that you may see your wretched state, the passion, the kindness and the wonderful works of God in his creatures, bodily and spiritual. And so it is no wonder that it increases your devotion as much as you say. But the use of it is evil when it is swollen with pride, and with the curiosity which comes from the subtle speculation and learning, such as theologians have, which makes them want to be known not as humble clerics and masters of divinity or of devotion, but proud scholars of the devil and masters of vanity and falsehood.[85] And in other men and women, whether they be religious or seculars, the use and exercise of this natural understanding is evil when it is swollen with proud and clever learning of worldly things and earthly ideas, for the coveting of worldly honours and rich possessions, and the pleasure and vainglory which comes from men's flatterings.

Next, you ask me why you should put down such thoughts under the cloud of forgetting, since it is true that they are good of their kind, and when well used they do you so much good and greatly increase your devotion. My answer is that you must clearly understand that there are two kinds of lives in holy Church.[86] One is the active life, and the other is the contemplative life. The active life is the lower and the contemplative life is the higher. Active life has two degrees, a higher and a lower; and the contemplative life also has two degrees, a lower and a higher. Further, these two lives

---

is assimilated to the God revealed in Christ by contemplating him: "... the soul who thus contemplates him is made like to him who is contemplated ..." (*Showings*, p. 164).

85. The author is here reflecting on the dangers that can accrue from attributing the "lights" granted in meditative prayer to one's own theological erudition. To accuse him of anti-intellectualism is to miss his point: namely that in the unitive prayer that is the "work of his book," theological erudition has of itself nothing, or worse than nothing, to offer. As R. M. frequently remarks, he is a master of hyperbole, and probably overemphasizes the spiritual dangers of academic learning.

86. The medieval Dionysians teach that the twofold knowledge of God—speculative and unitive—is at the basis of the distinction between the "two lives": and that the first will precede and ordinarily lead to the second. Cf. Introduction, supra, pp. 61–62.

are so joined together that though in part they are different, neither of them can be lived fully without having some part in the other. For the higher part of the active life is the same as the lower part of the contemplative life. Hence, a man cannot be fully active unless he is partly a contemplative, nor can he be fully contemplative here below unless he is in some way active.[87] It is the nature of the active life both to be begun and ended in this life. Not so, however, of the contemplative life, which is begun in this life and shall last without end. That is why the part that Mary chose shall never be taken away. The active life is troubled and anxious about many things; but the contemplative sits in peace, intent only on one thing.

The lower part of the active life consists in good and honest corporal works of mercy and of charity. The higher part of the active life, and the lower part of the contemplative, consists in good spiritual meditations and earnest consideration of a man's own wretched state with sorrow and contrition, of the passion of Christ and of his servants with pity and compassion, and of the wonderful gifts, kindness, and works of God in all his creatures, corporeal and spiritual, with thanksgiving and praise. But the higher part of contemplation, insofar as it is possible to possess it here below, consists entirely in this darkness and in this cloud of unknowing, with a loving impulse and a dark gazing into the simple being of God himself alone.[88]

In the lower part of the active life, a man is outside himself and beneath himself. In the higher part of the active

---

87. The implication is that the *ex professo* contemplative will have to return to a form of meditative reflection or imaginative contemplation recommended by the spiritual masters; he is not speaking only of those whose state precludes them from undertaking the "work of his book" regularly.

88. In this contemplative exercise, the affection as well as the intellect must be purified, so that the soul in its love might tend to God alone. The holy thoughts (as John of the Cross will also teach) are often desired because they bring sweetness and comfort to the soul, rather than because they lead to God. The soul must also purify herself "of everything that can be known according to its own proper

life, and the lower part of the contemplative life, a man is within himself and on a par with himself. But in the higher part of the contemplative life, a man is above himself and under his God. He is above himself, because he makes it his purpose to arrive by grace whither he cannot come by nature: that is to say, to be knit to God in spirit, in oneness of love and union of wills.

One can understand that it is impossible[89] for a man to come to the higher part of the active life unless he leaves, for a time, the lower part. In the same way, a man cannot come to the higher part of the contemplative life unless he leaves for a time the lower part. It would be a wrong thing for a man engaged on meditation, and a hindrance to him, to turn his mind to the outward corporal works which he had done or should do, even though in themselves they are very holy works. In the same way, it would be very inappropriate and a great hindrance to a man who ought to be working in this darkness and in this cloud of unknowing, with an affective impulse of love to God for himself alone, to permit any thought or any meditation on God's wonderful gifts, kindness or his work in any of his creatures, bodily or spiritual, to rise up in his mind so as to press between him and his God, even if they should be very holy thoughts, and give him great happiness and consolation.

This is the reason why I bid you put down any such clear and insinuating thought, and cover it up with a thick cloud of forgetting, no matter how holy it might be, and

---

form in her intellect" (*Mystical Theology*, chap. 1). This is Gallus's exegesis of the Dionysian *ab omni absoluto*. De Balma adds: "The limited is what is known in its own proper form as having distinct being." In the contemplative exercise such distinct knowledge darkens the mind.

89. R. M.: "He says that it is impossible, because 'for a time,' we are to understand an instant or a moment. However, with special grace and with the Holy Spirit's co-operation, it is not only possible but very easy to meditate on God whilst doing something else; though of course one should not presume to do this during the time of the divine office or any other spiritual exercise. However, in so far as in us lies, we should always and everywhere think of God with reverence and devotion."

no matter how well it might promise to help you in your endeavour. Because it is love alone that can reach God in this life, and not knowing.[90] For as long as the soul dwells in this mortal body, the clarity of our understanding in the contemplation of all spiritual things, and especially of God, is always mixed up with some sort of imagination;[91] and because of it this exercise of ours would be tainted, and it would be very surprising if it did not lead us into great error.

CHAPTER IX

During this exercise, the calling to mind of the holiest creature God ever made is a hindrance rather than a help.

The intense activity, therefore, of your understanding, which will always press upon you when you set yourself to this dark contemplation, must always be put down. For if you do not put it down it will put you down; so much so that when you imagine that you can best abide in this darkness, and that nothing is in your mind except God alone, if you take a close look, you will find that your mind is occupied, not with this darkness, but with a clear picture of something beneath God. If this is in fact so, then indeed that thing is above you for the moment, and between you and your God. So set yourself to put down such clear pictures, no matter how holy or how pleasant they may be.

One thing I must tell you. This blind impulse of love towards God for himself alone, this secret love beating on this cloud of unknowing, is more profitable for the salvation

---

90. R. M.: "Would that our intellectual force *(acumen ingenii)* were never occupied with vanities, but always with spiritual things and especially with God. However, the author is speaking here of the time of this exercise, when we possess the grace, though not in such abundance that we are carried above ourselves."

91. Cf. *The Ascent to Contemplative Wisdom*, p. 247.

of your soul, more worthy in itself, and more pleasing to
God, and to all the saints and angels in heaven; yes and of
more use to all your friends both bodily and spiritually, whether they are alive or dead. And it is better for you to experience
this spiritually in your affection than it is to have the eye
of your soul opened in contemplation either in seeing all the
angels and the saints in heaven, or in hearing all the mirth
or the melody that is amongst those who are in bliss.

Nor need you be surprised at what I say; for if you
could once see it as clearly as you can come by grace to
touch it and to experience it in this life, you would think
as I do.[92] But take it for granted that no man shall ever
have such clear sight here in this life; but the feeling—that
a man can have through grace, when God deigns to grant
it.[93] So lift up your love to that cloud; or rather, if I am
to speak more truthfully, let God draw your love up to that
cloud; and try, through the help of his grace, to forget every
other thing.[94]

A simple awareness of anything under God, which forces
itself upon your will and consciousness, puts you further away
from God than you would be if it did not exist; it hinders
you and makes you less able to feel, by experience, the fruit
of his love. How much more, then, do you think that an
awareness which is drawn to yourself knowingly and deliberately, will hinder you in your purpose? And if the consciousness of any particular saint or pure spiritual thing

92. R. M.: "One cannot handle spiritual things in a bodily way. The author
is speaking hyperbolically."

93. R. M.: "If there were no possibility of possessing it at all in this life,
then it could neither be known nor written about in any way. It is the fulness
of the knowledge which is reserved to the next life."

94. R. M.: "This exercise is sometimes called, among many other names,
a stillness *(vacatio)* or a being lifted on high *(sursumactio passive)*, or a forgetting
(oblivio). All these names and many others are used to describe the valiant efforts
the contemplative must make before he reaches the cloud of unknowing; for there
is nothing to be found therein which is knowable in itself, either actively or passively.
Hence it is written: Be still and see that I am God, etc. *(Vacate et videte quoniam
ego sum Deus*—Vulgate, Ps. 45:11)."

hinders you so much, how do you think that the consciousness of any living person in this wretched life or any corporal or worldly thing will hinder you and be an obstacle to you in this exercise?

I am not saying that any such simple, sudden thought of any good and pure spiritual thing under God which presses against your will or your understanding, or is wilfully drawn into your mind deliberately in order to increase your devotion, is therefore evil, even though it is a hindrance to this sort of exercise; and God forbid that you should understand it so! But I do say that in spite of its goodness and holiness, in this exercise it is more of a hindrance than a help—I mean during the time of the exercise. For certainly, he who seeks to have God perfectly will not take his rest in the consciousness of any angel or any saint that is in heaven.

CHAPTER X

*How to know when a thought is not sinful; and when
a sinful thought is capital or venial.*

But if any living person, man or woman, comes to mind, or any bodily or worldly thing whatever, the case is quite different.[95] A simple thought of any of these which comes up against your will and your consciousness, though it is not a sin imputed to you, it is the effect, beyond your control, of original sin from which you were cleansed in your baptism.

---

95. R. M.: "At the end of the preceding chapter, the author says that good thoughts, such as those on the passion of Christ or heavenly truths, in the context of the exercise described in this book, must be abandoned for the time, even though they inspire the contemplative to devotion and perhaps to tears. This is good advice, unless you are instructed differently by a special gift or the leading of the Holy Spirit; for then you ought not to reach out after them in respect of this exercise. But at the beginning of this chapter, the author intends to teach that the bad thoughts which infect the mind, for example, lustful thoughts, are much more to be rejected, especially when the good are to be rejected for the sake of the better."

Nonetheless, if this sudden impulse or thought is not beaten down straight away, your fleshly heart, because of its frailty, will be immediately affected with some kind of pleasure if the thing pleases you, or has pleased you before, or with some kind of resentment if it is a thing which you imagine upsets you, or has upset you before.[96] Such a sinful affection can be grave in worldly men and women who have been living in serious sin. But the same affection, which causes pleasure or resentment in the fleshly heart, is no more than venial sin in you and in all others who have, with a sincere will, forsaken the world and have bound themselves in any way, privately or openly,[97] to the devout life in holy Church, and therefore wish to be governed, not according to their own will and understanding, but according to the will and the counsel of their superiors whoever they are, religious or secular. This is because your intention[98] has been rooted and grounded in God from the time when you first began to live according to the state of life in which you now persevere.[99] But if it should happen that this affection which causes pleasure or resentment in your fleshly heart be allowed to remain there for any length of time without being repudiated, it will

96. Gallus, in his first commentary on the *Canticle of Canticles* (1:15) ("my mother's children have waged war on me"), says that these children are the uncontrolled impulses of the lower part of the reason, which always contradict the synderesis (the understanding and the will in its movement towards God); and in particular of the sensuality, which with its incessant clamouring draws the mind down from contemplation of heavenly things to that of creatures.

97. That is, monks or nuns who have made public profession by vows, and those who have bound themselves to religious, or to other superiors (e.g., bishops) by a promise or a *propositum*. Cf., Introduction, supra, p. 13.

98. Intention (ME "entent") also appears to be used technically in this context: the intention or *propositum* is made to God.

99. R. M.: "The cause of resistance against evil is the grace of God together with the free will. What the author means is that if a man has fixed his intention beforehand by grace and free will, it is obvious that he will consent to a good thought and fight against an evil one. But lovers of the world, on the contrary, oppose a good thought and accept an evil one." Methley is clarifying his author's teaching that bad thoughts have a more disastrous effect on those in mortal sin by referring to the Augustinian doctrine on grace and free will.

eventually become fastened to the spiritual heart (that is to say, the will) with full consent; then it will be deadly sin.

This happens when you, or any of those of whom I am speaking, wilfully bring up in their mind any living person, man or woman, or any bodily or worldly thing whatsoever: to the extent that if it is a thing which grieves or has grieved you before, there rises up in you a spiteful passion and an appetite for vengeance, then it is called wrath. Or else there rises up a fierce contempt and some kind of loathing for a person along with spiteful and disapproving thoughts; this is called envy. Or else a weariness and a repugnance for any good occupation, bodily or spiritual; this is called sloth. If it is a thing that pleases you, or has pleased you before, there rises up in you a keen delight in thinking about it whatever it is, so much so that you take your rest in that thought, and finally fasten your heart and will to it and feed your carnal love upon it. During that time you think that you covet no other wealth except always to live in this peace and rest with the thing that you are thinking about.[100] If this thought, which you bring to mind yourself in this way, or else take to yourself when it is brought to your mind and rest in it thus with delight, concerns natural or intellectual talents or worthiness of favour or of rank, or of comeliness or beauty, then it is pride. If it is a thought of any sort of worldly possessions, riches or cattle, or whatever man can possess or be master of, then it is covetousness. If it concerns delicacies in food or drink, or any sort of pleasure which comes from the sense of taste, then it is gluttony. If it concerns the pleasures of love or any kind of fleshly dalliance, for

---

100. R. M.: "To live always in this peace." He is not speaking of true peace, since according to the Lord's word, there is no peace for the wicked (Isaiah 48:22). It is called peace because the appetite of the fleshly heart is fixed in the lustful pleasure. By what follows—"natural or intellectual talent or beauty in yourself or anyone else"—the author means if the thought is an evil one. But notice carefully that if one does not consent to the sin, but merely feels the temptation, there is no sin at all, but merit."

the seduction or flattery of any living person, man or woman, then it is called lust.[101]

CHAPTER XI

Each thought and impulse is to be given its proper value; carelessness in venial sin is always to be avoided.

I do not say this because you, or any of the others I have mentioned, are guilty and burdened with any such sins, but because I want you to reckon each thought and each impulse at its proper value and to work earnestly to destroy[102] the first impulse and thought of those things in which you can thus commit sin. For there is one thing I must tell you: that he who takes no account of or pays little heed to the first thought, even though there is no sin in it for him, whoever he may be he cannot avoid carelessness with regard to venial sin. No one can keep absolutely clear of venial sin in this mortal life.[103] However, carelessness in venial sin should always be avoided by all true disciples of perfection.[104] Oth-

---

101. It is unknown when the catalogue of the seven or eight capital sins was first enunciated, but Evagrius Ponticus wrote a treatise, *De octo vitiosis cogitationibus,* in A.D. 383 (PG 40, 1271–73). Cassian seems to have brought the tradition to the West around the same time. "Deadly" or "mortal" is not quite an accurate description: They are not necessarily mortal sins but the sources of sin—as the author here makes plain. Hilton treats of them at great length in *Scale* I (Underhill, pp. 132–81).

102. R. M. says that he prefers to say abandon *(destitutionem)* rather than destroy *(destructionem)* here, following him who says that the first impulse towards something evil in the apprehension is meritorious or the opposite according to the value put on it. This is the author's own view in his treatise on the *Discernment of Spirits.*

103. Cf. 1 John 1:8.

104. This again appears to be a reference to religious life in the strictly canonical sense. The scriptural allusion is to Matthew 19:21.

erwise I would not be surprised if they soon commit grievous sin.[105]

CHAPTER XII

By means of this exercise sin is destroyed and virtues are acquired.

If, then, you are determined to stand and not to fall,[106] never cease from your endeavour, but constantly[107] beat with a sharp dart of longing love upon this cloud of unknowing which is between you and your God. Avoid thinking of anything under God and do not leave this exercise no matter what happens. For it alone, of itself, destroys the root and the ground of sin.[108] No matter how much you fast, or keep

---

105. This is the teaching of Saint Thomas; cf. *Summa Theologiae* 2a–2ae, 88, 3.

106. Cf. 1 Corinthians 10:12.

107. R. M., who tells us in his prologue that he has practised this exercise for about fourteen years, is disconcerted by his author's insistence that there can be no slackening off. So he comments here: "Never to leave off, but always to go on thrusting with the spiritual desire is impossible: first for those who are asleep, in so far as they are asleep, unless the exercise can be continued somehow or other through a dream; secondly, for those who are awake, it is impossible to weigh up every impulse of the mind. The exercise can, however, be practised all the time and everywhere in intention; and this is what the author means." Gallus, however, also insists that the contemplative effort is to be a constant occupation. In his third commentary on the last verse of the *Canticle* (8:13: "let me hear your voice") he observes that this is the final exhortation of the spouse to the soul, which "shows that nothing is more pleasing to God, nothing more perfect in the part of Mary, than to be exercised incessantly *(incessanter exerceri)* in the fervour of ecstatic desires and the divine rays by always striving upwards and never turning away *(semper in superius conando nec deinde proficiens)*." R. M. adds: "Fulfil all the duties of your state with a pure heart. But amidst them all, or some of them, in so far as you can, always have your soul reaching upwards towards God. And if you are rapt above your natural awareness *(super sensus)* do not doubt that the Lord will dispense on your behalf."

108. Cf. Romans 6:6.

watch, no matter how early you rise, no matter how hard your bed, no matter how rough your hairshirt;[109] yes and if it were lawful to do so, as it is not, even were you to put out your eyes, cut out your tongue from your mouth, stop up your ears and nose, though you were to cut away your private parts[110] and cause your body all the pain that you could think of; all this would be of no avail at all to you. The impulse and tendency to sin would still be in you.

Yes, and more than this. No matter how much you were to weep and sorrow for your sins, or for the passion of Christ, or be ever so mindful of the joys of heaven, what would it profit you?[111] Certainly it would be of great good, great help, great gain and great grace. But in comparison with that blind impulse of love, there is little it can or may do. This, without all those other things, is Mary's best part. Without it they profit little or nothing. Not only does it destroy the root and ground of sin, as far as that is possible here below,[112] but it also acquires the virtues.[113] For when it is truly implanted, all the virtues will be perfectly and delicately implanted, experienced and contained in it, without any mixture

---

109. ME: "were thou never so scharp."

110. Cf. Matthew 19:12, which, according to tradition, Origen took literally.

111. Cf. 1 Corinthians 13:3.

112. The author in this chapter is speaking of active and passive purification in the contemplative ascent, where the purgative and illuminative ways coalesce. It is a Dionysian principle that the purpose of purification is illumination; but Thomas Gallus adds, "purification is more powerfully effected by longing love" *(per suspirium amoris)*. Active purification is precisely this "constant endeavour" to cooperate with the contemplative graces (we are to remember that the soul begins to undertake the exercise only when she is assured in faith that she is called to contemplation), which cleanse by illumination; and this is passive purification: "The effort itself separates the soul from its contraries; once separated, it is purified from its own proper darkness, and restored to the pristine purity and innocence." Thus the root and ground of sin is destroyed. Cf. also De Balma: "The purgative way purifies by means of sorrow, frequent contrition, and tears. But purification through the ascent of ardent love is much more efficacious."

113. De Balma: "The divine wisdom disposes the soul to receive the gifts . . . whereby faith is established, hope corroborated, charity is enflamed; the mind is shaped by fortitude, perfected by temperance, and acquires justice."

of motive.[114] And no matter how many virtues a man may have, without this they will all be mixed with some crooked motive, and therefore they will be imperfect.

For virtue is nothing else than an ordered and controlled affection which has God for its single object, himself alone. For he himself is the pure cause of all the virtues; so much so that if a man is moved to any virtue by any other cause besides God, even though he is the chief cause, that virtue will be imperfect.[115] An example of this may be seen in one or two virtues, which can stand for all the others. The two virtues, meekness and charity, are good examples; for whoever can have these two, he would clearly need no others; he would have them all.

CHAPTER XIII

The nature of humility; perfect and imperfect humility.

Let us look first at the virtue of humility.[116] See how it is imperfect when it flows from any other source which mingles with the chief, though this be God; and how it is perfect when its single source is God himself. First, if the matter is to be truly apprehended and understood, we must

---

114. In *A Letter of Private Direction* the author says that this exercise is the divine Wisdom descending into man's soul. This infusion, says Thomas Gallus in his third commentary on the *Canticle of Canticles*, anoints the soul with the gracious sweetness of the spiritual virtues—those that justify and sanctify.

115. "Virtue is nothing else than the ordered and controlled affection of the spirit" *(Nihil aliud est virtus quam animi affectus ordinatus et moderatus)*: Richard of St. Victor, *Benjamin Minor*, VII. Richard follows Augustine here (cf. H., 39/17, 19, 23).

116. In the Western tradition, and particularly in monastic theology and that of the early scholastics, self-contempt is always prominent in the treatment of humility. This is due in no small measure to the Pauline comparison between Christ's self-emptying and Christian living (Philippians 2:3–8). Christian Dionysianism, on the other hand, must shift the emphasis from the efficient to the final cause—stressing the divine glory that is the purpose of humility (ibid., 9–11).

know what humility is in itself. Then we shall be able to understand more clearly in truth of spirit what its cause is.

In itself, humility is nothing else but a man's true understanding and awareness of himself as he really is. It is certain that if a man could truly see and be conscious of himself as he really is, he would indeed be truly humble.[117] There are two causes of this meekness: One is the foulness, wretchedness and weakness into which a man has fallen by sin. As long as he lives in this life, no matter how holy he is, he must always experience this in some measure. The other is the superabundant love and worthiness of God himself.[118] At the sight of this, all nature trembles, all learned men are fools, and all the saints and angels are blinded;[119] so much so that were it not for the wisdom of his godhead, whereby due proportion is set between their contemplation and their natural and grace-given capacity, I would be at a loss to say what would happen to them.[120]

This second cause of humility is perfect, because it will last forever. The first cause is imperfect: not only because it is to pass away at the end of this life, but also because it can often happen, through the abundance of the grace which increases its desire as often and for as long as God deigns to grant it, that a soul living in this mortal flesh may suddenly

117. The author indicates that there is a twofold source of humility: seeing and feeling. Gallus may be his source here, in distinguishing a humility of the knowing power and of the loving power (intelligentiae principalis affectionis). Cf. his third Commentary on the Canticle (lilium convalium, 2, 1). Richard of St. Victor, however, distinguishes between voluntary humility—when a man by the use of his reason sees how weak and sinful he is—and devout humility, which the perfect soul possesses by grace (Explicatio in Cantica Cant., chap. XIV).

118. De Balma: "Every creature who truly recognizes the source whence he originates reckons himself as nothing; and since he is created from nothing, is all the more aware of the splendour of the Creator".

119. R. M.: "Clerics are not idiots, nor angels and saints blind; but all this is true in comparison with God, whom they cannot comprehend."

120. It is a Dionysian principle that the divine light (which Gallus interprets as the contemplative grace) is always measured according to the capacities of those who receive it. And we must never presume to exceed the limits set by our own capacities and the grace granted. Cf. Explanation on the Divine Names, chap. 7.

lose and forget all awareness and experience of its own being, so that it takes no account of its holiness or its wretchedness. But whether this experience happens often or seldom to a soul so disposed by God, my belief is that the experience lasts only a very short while. During this time it is made perfectly humble, for it has neither knowledge nor experience of any cause but the chief one. But whenever it has knowledge and experience of the other, along with the chief cause, then its humility is imperfect.[121] It is, however, good, and we must always have it; and God forbid that you should understand it in any other way than I say.

Chapter XIV

In this life it is impossible for a sinner to reach the perfection of humility unless imperfect humility comes first.

I would rather have this true knowledge and experience of myself as the wretch that I am,[122] even though I call it imperfect humility, because I believe that it would quickly obtain for me the perfect cause and virtue of humility; sooner indeed than if all the saints and angels in heaven, and all men and women who are living on earth in holy Church,

121. R. M. points out here that this imperfect humility is so called by the author because its source is speculative knowledge: "It is known through the senses and the intellect. Perfect humility is known in an ineffable way through union with God which transcends speculation." Walter Hilton also employs the distinction between this perfect and imperfect humility (cf. *Scale II*, chap. 37). Hilton's source is certainly the chapter in Richard of St. Victor's commentary on the *Canticle,* referred to above (n. 117). The author appears to teach that perfect humility is an experience rather than a habit, achieved only in the moment of union, "which lasts only a very short while."

122. Julian of Norwich maintains that it is only "by the special gift of our Lord" that "we have knowledge and sight of our sin and of our wretchedness." "Our Lord of his mercy," she says, "reveals our sin and our feebleness to us by the sweet gracious light of his own self" (*Showings*, pp. 332–33).

religious or secular, in every degree of life, were all of them together to do nothing else but pray to God for me to obtain this perfect humility. Yes indeed. It is impossible for a sinner to obtain the perfect virtue of humility or to keep it when it is acquired, without the imperfect humility.

So labour and toil as much as you can and know how, to acquire for yourself the true knowledge and experience of yourself as the wretch that you are.[123] And then I think that soon after you will have a true knowledge and experience of God as he is: not as he is in himself, for no one can experience that except God himself,[124] nor as you shall experience him in blessedness, both body and soul together, but in as much as this is possible, and as it is his good pleasure to be known and experienced by a humble soul living in this mortal body.[125]

Nor must you think, because I set down two causes of humility, one perfect and the other imperfect, that I wish you to leave off striving for imperfect humility, and concentrate entirely on acquiring the perfect. Indeed, I do not believe that you could ever so acquire it. But I write as I do with the intention of letting you know and showing you the worthiness of this spiritual exercise above every other bodily or spiritual exercise which man can or may perform by grace: how that hidden love, raised up in purity of spirit upon this dark cloud of unknowing between you and your God, delicately and perfectly contains in itself the perfect virtue of humility, without any particular or clearly defined

---

123. Thomas Gallus insists that the proximate preparation for unitive contemplation demands a constant and strenuous effort: the soul must sweat and dig out the heavenly secrets from the hard rock, slowly and laboriously (the Third Commentary on the *Canticle*, on the text *in foraminibus petrae* 2, 14). In this comparison between perfect and imperfect humility our author, like Gallus, may also be inspired by Richard of St. Victor, who says that "it is arduous and difficult to win the necessary grace in the higher reaches of contemplation: and compunction of heart, sighs and groans will be of more avail than a welter of investigation and reasoning" (*Benjamin Maior* IV).

124. Cf. John 1:18.

125. Cf. Matthew 11:27–30

sight of anything under God. And also I wish you to know what perfect humility is, and set it as a sign upon the love of your heart,[126] and do so both for you and for me; since it is my wish, by this knowledge, to make you more humble. For it often happens that a lack of knowledge is the cause of great pride, or so it seems to me.

Again, it might be that if you did not know what perfect meekness is, you might think, because you had a little knowledge and experience of what I call imperfect humility, that you had almost reached perfect humility. So you would deceive yourself, thinking that you were very humble, when in fact you were wrapped around in foul stinking pride. So set yourself to labour for perfect humility; because its nature is such that if a man has it, and as long as he has it, he will not sin: and afterwards, only a little.[127]

CHAPTER XV

A brief refutation of the error which maintains that there is no better means of humbling oneself than by calling to mind one's own sinfulness.

Have a steadfast trust that there is the sort of perfect humility mentioned above, and that through grace it can be acquired in this life. I say this to refute the error of those who declare that there is no more perfect cause of humility than that which springs from the awareness of our wretchedness and of our past sins.

---

126. Cf. Canticle of Canticles 7:6.

127. R. M.: "This true humility is in love, which is perfect in the highest union that is possible in this life. But until this is certainly revealed to you by the Lord, be on your guard against thinking that you are possessed of this highest humility, charity and union. What is said here about not sinning—that is, mortally—is not a general rule for everyone, but for the chosen, as is believed of the apostles after Pentecost, and of others specially chosen. For David and Solomon were contemplatives, yet they sinned mortally."

I readily grant that for those who sin habitually, as I do myself and have done, here is the most necessary and expedient cause: to be humbled under the awareness of our wretchedness and of our past sins, until such time as the complete rust of our sins is for the most part scrubbed away,[128] according to the witness of our conscience and our spiritual director.[129]

But to others who are to all intents and purposes innocent, who have never sinned seriously with determined will and awareness, but only through frailty and ignorance, and who set themselves to be contemplatives, and to both of us as well, if our spiritual director and our conscience alike bear witness to our proper amendment in contrition, and confession and satisfaction according to the law and ordinance of holy Church,[130] and as long as we are aware that we are moved and called by grace to be contemplatives—there is then another cause for being humbled. This is as far above the first as is the life of our Lady, Saint Mary, above that of the most sinful penitent in holy Church, or as the life of Christ is above that of any other man in this life,[131] or as that of an angel in heaven who never experienced weakness, nor ever shall, is above the life of the frailest man here in this world.

For if there were no more perfect cause of humility than

---

128. De Balma, speaking of the purgative way, says that the soul must humble itself first by recalling its sins, sighing and crying to God: "For just as a file is applied to iron, so that by this special friction the rust on the iron is removed, so after the infusion of grace, this humility gets rid of the rust left by sin."

129. R. M.: "Our conscience is purified and illumined by God's grace, and becomes one with the conscience and counsel of those who possess the highest virtue of discretion (*Virorum discretissimorum*), whom before we obeyed by faith. No one whose conscience is not purified and illumined can rely on his own counsel."

130. There is an allusion here to the *forti contritione* of Denis, which our author, like Gallus, interprets in the sacramental sense; and it is always "by the impulse of grace" that "you apply yourself to the exercise of this dark contemplation." Cf. *Mystical Theology*, chap. 1.

131. Gallus says, of contemplative humility, that it was this that brought the wisdom of God to earth (*humilitas deposuit sapientiam Dei in terram*), citing Philippians 2, "let that mind be in you which was in Christ Jesus, etc." (third commentary on the *Canticle*).

to see and experience one's wretchedness, I would like to ask those who allege this to be true, under what cause were they humbled who never saw nor experienced wretchedness nor stirring of sin, nor ever shall: as it is of our Lord, Jesus Christ, our Lady Saint Mary and all the saints and angels in heaven. It is to this and to every kind of perfection that our Lord Jesus Christ himself calls us in the gospel, where he tells us that we are to be as perfect by grace as he himself is by nature.[132]

CHAPTER XVI

By means of this exercise, the sinner who is truly converted and called to contemplation reaches perfection more quickly than by any other exercise: and obtains from God a most speedy forgiveness of his sins.

No man should think it presumptuous, because he is the most wretched sinner alive, to dare take upon himself—after he has made lawful amendment, and has felt himself called to the life that is termed contemplative with the agreement of his spiritual director, and in accord with his own conscience—to offer a humble impulse of love to his God, knocking secretly on the cloud of unknowing between him and his God. Our Lord said to Mary, who stands for all sinners that are called to the contemplative life: "Your sins are forgiven you."[133] This was not because of her great sorrow, nor for her awareness of her sins, nor yet for the humility that she had at the sight of her wretchedness. It was because, surely,

---

132. Matthew 5:48, "Be perfect as your heavenly Father is perfect." The exegesis of the text is that of the fourth Lateran council (A.D. 1215): "Be perfect by the perfection of grace as your heavenly Father is perfect by the perfection of nature."

133. "Therefore I tell you, her sins, which are many, are forgiven, for she loved much. . . . And he said to her, your sins are forgiven" (Luke 7:47–48).

that she loved much.[134] Here then can men see what this hidden impulse of love can win from our Lord, over and above every other exercise that a man may think to perform.

Yet I readily agree that she had great sorrow, wept very bitterly for her sins,[135] and that she was greatly humbled by the awareness of her wretchedness. We should do likewise, who have been wretches and habitual sinners all our life long; our sorrow for our sins should indeed be exceedingly great, and we should be deeply humbled in the awareness of our wretchedness.[136]

How? Surely, just as Mary did. For although she could never rid herself of the deep sorrow of her heart for her sins, all her lifetime she carried them with her wherever she went, as it were in a bundle bound together and stored secretly in the cavern of her heart,[137] in a way that could never be forgotten. Yet it still can be said, and is affirmed by holy scripture, that she had a greater sorrow of heart for her lack of love than for any awareness of her sins. She had a more sorrowing desire, a deeper sighing; she languished almost to the point of death for her lack of love, though she had very great love. And we are not to wonder at this; for it is the nature of a true lover that the more he loves the more he longs to love.

Yet she knew well, by her own experience in sober truth,

---

134. R. M.: "God forgave her many sins, not only nor chiefly for her great sorrow, etc., but because she loved much. The source of this love was God's grace, for he loved us first, and gave us grace that we might love him. We ought to have particular sorrow for our sins whenever they come to mind in any special way. But in this contemplative ascent it is undesirable to delay over them in actual sorrow, except when we are especially moved to do so; but since they are an obstacle to the higher, we can only know through the Holy Spirit if we should follow our instinct. For the rest, because of our feeble human nature, to recall one's special sins on occasion (though not during the contemplative exercise) is good and for some people necessary, lest they fall into pride, and forget whence they came, where they are and whither they go."

135. Luke 7:37–38. Cf. Luke 22:61–62.

136. Cf. Psalm 50:10; Psalm 130:2; Luke 15:18; 18:13–14, etc.

137. Cf. Canticle of Canticles 1:12; 2:14.

that she was a viler wretch than anyone else, and that her sins had made a division between her and her God whom she loved so much; and also that they were in great part the cause of this lingering sickness through lacking of love. What then did she do? Did she for this reason come down from the heights of her desire to the depths of her sinful life, and search about in the foul malodorous bog and dunghill of her sins, dragging them up one by one with all their circumstances, and sorrowing and weeping upon each one of them?[138] No, indeed, she did nothing of the sort. And why? Because God made her understand, by the grace within her soul, that she would never achieve anything thus. She was more likely by these means to raise up in herself a tendency to sin again, rather than to obtain by such methods a true forgiveness of all her sins.

So she hung up her love and her longing desire in this cloud of unknowing, and learned to love what she could not see clearly in this life by the light of understanding in her reason, or yet truly experience in sweetness of love in her affection;[139] so much so that often enough she paid but little attention to whether she had been a sinner or not. Yes indeed; I expect that very often she was so deeply moved in her affection by the love of his godhead that she had no eyes for the beauty of his precious and blessed body as he sat in his loveliness, speaking and preaching to her; nor of anything else, corporal or spiritual.[140] That this is true, the gospel appears to be witness.

---

138. The language here is reminiscent of the *Stimulus Amoris* of James of Milan, typical of the medieval approach to our author's imperfect humility. Cf. *The Goad of Love*, ed. C. Kirchberger (London, 1952), *passim*.

139. De Balma: "The whole of this wisdom reaches fulfilment only by the shearing away of all intellectual activity; when the loving power in its sovereign point desires nothing else than to be united with God alone."

140. Cf. Luke 10:39–42.

CHAPTER XVII

*The true contemplative has no desire to concern himself
with the active life, nor with what is done or spoken
against him; he must not try to explain himself to
his detractors.*

In the gospel of Saint Luke it is written that when our
Lord was in the house of Martha,[141] all the time that Martha
was busying herself with the preparation of his food, her
sister Mary sat at his feet. In listening to him, she had no
time for the busy activity of her sister; even though this activity
was very good and holy, for it is the first part of the active
life. Nor was she paying attention to the preciousness of his
blessed body, nor to the sweet voice and words of his manhood;
though this is better and holier, for it is the second part
of the active life and the first of the contemplative life.[142]
She was contemplating, with all the love of her heart, the
supreme and sovereign wisdom of his godhead, clothed in
the dark words of his manhood.[143] She had no desire to leave

---

141. "Now as they went on their way, he entered a village; and a woman
named Martha received him into her house. And she had a sister called Mary,
who sat at the Lord's feet and listened to his teaching. But Martha was distracted
with much serving; and she went to him and said, Lord, do you not care that
my sister has left me to serve alone? Tell her to help me. But the Lord answered
her: Martha, Martha, you are troubled about many things; one thing is necessary.
Mary has chosen the best part, which shall not be taken away from her" (Luke
10:38–43). On the Dionysian exegesis of the "two lives" and the "best part," cf.
Introduction, supra, pp. 62, 66–68.

142. Guigues du Pont, speaking of the immediate preparation for anagogical
contemplation, says: "Just as in the first degree (the devoted soul) concentrates more
and gazes upon the man rather than God—that is, the humanity rather than the
divinity of Christ, although it sees both together, now the situation must be reversed.
In so far as is possible the object of his concentration must be the Godhead rather
than the humanity. He must take hold of God by the handle of his humanity,
and embrace rather the feet of God" (*De Contemplatione*, MS Stonyhurst LXXVII
f. 43r.).

143. For Thomas Gallus, the *Benjamin maior* of Richard of St. Victor is a
tract that expounds the sixth and highest grade of contemplation, which is "the
work of this book." Richard, after pointing out that the gift of contemplation resides

off, not for anything that she saw or heard spoken going on around her. But she sat unmoving, sending up many a sweet and longing impulse of love, to beat upon that high cloud of unknowing between her and her God.

For one thing I must tell you. There never yet existed, nor ever shall, so pure a creature, one so ravished on high in contemplation and love of the godhead, who did not find this high and wonderful cloud of unknowing between him and his God.[144] It was in this cloud that Mary was occupied, sending forth her hidden impulses of love. Why? This is the best and holiest part of contemplation that may be had in this life; and it was her desire never to leave this part for anything; so much so that when her sister Martha complained about her to our Lord, and bade him command her sister to get up and help her, and not to leave her to work and labour by herself, Mary sat in silence and answered not a word. She did not offer so much as a frown towards her sister, for any complaint that she could make.[145] And no wonder: because she had another work to do, of which Martha knew nothing. Therefore she had no leisure to listen to her or to answer her complaints.

---

in the mystical ark of Moses (cf. infra, chaps. 73 and 74) proceeds to the contemplative exegesis of the two lives exemplified in Martha and Mary: "For whilst Martha, as Scripture teaches, was occupied in serving, Mary sat at the Lord's feet, listening to his words. In this way, as she sat and listened, she understood the highest wisdom of God hidden in the flesh, which she gazed upon with her physical eye" (*Benjamin Maior* 5, 1).

144. R. M.: "As often as we are completely rapt into the Cloud of Unknowing, which is the author's subject here, our ravishing, in comparison with that of the blessed in heaven who see, is a sort of cloud, though it is luminous. Further, though God is clearly seen by the blessed in heaven, he is still far above their comprehension, otherwise he could not be said to be immense. From this point of view, the blessed in heaven are also in a cloud, even though he is seen most clearly according to each one's capacity."

145. Methley here introduces a lengthy "moral" exegesis on 1 Kings 13:19: "The Philistines took steps to prevent the Hebrews making swords and spears; but every Israelite went down to them to sharpen his ploughshare, mattock, axe and sickle." The Philistines are the proud and worldly men who prevent the Hebrews—the contemplatives—from answering modestly the attacks (these are their lances and spears) of the worldly. "And we follow Mary in truth when we make no attempt

You see, my friend, all these works, words and looks that passed between our Lord and these two sisters are given as an example of all actives and all contemplatives that have lived in holy Church since that time, and shall live, until the day of judgement. For Mary stands for all contemplatives, who should conform their behaviour to hers; and in the same way Martha stands for the actives, according to the same comparison.

CHAPTER XVIII

Actives still complain about contemplatives, as Martha complained of Mary: the cause of these complaints is ignorance.

Just as Martha complained about her sister Mary, in the same way, even to this day, all actives complain about contemplatives.[146] Whenever a man or a woman living in any company in this world—whether it be religious or secular, it makes no difference—is aware that he is being moved through grace and with the advice of his director to forsake all outward business and set himself entirely to live the contemplative life,[147] as best he knows how, and according as

---

to defend ourselves against our detractors, passing over what is transitory." This is a *locus classicus* in medieval exegesis not only on the two lives, but on the "mixed life" of prelates and preachers. Cf. Gregory the Great, who teaches that to go down to the Philistines means to learn the liberal arts, which will help our understanding of Scripture *(In Ium Regum Expositiones)* III, 2: PL 79, 355–57).

146. R. M.: "The author is speaking in general terms; for not everyone is against good people all the time. May be some openly side with contemplatives; certainly others do, but 'secretly, for fear of the Jews.'" The scriptural allusion is to John 19:38.

147. It is noteworthy that the early Carthusians whose writings have been identified, including Saint Bruno himself, find themselves having to emphasize that the solitary life has its true place in the life of the Church. So Saint Bruno himself wrote to Raoul de Verde, the future Archbishop of Rheims (cf. *Lettres des premiers*

his conscience and his spiritual director advise him, then straightway his brothers and sisters, all his best friends, and many others who are ignorant of his inward movements and of that manner of life which he sets himself to live, turn upon him with many complaints. They reprove him sharply, saying that what he is doing is nothing; and they begin to tell him stories, true as well as fictitious, of men and women who have fallen away after giving themselves to the contemplative life; but they never say anything about those who persevere.

I agree that there are many who appear to have forsaken the world, who do fall away and have fallen away in the past; and instead of becoming God's servants and his contemplatives, have become the devil's, because they would not permit themselves to be governed by true spiritual counsel. And so they turn out to be hypocrites or heretics, or they fall into frenzies and many other kinds of misfortune, to the scandal of all holy Church.[148] But I shall say no more of them at this time, lest we digress. Later on perhaps, God willing and if need be, we may say[149] something about the nature and causes of their falling away. Let us leave them for the moment, and get on with our subject.

Chartreux, Sources Chrétiennes 88, Paris, 1962, p. 77). It is a point made with all emphasis in the *Consuetudines* of the Order. So Walter Hilton writes to Adam Horsley, then an official of the Exchequer, in praise of the solitary life. As we have seen, it is the burden of Methley's approach to *The Cloud* that the solitary, Carthusian life is intended to be that of the perfect.

148. De Balma writes in his prologue that "some religious, like the Israelites of long ago, have deserted the worship of their Creator, and have given themselves to the service of man-made idols". Cassian speaks of the neglect of contemplation as fornication (*Collationes* I, 13; PL 49, 499).

149. The main stream of the MSS in H.'s text appear to read "*men* mowe sey"; but it is significant that she does not cite the reading of Do as well as Pa, "we"; and both the Latin versions read *possumus*, "we can."

CHAPTER XIX

*A brief apology by the author of this book; all con-
templatives must wholly excuse all actives for their
complaints of word or deed.*

Some may think that I do little honour to Martha, that
special saint, because I draw a parallel between her complaints
against her sister with wordly men's words, or theirs with
hers. But truly I do not mean any dishonour to her or to
them. God forbid that in this book I should say anything
that might be taken as a rebuke to any of the servants of
God in any degree, particularly of his special saint. For I
believe that every excuse should be made for her complaining,
if we take into account the time and the way in which she
spoke. Her ignorance was the cause of what she said. It is
no wonder that she did not know, at that time, how Mary
was occupied; for I believe that up to then she had heard
but little of this perfection.[150] Also, what she said was said
courteously and in a few words; therefore there is every excuse
for her.[151] Similarly, it seems to me that men and women
living the active life in the world should also have every excuse
made for them when they complain in the manner we have
mentioned before, even though what they say is said rudely;
for we must make allowance for their ignorance. Just as Martha
had very little knowledge of what her sister Mary was doing,
when she complained of her to our Lord; in the same way
these people nowadays have little or no knowledge of what
these young disciples of God are about, when they turn from

---

150. The author doubtless has in mind Martha's later "confession of faith"
in response to the Lord's spiritual questioning, "I am the resurrection and the life. . . .
Do you believe this?" and her "secret" calling of her sister Mary. Cf. John 11:20–
29.

151. R. M.: "Martha and many others are to be considered in good faith.
But those who have knowledge either full or in part, or according to our text
who should have it and refuse to acquire it when they can, are culpable in so
far as they blame contemplatives maliciously."

the business of this world and dispose themselves to be God's special servants in holiness and righteousness of spirit. If they did know, I daresay that they would neither do nor say as they do. So it seems to me that we must always make every excuse for them, because they know no better way of life than that which they live themselves. Furthermore, when I reflect on my own innumerable faults which I have committed myself in time past, both by word and deed, because of my ignorance, it seems to me that if I myself would have God excuse me for faults I have committed in ignorance, then I should in charity and compassion always excuse the ignorant words and deeds of other men. Otherwise I am not doing to others as I would that others did to me.[152]

CHAPTER XX

Almighty God will answer well enough for those who have no desire to leave their occupation of loving him in order to make excuses for themselves.

So it seems to me that they who are set on being contemplatives should not only make excuses for active men who complain about them, but it seems to me also that they should be so occupied in spirit that they take little or no heed of what men might do or say concerning them. That was what Mary did, who is an example for us all, when her sister Martha complained to our Lord. And if we do that sincerely, our Lord will do now for us what he did then for Mary.

What was that? It was this. Our loving Lord Jesus Christ, to whom nothing is secret, though Martha asked him to act as judge, and to bid Mary rise up and help her to serve him, yet because he saw that Mary was fervently occupied in spirit

---

152. The "golden rule" as enunciated in Matthew 7:12: "All things therefore whatsoever you would that man should do to you, do you also to them. For this is the law and the prophets."

with the love of his godhead, he answered courteously and reasonably, as became him, on behalf of her who would not leave his love in order to excuse herself. And how did he answer? Indeed, not merely as a judge to whom Martha had appealed, but as an advocate he lawfully defended her who loved him. And he said, "Martha, Martha." In his urgency he called her name twice, because he wanted her to hear him and to take heed of his words. "You are much occupied," he said, "and troubled about many things." For they who are actives must always be occupied and busy about many different things, which are given to them first for their own use, and then for acts of mercy towards their fellow-Christians, as charity demands. This our Lord said to Martha because he wished to let her know that her business was good and profitable for her soul's salvation. But lest she should think that this is the best work that a person might do, he added these words: "Only one thing is necessary."

What is that one thing? Surely that God may be loved and praised for himself, above all other business, bodily or spiritual, that man can do. And lest Martha might think that she could both love and praise God above all other business, bodily or spiritual, and at the same time be busy about the necessities of this life, he wished to make it clear to her that she could not serve God both in corporal works and in spiritual works together perfectly (imperfectly she could, but not perfectly). So he added to what he had said: that Mary had chosen the best part, which would never be taken away from her.[153] Because that perfect movement of love which is begun here

---

153. "All the just love God, but there is a special and pre-eminent love of God in perfect spiritual men, which by its excellence outstrips reason and understanding. This love is called ecstatic, or producing ecstasy, because it raises the sovereign point of the loving power (*affectus*) above all intellectual knowledge. On this love is founded the best part of Mary, which shall never be taken from her (Luke 10) because charity never falls away (1 Corinthians 13)" (Thomas Gallus, in his Explanation on the *Divine Names*, chap. 4).

THE CLOUD OF UNKNOWING

is equal in all respects with what shall last without end in the bliss of heaven; they are both one.[154]

CHAPTER XXI

The correct interpretation of the gospel text "Mary has chosen the best part."

What is the meaning of "Mary has chosen the best"? Wherever the best is declared or named it demands that these two things should precede it: a good and a better; in order that itself may be the best, the third in number. What are these three good things, of which Mary chose the best? Three lives they are not, for holy Church only takes account of two, the active life and the contemplative life.[155] These two lives are allegorically understood in this gospel story of these two sisters, Martha and Mary: by Martha the active, by Mary the contemplative. Outside of these two lives, no man can be saved;[156] and where there are no more than two, no man can choose the best.

But though there are only two lives, yet in these two there are three parts, each one better than the other. And these three have been set out specifically in their places earlier

---

154. "The perfection of unitive love is precisely the same union as in heaven; but here below separation is still possible." So Gallus, in his third commentary on the Canticle (3:11 "in the day of the espousals"). Our author, in his *Letter on Prayer*, calls it the oneness of love and union of wills "where a marriage is made between God and the soul." R. M. qualifies this: "Though the anagogical impulses of love in the perfect are numberless, yet they are called one and the same, because in some fashion they are the same movement here below as they will be there. Here in a more hidden way; there, more clearly." However, the question here does not refer, as R. M. translates *(equalis est in numero)*, to the frequency of the "stirrings," but to the quality of the contemplative love.

155. Cf. Introduction, supra, pp. 61ff.

156. Guigo du Pont: The Church approves two forms of life, the active and the contemplative ... outside these two lives, there is nothing truly good (*De Contemplacione*, MS cit., f. 44r.).

on in this book.[157] For, as we have said, the first part consists in good and honest corporal works of mercy and charity. This is the first degree of the active life, as was noted above. The second part of these two lives consists in good spiritual meditations on a man's own wretchedness, on the passion of Christ and the joys of heaven. The first part is good, but this part is better; for this is the second degree of the active life, and the first of the contemplative life. In this part the contemplative life and the active life are joined together in spiritual relationship. They are made sisters after the example of Martha and Mary. An active may make progress in contemplation thus far and no further, unless very seldom, and by a special grace. A contemplative may not descend any lower towards active life than this, except very seldom and when there is great need.

The third part of these two lives stands in this dark cloud of unknowing, with many secret impulses of love towards God himself. The first part is good, the second is better, but the third is the best of all. This is Mary's best part; and therefore it is clearly to be understood that our Lord did not say, "Mary has chosen the best life"; for there are only two lives, and of two no man can choose the best. But of these two lives, "Mary has chosen," he said, "the best part, which shall never be taken away from her." The first part and the second, although both are good and holy, yet they end with this life. For in the other life, it will not be necessary to exercise ourselves in the works of mercy, or to weep for our wretchedness or for the passion of Christ. For then no one shall be hungry or thirsty, no one shall die for cold, or be sick or without lodging or in prison or need burial,[158] for then no one shall die anymore.[159] But the third part,

---

157. Cf. supra, chap. 8, pp. 135–39.
158. Cf. Matthew 25:35–36.
159. Apocalypse 21:4: "He will wipe away every tear from their eyes; and there will be no more death, or mourning, or cries of distress, no more sorrows: these old things are passed away."

which Mary chose, let those choose who are called to it by grace; or to speak more truly, let those who are chosen for it by God tend towards it with desire. For that shall never be taken away; if it begin here, it will last without end.

So let the voice of our Lord cry to these actives as if he were speaking now to them on our behalf, as he did then for Mary to Martha. "Martha, Martha": "Actives, actives, busy you now as best you can in the first part and in the second, now in the one and now in the other; and if you so desire and feel yourselves so disposed, in both at once. But do not meddle with contemplatives, you do not know what they are about. Let them sit at their rest and at their play,[160] with the third and the best part of Mary."

CHAPTER XXII

The wonderful love of Christ for Mary, who represents all sinners truly converted and called to the grace of contemplation.

Sweet was that love between our Lord and Mary. She had great love for him; but his for her was greater. And if a man would contemplate aright all the looks that passed between him and her, not according to the words of a gossip, but according to the witness of the gospel story which cannot in any way be false, he will find that her heart was so set on loving him that nothing beneath him could bring her comfort, nor keep her heart from him. This is she, that same Mary, who, when she sought him at the sepulchre with tears running down her face, refused to be comforted by angels.[161] For when they spoke to her with such sweetness and such love, and said: "Do not weep, Mary, because our Lord whom

---

160. R. M. translates the ME "in here rest and in here pley" (cf. H., 55/5) as *in sua quiete et suo solacio.*

161. Cf. John 20:7–18.

you seek is risen, and you shall possess him, and see him alive in all his beauty amongst his disciples in Galilee, as he said," she would not go away on that account, because it seemed to her that when people truly seek the king of angels, they ought not to leave off because of angels.[162]

Furthermore, whoever will examine carefully the gospel story, he will find many wonderful examples of perfect love written about her for our instruction[163] which are also in accord with the exercise described in this book, as though they had been set down and written for this very purpose. And, indeed, so they were, if anyone can rightly understand them.

If anyone wants to see in the gospel account the wonderful and special love that our Lord had for Mary, who stands for all habitual sinners truly converted and called to the grace of contemplation,[164] he will find that our Lord could not allow any man or woman, not even her own sister, to speak a word against her, without himself answering for her. Furthermore, he reproached Simon the leper in his own house, because his thoughts were against her.[165] This was great love; this was surpassing love.

---

162. Cf. Matthew 28:1; John 20:11.

163. Cf. Matthew 19:12.

164. When Julian of Norwich writes of "the sinners . . . known to Holy Church, on earth and also in heaven, by their surpassing honours," she tells us that "God joyfully . . . brought to my mind first Magdalen" (*Showings*, p. 242).

165. Cf. Luke 7:36ff.; Mark 14:3. The author takes for granted the traditional identification of the "three Maries": the woman who was a sinner, Mary of Bethany, and Mary Magdalen.

CHAPTER XXIII

It is God's will spiritually to provide and answer
for those who have no desire to provide and answer
for themselves, because of their preoccupation with his
love.

Truly, then, if we are ready to conform our love and
our living, insofar as is possible for us by grace and by direction, to the love and the living of Mary, there is no doubt
that he shall answer now for us spiritually, in the same way,
every day, in the hearts of all those that either speak or think
against us. And not but what there will always be someone
to think or speak something against us as long as we live
this life of travail, even as they did against Mary.[166] But I
say that if we pay no more heed to what they say or think,
and do not give up this hidden ghostly work because of their
words or their thoughts, anymore than she did, our Lord,
I say, will answer them in spirit, as long as all is well with
them who so think and speak, to such effect that within a
few days they will be ashamed of their words and their
thoughts.[167]

Just as he will answer for us in this way in spirit, so
he will direct other men in spirit to provide us with all that
is necessary for this life, such as food and clothes and everything else, when he sees that we refuse to leave off the
work of his love to busy ourselves about those things. I say
this in refutation of their error who maintain that it is not
lawful for men to devote themselves to the service of God
in the contemplative life, unless they are assured beforehand
of having what is necessary for the body.[168] For they say

---

166. Cf. Matthew 5:11–12.
167. Cf. Psalm 6:11.
168. Cf. Matthew 6:31–33.
169. At the foot of the page (f. 17b.) in Do, the Latin hexameter is quoted
(written in James Grenehalgh's hand): *Dat Deus omne bonum, sed non per cornua taurum.*

THE CLOUD OF UNKNOWING

that God sends the cow, but not by the horn.[169] Now they
are wrong to say this of God, as they well know.[170] For
if you, whoever you are, have been sincerely converted from
the world to God, you must trust steadfastly that God will
give you, without your attending to it, one of two things:
either an abundance of what is necessary,[171] or strength in
body and spiritual patience to put up with the lack of them.[172]
What then does it matter which of these two a man has?
For true contemplatives it is all the same. And whoever is
doubtful of this, either the devil is in his heart and robs
him of his faith, or else he is not yet as truly converted
to God as he should be; no matter how clever or holy the
reasons which he puts up against it, whoever he may be.

So you who set yourself to be a contemplative as Mary
was, choose rather to be humbled under the wonderful height
and worthiness of God,[173] which is perfect, rather than under
your own wretchedness, which is imperfect. That is to say,
take care that you make the worthiness of God the object
of your special contemplation, rather than your own wretchedness. For they who are perfectly humble shall never lack

---

170. This is the teaching of the *Ladder*, "He [God] acts like a prodigal father";
or as the proverb has it, "He gives the ox by the horn" (ed. cit., p. 95).

171. The author of the *Ancrene Riwle* takes it for granted that his anchoresses
will be reasonably provided for, to the extent that they need to live as frugally
as they can on the alms that they, apparently, liberally receive (Salu, pp. 183–84).
He is speaking in the context of the contemplative life, and his text is Martha
and Mary, Luke 10:42. In fact, as H. (p. 192) indicates, citing R. M. Clay, "The
Bishop was careful not to licence anyone unless he was satisfied that sustenation
was secure and permanent" (*Hermits and Anchorites of England* [London, 1913], p.
103); and that this was the general practice, Aelred of Rievaulx's *De Institutione
Inclusarum* (VI, XI) is sufficient witness. R. M.'s Charterhouse of Mount Grace was
a royal foundation under Richard II, and they were granted the profits of the lead
mines on their estates (cf. E. M. Thompson, *The Carthusian Order in England*, pp.
229ff.), but it had fallen on hard times before the end of the fifteenth century
(ibid., p. 232).

172. Spiritual patience, one of the fruits of the Holy Spirit according to the
Pauline list in Galatians 5:22, is constantly stressed in both Old and New Testaments,
particularly in the context of persecution. Cf. NCE, vol. 8, 1087ff.

173. "Be humbled under the mighty hand of God, that he may exalt you
in the time of his visitation" (1 Peter 5:6).

anything, neither corporal nor spiritual.[174] The reason is that they have God, in whom is all abundance; whoever has him, indeed, as this book says, needs nothing else in this life.[175]

CHAPTER XXIV

The nature of charity; it is subtly and perfectly contained in the exercise described in this book.

We have said that humility is subtly and perfectly contained in this little blind impulse of love as it beats upon this dark cloud of unknowing, with all other things put down and forgotten. The same is to be understood of all the other virtues, and particularly of charity. We are to understand that charity means nothing else than the love of God for himself above all creatures, and the love of man equal to the love of yourself for God's sake.[176] It is very obvious that in this exercise God is loved for himself above all creatures. For, as was said before, the essence of this exercise is nothing else but a simple and direct reaching out to God for himself.[177] I call it a simple reaching out because in this exercise the perfect apprentice does not ask to be released from pain or for his reward to be increased; in a word, he asks for nothing but God himself; so much so that he takes no account or regard of whether he is in pain or in joy,[178] but only that the will of him whom he loves be fulfilled. It is evident, then, that in this exercise God is perfectly loved for himself,

---

174. This is the burden of the *Magnificat;* cf. Luke 1:46–53.

175. The sentiments of the great prayer of Julian of Norwich: "God of your goodness give me yourself, for you are enough for me . . ." (*Showings*, p. 184).

176. The author's version of the "great commandment": Cf. Deuteronomy 6:5; Leviticus 19:18; Luke 10:27. H. cites Augustine's version in his *De Doctrina Christiana,* III, 16.

177. Guigo du Pont: "When he begins to draw more often and more earnestly from the God-man these burning impulses, he immediately sends them up to God, without subjecting them to any other reflection or meditation" (MS cit., f. 43r.).

178. Cf. *The Ascent to Contemplative Wisdom*, p. 247.

and above all creatures. In this exercise, the perfect worker will not permit his awareness of the holiest creature God ever made to have any share.

Experience shows that in this exercise, the second, the lower branch of charity, that for your fellow-Christian, is truly and perfectly fulfilled. For the perfect worker here has no special regard for any individual, whether he is kinsman or stranger, friend or foe.[179] For he considers all men alike as his kinsmen, and no man a stranger to him. He considers all men his friends and none his foes. So much so that he considers all those that cause him pain and do him mischief in this life to be his very special friends, and he considers that he is being moved to wish them as much good as he would to the dearest friend he has.[180]

Chapter XXV

During the time of this exercise, the perfect soul has no special regard for any particular person in this life.

During this exercise, I say that he must not have any special regard for anyone alive, whether friend or foe, kinsman or stranger. For if this exercise is to be done perfectly, that cannot be, as it is when all things under God are entirely forgotten; which is fitting for this exercise. But I avow that he shall be made so virtuous and so charitable by reason of this exercise that when he comes down to frequent the company of or to pray for his fellow-Christians, his will shall

---

179. "If the mind would achieve the perfection of its desire, it must imitate the divine attitude: that of the spiritual sun which sends down the radiance of his bounty on good and evil alike. Thus we are to beseech the Saviour's mercy not only for our relatives, but for all; just as he himself wishes to sustain with his merciful love all human kind, without discrimination.... We must imitate him who showers down his most blessed love on all alike" (De Balma).

180. Cf. Matthew 6:44–48.

be directed as particularly towards his foe as towards his friend, towards the stranger as towards his kinsman. I do not mean that he comes down from this work completely, for that cannot be without great sin, but from the height of the contemplative exercise, which he must do sometimes when it is expedient and necessary according to the demands of charity.[181] Yes, and sometimes his will must be directed rather to his foe than to his friend.[182]

It must be said, however, that in this exercise he has not the leisure to consider who is his friend or foe, kinsman or stranger. I am not saying that he is not to feel sometimes, and even often, that in his affection he is more drawn to one or two or three than to all the rest; that is lawful for many reasons, and as charity demands.[183] Such special affection Christ our Lord had for John and Mary and Peter before many others.[184] What I say is that in the time of this exercise all alike should be dear to him; because then he will experience no cause for affection, except God alone. Thus, all will be loved plainly and simply for God, and in the same degree as he loves himself.

For as all men were lost in Adam,[185] and as all men who bear witness to their desire of salvation by good works

<hr/>

181. The author's casual reference here indicates the commonplace nature of the problem. Guigo the Angelic, in the *Ladder*, equally takes for granted the superiority of the contemplative life and the exercises proper to it; of the four obstacles to the continual occupation of the contemplative he simply says that unavoidable necessity is the first (op. cit., p. 97). The problem was a more serious and practical one for Gregory the Great, and he deals with it at length in his *Regula Pastoralis* [Pastoral care]. His principle is that preachers and pastors must aim at the union of the two lives; but contemplatives should undertake external works only with reluctance—an unwilling obedience (op. cit., I.6).

182. Cf. Luke 6:27–36.

183. The *locus classicus* for this teaching is Origen's comment on Canticles 2:4: "He set in order charity in me" (*Hom. in Cant.* 3, V, 4; PG 13, 156).

184. Cf. John 13:23; 19:26; 20:2, 21:15–17. "Mary" here refers to Mary Magdalen: cf. supra, chap. 22, p. 165.

185. The passage is repeated in the author's letter *Private Direction (Privy Counsel)*: cf. Romans 5:12–21.

are saved and shall be by the power of Christ's passion alone,[186] a soul whose affection is perfectly extended in this exercise and thus united to God in spirit, not exactly in the same way, but as it were in the same way, does all that in it lies, as the experience of this exercise bears witness, to make all men as perfect in this work as it is itself. For just as when a limb of our body feels sore, all the other limbs are in pain and ill-affected on that account,[187] or when one limb is in good health, all the rest are likewise in good health; so it is, spiritually, with all the limbs of holy Church. For Christ is our Head and we are the limbs, as long as we are in charity.[188] And whoever desires to be a perfect disciple of our Lord is called upon to lift up his spirit in this spiritual exercise for the salvation of all his natural brothers and sisters, as our Lord lifted up his body on the cross.[189] And how? Not for his friends and his kinsfolk and for those who love him dearly, but in general, for all mankind, without any special regard for one more than for another. For all those who desire to forsake sin and ask for mercy are to be saved through the power of his passion.[190]

What has been said of humility and charity is to be un-

---

186. Cf. Denzinger-Schönmetzer, 624.

187. Cf. 1 Corinthians 12:12, 22.

188. Cf. Ephesians 5:23.

189. Cf. John 10:35. It is Thomas Gallus who reduces the Dionysian extension to the following of Christ, especially of Christ suffering: e.g., in his Explanation on the *Ecclesiastical Hierarchies*, chap. 3, where the text reads, *divina benignitas ordinans substantiam nostram et formans deiforme archetypis pulchritudinibus*—"the divine goodness benignly directs our substance and fashions it in his own form by the archetypal beauties." Gallus's comment is: "directing our *substance:* that is, our heart, our whole life and living, words and deeds, *benignly,* that is, in imitation of the loving Jesus Christ who shows us so much love, *and fashions it in his own form* by means of the *archetypal* beauties: that is, makes us like to God through the beautiful works of Christ, which are the exemplars of all our living: 1 Peter 4, 'Christ suffered for us leaving us an example'; John 3:14, 'As Moses lifted up the serpent in the wilderness, so must the Son of Man be lifted up'; 1 Corinthians 2:2, 'For I decided to know nothing among you except Jesus and him crucified.' The mysteries of the divine humanity provide a kind of ladder to the contemplation of his Godhead."

190. Cf. Julian of Norwich: "All will be turned to our honour and profit by the power of his passion" (*Showings*, p. 227).

derstood of all the other virtues; for they are all subtly contained in this little impulse of love mentioned before.

CHAPTER XXVI

This exercise is extremely laborious except with very special graces, or habitual cooperation with ordinary graces over a long period; the distinction in this exercise between the activity of the soul supported by grace, and the activity of God alone.

So now labour earnestly for a short while, and beat upon this high cloud of unknowing, and then take your rest. For whoever is to become accustomed to this exercise will have hard labour;[191] yes, and very hard labour indeed, unless he receive a very special grace, or else it has become a habit with him over a long period.[192]

But, you may ask, in what does this labour consist? Surely not in that devout impulse of love that is continually worked in the will, not by the soul itself but by the hand of almighty God, which is always ready to perform this work in every soul that is disposed for it,[193] and does all that it can, and has done for a long time, to make itself ready for this exercise? And so, you may ask, where precisely is the labour? The work consists in the treading down of the awareness of all the creatures that God ever made, and in keeping them under

191. The author seems to be recalling the necessary abandonment of the "knowing power" in this exercise. As De Balma says: "This attachment (of the intellect to the affection) has to be rejected by great labour *(nonnisi per magnum exercicium et laborem);* for the intellect's apprehension is by means of the imagination and fancy . . . and . . . He is unknown to the intellect."

192. Cf. *The Ascent to Contemplative Wisdom*, p. 249.

193. Love of God is the first impulse implanted in the minds of those who are incorporated into Christ by baptism: "Through this love the mind tends directly into God and is extended towards union with him" (Gallus, Explanation on the *Ecclesiastical Hierarchy*, chap. 2). He points out, in the same chapter, that "every soul who truly loves God is united to him, though he may not know it."

the cloud of forgetting, as we mentioned before.[194] Here is all the labour; for this, with the help of grace, is man's work. And the other beyond this, the impulse of love, this is the work of God alone. So press on with your own work, and he, I promise you, will certainly not fail in his.

Press on then earnestly, and show your mettle. Do you not see how he is standing waiting for you? For shame! Labour earnestly for a little while, and you will soon find rest from the severity and the hardship of that work.[195] For though it is hard and constraining in the beginning,[196] when you have no devotion, nevertheless afterwards, when you have devotion it shall become very restful and very easy for you, though it was so hard before.[197] Then you shall have very little labour, or none at all. For then God will work sometimes all by himself; but not always nor even for a long time together, but when it pleases him and as it pleases him; then it will seem to you a joyful thing to leave him to get on with it.[198]

Then perhaps it will be his will to send out a ray of spiritual light, piercing this cloud of unknowing between you and him, and he will show you some of his secrets, of which

194. "When the soul intent on union first extends itself towards the divine light, it is infected by all sorts of fancies, which threaten to deprive it of the sweet fruits of union; but because of its training in spiritual warfare it courageously passes through them, and treads them stoutly underfoot" (Gallus, first commentary on the Canticle, Pez, 530).

195. Cf. Matthew 11:27.

196. De Balma: "If at first the hardship done to the flesh seems insupportable, you will soon find the rest you are looking for in the joy of the Beloved".

197. "Union means that the devout mind enjoys God's company, and takes its joyous repose in him. We must realize that the way of this upward contemplation consists in the filial affection of blessed devotion. There is no other road to it" (Guigues du Pont, MS. cit., f. 42v.).

198. Guigues du Pont adds: "God, the Father of mercies, and the One who bestows all consolation, in his loving goodness, frequently finds a chink in that cloud on behalf of that soul who seeks him. It is through these chinks that God in his goodness is now and then touched by secret aspirations: that is, he pours himself out on the souls who penetrate his cloud with the sharp arrows of their loving affection."

man may not or cannot speak.[199] Then you shall feel your affection all aflame with the fire of his love, far more than I know how to tell you or may or wish to at this time.[200] For I dare not take it upon me to speak with my blabbing, fleshly tongue of the work that belongs to God alone; and, to put it briefly, even though I dared so to speak I would not wish to. But I am very pleased to speak to you of the work that falls to man, when he feels himself moved and helped by grace; for it is less hazardous to speak of this than of the other.

CHAPTER XXVII

Who should undertake this grace-giving exercise.

First and foremost, I will tell you who should give himself to this exercise, and when and by what means; and what discretion you ought to have in it. If you ask me who should give himself to it, I answer, all who have with a sincere will forsaken the world, and who give themselves not to the active life,[201] but to that life which is called the contemplative. All these should give themselves to this grace and to this exercise, whoever they are, whether they have been habitual sinners or not.

---

199. Cf. 2 Corinthians 12:4.

200. For a discussion of this passage, cf. Introduction, supra, p. 72.

201. On the exception he does make in favour of some actives, cf. his Prologue, supra, p. 103, and Introduction, supra, p. 14.

CHAPTER XXVIII

No one should presume to undertake this exercise until he has been lawfully absolved in his conscience of all his particular sins.

If you ask me when they should begin to undertake this exercise, I answer you and say, not before they have cleansed their conscience[202] of all the particular sins that they have committed beforehand, according to the ordinary direction of holy Church.[203]

In this exercise the whole root and the ground of sin which always remains in a soul after confession, no matter how earnest it has been, all withers away.[204] Whoever, then, wishes to undertake this exercise, let him first purify his conscience; and then when he has done all that he can in fulfilment of the Church's law, let him dispose himself boldly but humbly for this exercise. Let him consider that he has been kept from it for too long; for this is the exercise in which a person should labour all his lifetime, even though he may never have sinned seriously.

As long as a man lives in this mortal flesh, he will always see and feel this thick cloud of unknowing between himself and God. And not only that, but it is one of the painful

---

202. The bride does not seek union at the beginning of the *Canticle* until she has purified herself completely, according to the direction of the wise man, "I purified myself thoroughly in order to know and seek wisdom" (Ecclesiasticus 7:26). Gallus in the Prologue to his third commentary.

203. R. M.: "To call to mind all one's particular sins is difficult or impossible. But a person cleanses his conscience of each separate sin, through the absolution *(secundum effectum remissionis)* by confessing as fully as he can: that is, when nothing which ought to be confessed is kept back. And so the author adds: according to the ordinary direction of holy Church."

204. R. M.: "As long as you live this mortal life, you will be impeded by original sin. But as far as human exercises are concerned, there is none more powerful, for those who have taken the necessary steps, than the one in question, according to the directions given."

results of original sin that he will always see and feel that some of the many creatures that God made, or some of their works, will always be inserting themselves in his awareness, between himself and God.[205] This is the just judgment of God: that man, when he had the sovereignty and lordship over all other creatures, wilfully made himself subservient to the desires of his subjects, forsaking the commandment of his God and maker.[206] In the same way, now that he wishes to fulfil the commandment of God, he sees and feels that all the creatures that should be beneath him are proudly pressing above him, between himself and his God.

CHAPTER XXIX

A man must labour at this exercise perseveringly, enduring the pain of it and judging no one.

Therefore, whoever desires to come to the purity which he lost because of sin, and to arrive at that well-being where all sorrow passes away, must persevere in the labour of this exercise and endure the pain of it, whoever he be; whether he has been an habitual sinner or not.

All men find this exercise laborious, both sinners and those innocents who have never sinned grievously. Those who have been sinners find it much more laborious than those who have not; and that is very reasonable. And yet it often happens that some who have been wicked and habitual sinners come more quickly to the perfection of this exercise than those who have not. This is a miracle of mercy from our

---

205. There is, says Gallus, a double cloud between the self and God, who dwells in inaccessible light: This is due to the common blindness through the sin of Adam, and to the condition of our nature (on the *Canticle* 2, 9: "he stands behind our wall").

206. Cf. Genesis 2:19; 3:11.

Lord,[207] who gives his grace in this special way, to the wonder of all the world. But truly, I look forward to the delight of judgment day when God and all his gifts shall be seen clearly.[208] And then some who are now despised and considered as of little or no account, as common sinners, and perhaps some that are now wicked sinners, will take their rightful place in his sight with the saints; and some of those who now appear to be very holy and are honoured by men for their angelic behaviour, and some of those who perhaps have never sinned seriously, will have their place in sadness amongst the calves of hell.[209]

From this you must see that no man should be judged by others here in this life, neither for the good nor the evil that they do.[210] Of course it is lawful to judge whether the deeds are good or evil, but not the men.[211]

CHAPTER XXX

Who should judge or reprehend the faults of others.

And who, I pray, are to judge the deeds of others?[212] Surely those who have power over and care of their souls,

---

207. R. M.: "Properly speaking, a miracle is an event above nature; but our author is speaking more loosely, taking into account nature as it was before Adam sinned."

208. Our author may appear less sensitive than is Julian of Norwich concerning the delight on judgment day in the punishment of the wicked. Cf. *Showings*, p. 233.

209. Cf. Psalm 105:20.

210. Cf. Matthew 7:1.

211. R. M.: "It is lawful for us to pass judgment on those deeds which clearly cannot have come from a good conscience. But such a judgment cannot be inflexible, since the sinner can make amends."

212. R. M. cites Ecclesiasticus (17:12): "And he (sc. God) gave to everyone of them commandments concerning his neighbour," and comments: "In every walk of life, religious, cleric, or lay, we have to pass judgment with charity—religious on their brethren, clerics on their fellows, layfolk on their neighbour. But note that I say 'with charity.' And perfect charity takes into account time, place and

whether this power is given externally by the statute and the law of all holy Church, or else interiorly in spirit by the special impulse of the Holy Spirit in perfect charity.[213] Every man must take care not to presume to arrogate to himself the condemnation or reprehension of the faults of other men, unless he feels truly that he is led in this work, interiorly, by the Holy Spirit. Otherwise he may very easily err in his judgments. And therefore beware. Judge yourself as you like; it is a matter between you and your God, or between you and your spiritual father; but leave other men alone.[214]

CHAPTER XXXI

How to conduct oneself, when first undertaking this exercise, against all sinful thoughts and impulses.

When once you feel that you have done all that is in your power to make amends according to law by the judgement of holy Church, then you must begin to dispose yourself earnestly for the labour of this exercise. If it happens that

circumstances. In this life, charity is perfect only when it never fails (1 Corinthians 13:8); whilst in heaven it need not grow because it is always exercised perfectly. No-one knows by experience that he is truly moved by the Holy Spirit except through the Spirit himself."

213. Walter Hilton also has a chapter with this title; he does not however mention the special impulse of the Holy Spirit, but contents himself with saying that to reprove another from charity alone is not the task of the contemplative, "unless there is very great need, so that a man would perish if he went unreproved" (*Scale of Perfection* I, chap. 17).

214. R. M.: "The apostle says, 'neither do I judge my own self' (1 Corinthians 4:3). But if it is lawful for us to pass judgment on acts which clearly cannot be done with a good conscience, then it is much more so in the case of our own sins, whether they are openly committed or known only to God and ourselves. Note, however, that the author is speaking of the *ex professo* contemplative, who is in danger of sinning if he judges definitively and without discernment on uncertain or obscure matters; unless he has the Holy Spirit for witness. If you are someone's superior, and you must make a judgment, pray to God to be enlightened so that you can understand aright the statutes of the Church or of your Order. But beware of making a definitive judgment; this belongs to God alone."

particular sins which you have committed are always inserting themselves, in your awareness, between you and your God, or any new thought or impulse concerning any other sin, you are bravely to step above it with a fervent impulse of love, and tread it down under your feet. And try to cover them with a thick cloud of forgetting, as though they had never been committed by you or by any other man. And if such thoughts often arise, put them down often; in short, as often as they arise, as often put them down. And if it seems to you that this is very laborious, you can look for tricks and devices and secret subtleties or spiritual tactics,[215] by which you can put them away. These tactics are better learned from God than from the experience of any man in this life.

Chapter XXXII

Two spiritual devices helpful to the beginner in this exercise.

However, I would like to tell you something about these devices, according to my experience.[216] Put them to the test, and if you can do any better, well and good.[217]

You are to do all that in you lies to act as though you

---

215. ME: "sleiʒtes and wiles and priue sotiltees of goostly sleiʒtes" (H., 66/ 9–10). R. M.'s Latin version reads "industrias et machinas et secretas subtilitates vel spirituales practicaciones" (f. 20a.).

216. This chapter illustrates vividly the author's power of imagination, and his ability to suit it to his style. Cf. Preface, p. xiff.

217. Gallus, in the prologue to his third commentary on the *Canticle*, says that the contemplative soul (the bride of the *Canticle*), in her desire to be caught up to union, uses three devices *(tribus utitur artificiis):* most chaste prayer, revelation of the mind, and aptitude for union. Prayer is most chaste when the bride asks not for the spouse's gifts but for the spouse himself. *Revelatio mentis* is the mind's divesting itself of the obstacles to union enumerated in *Hidden Theology*, chap. 1. Aptitude for union is obtained through *affluentem devotionem et resolutionem:* "my soul has melted" (Cant. 5:4).

did not know that they are pressing very hard upon you and coming between you and your God. Try to look over their shoulders, as it were, as though you were looking for something else: that something else is God, surrounded on all sides by the cloud of unknowing.[218] If you do this, I am sure that within a short time you will find your burden easier. I believe that when this device is well and truly understood, it is nothing else but a longing desire for God, to experience him and see him as far as may be possible here below. This desire is charity, and it always wins easement.

There is another device, which you can put to the test if you so wish. When you feel that you can in no way put down these thoughts, cower down under them like a poor wretch and a coward overcome in battle, and reckon it to be a waste of time for you to strive any longer against them. In this way, though you are in the hands of your enemies,[219] you give yourself up to God; feel as though you were hopelessly defeated. Pay particular attention to this device, I pray you, for it seems to me that when you put it to the test you will find yourself melting as though to water.[220] And truly it seems to me that if this device is properly understood in its subtlety, it is nothing else but a true knowledge and experience of yourself as you are, a wretch, filth, far worse than nothing.[221] This knowing and experience is humility. This humility merits to have God himself coming down in his power to avenge you against your enemies, to take you up, to cherish you and to dry your spiritual eyes,[222] as the father does for the child that was in danger of death under the mouths of wild boars or mad, biting bears.

---

218. Cf. Exodus 20:22 (Vulgate).

219. Cf. Jeremiah 12:7.

220. Canticle 5:4 Cf. supra, note 217 .

221. "And the base things of the world and the things that are contemptible, hath God chosen; and things that are not, that he might bring to nought things that are . . ." (1 Corinthians 1:28ff. [Douai]).

222. Cf. Apocalypse 21:4; Isaiah 61:13.

Chapter XXXIII

*In this exercise a soul is absolved of his particular
sins and the punishment due to them; and yet there
is no perfect rest in this life.*

I am not going to speak to you of more devices at this
time; for if you have the grace to put these to the test by
experience, I believe that you will be able to teach me better
than I can teach you.[223] And even though it might happen
thus, truly it seems to me that I am very far from arriving
there. So I pray you to help me, and work both on your
own behalf and mine as well.

Press on, then, and labour earnestly for the time, I pray
you. Endure the pain humbly, if you cannot quickly acquire
these tricks. For truly this is your purgatory. But when your
pain is all over, and God has given you these devices, and
you have acquired the habit of them through grace, then I
am sure that you will be purified, not only from sin but
also from the pain attaching to it. I am speaking of the pain
of your own special past sins, not of the pain of original
sin. For that will always be with you to your dying day,
no matter how earnestly you labour. Nevertheless it shall
trouble you little, in comparison with the pain of your own
particular sins. And even so, hard labour will always be yours.
For new and fresh impulses towards sinning are always springing up out of this original sin, which you must always smite
down and earnestly cut away with the sharp, two-edged, awesome sword of discretion.[224] From this you can understand
and learn that there is no absolute security nor any true rest

223. "I decided to send you my thoughts ... so that you who have come
to know more about these matters by your experience than I have by theorizing
about them may pass judgment on my thoughts and amend them" (*Ladder*, p. 81).

224. "For the word of the Lord is sharper ... than any two-edged sword
... discerning the thoughts and intentions of the heart" (Hebrews 4:12). Fear of
the Lord is the beginning of wisdom, and discretion is a virtue without which
contemplation is impossible.

in this life. But you must not turn back because of this, or be too fearsome of falling. For if it happens that you receive grace for the destruction of the pain of your own particular sins of the past, in the way I have described, or better if you can, you may be sure that the pain of original sin, or else the new impulses to sin that are to come, will be able to trouble you hardly at all.

CHAPTER XXXIV

God gives this grace freely without any preceding cause;
it cannot be achieved by any particular means.

If you ask me by what means you are to come to the practice of this exercise, I beseech almighty God out of his great grace and great courtesy to teach you himself.[225] For it is right for me to let you know that I cannot tell you; and no wonder. Because this is the work of God alone, brought about in a special way in whatever soul that pleases him,[226] without any merit on its part. For without this divine work neither saint nor angel can ever hope even to desire it.[227] And I believe that our Lord will deign to effect this work in those that have been habitual sinners, particularly and as often, yes, and perhaps even more particularly and more often,

---

225. Cf. John 6:45; Isaiah 54:13.

226. "But this contemplative grace cannot be communicated in word or writing, for no one knows it except he who receives it, though he who possesses it can speak of it to someone else who has it" (Gallus, Explanation on the *Divine Names*, chap. 1).

227. R. M.: "The saints and angels in heaven do not see in a mirror dimly, but clearly, simply and openly, face to face; though they also see God in creatures. But what the author seems to be implying is this: since God is incomprehensible, it would never be possible to be carried above natural knowledge to the incomprehensible God, except by the hand of God. When the author says, 'without any merit,' we are to understand without sufficient or condign merit from every point of view. For we merit whenever we do good." De Balma: "No mind can perceive these things except by the divine visitation ... for this knowledge through ignorance is taught by God alone."

in those who have been habitual sinners,[228] than in others who, comparatively speaking, have never caused him great grief. It is his will to do this because he wishes to be seen as all merciful and almighty; he wishes us to see that he works as it pleases him, where it pleases him and when it pleases him.[229]

At the same time, he does not give this grace, nor does he accomplish this work in any soul who has not the capacity for it.[230] And yet there is no one lacking this grace who has not the capacity to receive it,[231] whether he be sinful or innocent. For the grace is not given because of innocence, nor is it withheld because of sin. Take careful notice that I say "withheld," and not "withdrawn."[232] You must beware of error here; for the nearer we come to the truth, the more we must be on our guard against error; and this is my intention. If you cannot understand what I say, lay it aside

---

228. Julian of Norwich says of the great penitents, such as David and the Magdalen (and amongst whom she includes herself): "And also God in his special grace visits whom he will with such great contrition, and also with compassion and true longing for him, that they are suddenly delivered ... and made equal with the saints" (*Showings*, p. 244–45).

229. Cf. John 3:8.

230. De Balma: "So it comes about by the divine mercy, and according to the capacity of the person, when the mind has aspired for a long time to be fastened more securely to the beloved by the knot of burning love, the blessed vision is granted to him, for a brief time—as it must be in rapture, according to his capacity.... In this supreme elevation, it is grace alone which is working" (*The Ascent* ... p. 249).

231. In a long passage on passive purification, in his Explanation on the *Divine Names*, chap. 4, Gallus notes that the eyes of the mind (the intellect and the affection) are closed by the after-effects of sin, actual and original, and by inordinate desires and fancies; and that they can be opened only by the divine illuminative grace. This grace sets the affection on fire and gives the soul a capacity and a taste for union.

232. R. M.: "*Withheld* and *withdrawn*, according to the author, differ in this way: a sinner, no matter how wicked he has been, when he is truly converted, becomes a persevering seeker after God, who does not withhold any gift of contemplation from him permanently. Such grace is given when it is most opportune, all circumstances considered; as is clear with the great priest Paul, the Magdalen and others; although it may be withdrawn for a time because of sin, as happened with David, who said 'Give back to me the joy of your salvation' (Psalm 50:14). For he who says 'Give back' indicates that he had it before."

until God comes and teaches you. Do this, and keep out of harm's way. Be on your guard against pride, because it blasphemes God in his gifts and makes sinners arrogant. If you were truly humble, you would have the right feeling for this divine work, even as I say: that God gives it freely without any meriting. The nature of this work is such that its presence gives the soul the capacity to possess it and to experience it; and no soul can have this capacity without that presence.[233] The capacity for this exercise is inseparably united to the exercise itself. The two cannot be divided. So whoever experiences this divine work is able for it, otherwise not; insomuch that without this divine work a soul is as it were dead and cannot covet it or desire it. For as long as you have a will for it and a desire for it, insomuch you possess it, neither more nor less. Yet it is not a will nor a desire, but something which you are at a loss to describe, which moves you to desire you know not what. You must not care if you understand no more of it; just press on with the exercise more and more, so that you are always engaged in it.[234]

To put it more clearly, let it do with you and lead you as it will. Let it be the one that works; you simply must consent to it.[235] Simply look at it, and just let it be. Do not interfere with it, as though you wished to help it on, lest you spill it all. Try to be the wood and let it be the

---

233. Gallus: "The divine goodness conforms us to himself according to our capacity" (Prologue to the Explanation on the Angelic Hierarchies). "Here the mind does not act but is acted upon" (the Gloss on *Draw me after thee* (1, 3) in the third commentary on the Canticle). "The eternal power of Christ, with whom I am united (by dark contemplation) gratuitously vivifies me and disposes me" (from the Explanation on the *Divine Names*, chap. 4). "It is through the power of charity that the soul in the sovereign point of the spirit is extended" (ibid., chap. 7). "The rational soul is personally united to the Word, supernaturally and gratuitously" (ibid., chap. 4). "This contemplation is a grace; to strive after it is not a precept but a counsel. Yet it is a precept when God commands that the grace granted be shown to him" (ibid.).

234. Gallus: "The grace of contemplation is given, not that the soul may exercise herself in it occasionally, but that often and with full deliberation she may seek to dwell in heaven" (Explanation on the *Divine Names*, chap. 1).

235. Cf. supra, note 233.

carpenter;[236] the house, and let it be the husbandman dwelling in the house. During this time be blind, and cut away all desire of knowing;[237] for this will hinder you more than it will help you. It is enough for you that you feel moved in love by something, though you do not know what it is; so that in this affection you have no thought of anything in particular under God, and that your reaching out is simply directed to God.[238]

If this is the way of it, then trust steadfastly that it is God alone who moves your will and your desire: he alone, entirely of himself, without any intermediary, either on his part or on yours.[239] And do not be afraid of the devil, for he cannot come so close. He can never come to move a man's will except very rarely, and very indirectly, no matter how clever he is. Nor can a good angel move your will effectively without an intermediary.[240] In short, nothing can move it except God.

By what I have said here you may understand a little, but much more clearly by experience, that in this exercise

---

236. Cf. the elaborate image in *Hidden Theology*, chap. II.

237. *The Ascent*: "Because it is difficult to abandon all those things [i.e., sensible and intellectual operations and objects], we are directed to shear them away" (p. 246). The textual source is Thomas Gallus who, in his Explanation on the *Divine Names* (chap. 1) concerning the silencing of the lower faculties, alters the Latin of his text from *sedantes* or *requiescentes* ("resting") to *secantes*, "cutting." The intellectual operations in this exercise must be cut away because the end of the operation is union, in which all knowledge is terminated. A point is reached in the ascent when the intellectual eye is deprived of sight.

238. Gallus: "It is permissible and safer and more useful, above all other exercises, for the soul to extend herself lovingly and devoutly to receive the divine visitation and always to desire an increase of divine knowledge. In this extension there is scarcely any labour or danger for the pure and loving soul. It is an extremely useful exercise, even when the mind is investigating nothing, and is not contemplating any particular facet of the divine wisdom" (Explanation on the *Divine Names*, chap. 1).

239. Ignatius Loyola synthesizes the traditional doctrine alluded to here, in his "Rules for the Discernment of Spirits (second week)" (*Exx* 329–331).

240. Cf. Saint Thomas Aquinas, *Summa Theologiae* I, 99. 111 and 114. Our author is well versed in Thomistic teaching. Cf. Introduction, supra, p. 40.

men must use no intermediaries, nor can they come to it through intermediaries. All good intermediaries depend on it, but it depends on none of them; nor can any intermediary lead you to it.[241]

CHAPTER XXXV

The threefold occupation of the contemplative-apprentice: reading, reflecting and praying.

Nevertheless, there are certain preparatory exercises which should occupy the attention of the contemplative apprentice:[242] the lesson, the meditation and the petition.[243] They may be called, for a better understanding, reading, reflecting and praying.[244] You will find a much better treatment of these three than I can manage in the book of another author. So I need not rehearse their qualities here.[245] I will, however, make the point—for those who are beginners and

241. Julian of Norwich expresses this teaching very beautifully and simply (*Showings*, chap. 6, pp. 184ff.).

242. For our author, the exercises preparatory to his "work," the dark contemplation, or rather this kind of contemplative effort, is what Thomas Gallus calls antecedent or speculative contemplation, "which is learnt as well by meditating as by reading or listening" (*Prologue* to the third commentary on the *Canticle*).

243. James Grenehalgh, in his annotations to *The Cloud* in MS Douce 262, cites this passage as evidence that the "disciple" was unlettered, i.e., did not know Latin. Initially, he may have been; but if, as is likely, he was a Carthusian "beginner," he would have learned his Latin in the interval of reflecting on *The Cloud*, and the receipt of the "Letter of Private Direction" *(Privy Counsel)*, with its liberal sprinkling of citations from the Latin Vulgate. Cf. Introduction, supra, pp. 9–11.

244. The first three terms—ME "Lesson, Meditacion, Oryson" (H.71/12) are immediately derived from church Latin: *Lectio, Meditatio, Oratio*. Of the second three, "Redyng" and "thinking" are from OE, though "preiing" is obviously derived from the Latin *precari*, "to entreat"; its first use in English according to NED is in 1303. R. M. translates both "Oryson" and "preiing" as *oracio*.

245. It is highly probable that the book here is Guigo II's *Ladder* (cf. pp 18, 19, 39–51)—reading, reflecting and praying are its first three rungs, the fourth is contemplation itself. Cf. Introduction, supra, pp. 78–79.

proficients,[246] but not for the perfect, insofar as there are such, here below—that these three are so linked together that there can be no profitable reflection without previous reading, or hearing.[247] (Reading and hearing come to the same thing: the clerics read the books, and the layfolk read the clerics when they listen to them preaching the word of God.[248]) Nor will beginners or proficients come to true prayer without previous reflection. See how this is demonstrated in this same book.[249]

God's word, whether written or spoken, is like a mirror.[250]

---

246. Guigo writes: "The first degree is proper to beginners, the second to proficients, the third to devotees" (p. 93). The suggestion that *The Cloud* author is referring to Hilton's Latin treatise on the same subject, "Letter to a Hermit"—*Epistola ad quemdam solitarium de lectione, intentione, oratione et aliis* (cf. *The Way* VI [July 1966] pp. 230–41), and/or to certain chapters in his *Scale of Perfection*, is obviously less likely. Cf. Introduction, p. 78ff. For the medieval monastic writers, the "beginners" *(incipientes)* are the novices, the proficients *(proficientes)* are the professed, and the perfect, "insofar as there are such, here below," are the *seniores*. Cf. Introduction, supra, p. 79.

247. *The Ladder*, after the summary statement "You can see ... how these degrees are joined to each other" (p. 92), goes on to elaborate how they are linked together (pp. 93–95).

248. "Listening is a kind of reading, and that is why we are accustomed to say that we have read not only those books which we have read to ourselves or aloud to others, but also those which our teachers have read to us" (*Ladder*, pp. 93–94).

249. ME: "See by þe preof in this same cours." McCann (ed. cit., p. 88) indicates the uncertainty of interpretation, as does H. (72/2–3). What they have perhaps failed to notice is that Guigo, in his chapter "How these degrees are linked to one another" (*Ladder*, p. 93), uses the example of the dialogue between the Samaritan woman (who was living with a man not her husband—John 4:6ff.) and Jesus at Jacob's well, and the woman's plea for "the water of life." "When the woman heard this, it was as if the Lord had read it to her and she meditated on this instruction in her heart, thinking that it would be profitable for her to have this water. Fired with the desire for it, she had recourse to prayer, saying, 'Lord, give me this water. . . .' You can see that it was because she had heard the Lord's word and then meditated on it, that she was moved to prayer" (p. 94).

250. The references above to "well" and "water" might have recalled to the author's mind the traditional image of scripture as a mirror. H. (p. 195) refers to Augustine and to the well-known passage from Gregory's *Moralia* II, 1: "Holy Scripture brings as it were a mirror before the eyes of the mind, so that we may see our spiritual face in it, and notice our dirtiness or comeliness."

The spiritual eye of your soul is your reason.[251] Your spiritual face is your consciousness. And just as your bodily eyes cannot see where the dirty mark is on your bodily face, without a mirror, or without someone else telling you where it is, so with your spiritual faculties.[252] Without reading or listening to God's word, it is not possible for the understanding, when the soul is blinded by habitual sin, to see the dirty mark on his consciousness. It follows, then, that when a person sees in the bodily or the spiritual mirror, or knows by the information he gets from someone else, just where the dirty mark is on his bodily or spiritual face, he goes to the well to wash it off—and not before. Now if this mark is a particular sin the well is holy Church, and the water is confession, with all its elements. And if the mark is simply the blind root with the impulse to sin, then the well is the merciful God, and the water is prayer, with all its elements.

And so you can see that beginners and proficients cannot come to proper reflection without previous reading or listening, or to prayer without previous reflection.

---

251. R. M.: "The human soul has many eyes according to various meanings, but in contemplatives, the affection which has the power of wounding is called the eye of the soul, according to the scripture, 'You have wounded my heart my sister, my bride, you have wounded my heart with one of your eyes, etc.' (Canticle 4:9)." Hugo de Balma, in speaking of the contemplative exercise, says "In the actual exercise itself, the speculative understanding must not think of anything. This is the eye by means of which, according to the Canticle, the spouse is wounded by the bride . . .' " (*The Ascent to Contemplative Widsom*, p. 244).

252. It is clear from the course of the argument that the author has in mind the definition of prayer which he gives later on: "A devout intent of the mind reaching out to God, in order to attain the good and to avoid evil" (chap. 39). We cannot pray to be rid of sin unless we know what it is. "The soul blinded in habitual sin" is of course the beginner, who is meditating on his past iniquity. The proficient is concerned with the hidden roots of the faults that remain in him.

CHAPTER XXXVI

The meditations of those habitually occupied in the exercise described in this book.

However, things are different for those habitually occupied in the exercise described in this book. Their meditations are, so to speak, sudden awarenesses and obscure feelings of their own wretchedness, or of God's goodness, without any previous reading or listening, or of a special sight of anything under God. These sudden intuitions and obscure feelings are more quickly learned from God than from man.[253]

It would not bother me at all if at this time your meditations on your own sinfulness or God's goodness—given of course that you feel yourself moved to it by grace, in accord with your spiritual counselling[254]—amounted to nothing other than what you find in the word "sin" or "God" or some similar word which took your fancy. For here it is not a question of analysing or elucidating these words rationally or listing their various meanings in the hope that such consideration would increase your devotion.[255] I do not believe this to be so, or that it could ever happen in this exercise. These words must be held in their wholeness. By "sin" you must mean some sort of undefined lump: nothing else, in fact, than yourself.[256] It is my belief that in this obscure look-

---

253. Cf. *The Ascent to Contemplative Wisdom*, p. 248.

254. "By counseyl" (ME). The author repeats his *caveat* that no one should undertake the contemplative exercise proper without the consent of an experienced spiritual father.

255. The author is again concerned with the discernment of spirits or impulses, or with the consolation and desolation proper to contemplatives: the careful and attentive reading of scripture, followed by the rumination and mastication of the "sweet kernel" (the *Ladder*'s description of meditation) does not of itself achieve self-awareness, or the awareness of God; this is caused directly by God.

256. "The soul is prevented from seeing God by its own proper darkness, which envelops it on all sides. This darkness is the result of original sin and actual sins, negligence, and also the oppression of the bodily dwelling. The divine light, i.e., special contemplative graces, gradually disperses this darkness and opens the eyes of the soul." So Gallus, in his Explanation on the *Divine Names*, chap. 4. Walter

ing at sin, as a congealed mass which is none other than yourself, there should be no need to look for anything to hold down during this time more irrational than yourself.[257] And yet anybody looking at you would see you quite co-ordinated in your bodily movements, and nothing remarkable in the way you kept your countenance, whether you were sitting, walking, lying down or leaning on something, or stand-ing or kneeling—sober and restful.

CHAPTER XXXVII

The special prayers of the habitual workers in the exercise of this book.

Just as the meditations of those habitually exercised in this grace and in this book are sudden intuitions without previous causes, it is the same with their prayers. I am speaking of their personal prayer, and not of those ordained by holy Church.[258] For those who are truly exercised in this work have more regard for the Church's prayer than for any oth-er.[259] And they perform them in the manner and according

Hilton (*Scale of Perfection*, I, chap. 52), speaking of this same darkness, says that it is "a dark and painful image of your own soul which lacks the light of knowing and the experience of loving, all wrapped around with the black stinking clothes of sin" (Underhill, p. 126).

257. R. M. considers that the author is here speaking about spiritual inebri-ation—being beside oneself in spirit. However, it is clear from other references that the author has in mind the intense sorrow which this awareness of the sinful self causes, and its almost intolerable burden. Cf. chaps. 43–44, infra, pp. 201ff. and *Private Direction*. Cf. also Julian of Norwich, *Showings*, chap. 39, p. 244: "Sin ... belabours ... breaks a man and purges him in his own sight so much that at times he thinks himself not fit for anything but to sink into hell."

258. This is one of the passages that most probably indicate that the author and his disciple belong to a religious order, since the prayers laid down by "holy Church" are obviously the divine office, and there is no indication that the author is thinking merely of the recitation of the office obligatory on secular priests. Similarly, the reference to "form and rule" and "holy fathers" would seem to refer to the rubrics for the monastic chanting of the office.

259. Hilton makes the same point in his *Letter to a Hermit*, MS P.R.O.1/239ff, 237–38.

to the rubrics ordained by the holy fathers who have gone before us. Their personal prayers, however, always rise directly to God without any intermediaries or previous or concomitant meditation.[260] And if words are used—and this happens rarely—they are very few indeed; in fact, the fewer the better. And it is my belief that a little word of one syllable is better than of two, and more in accordance with the work of the Spirit.[261] This is because a spiritual worker in this exercise should always find himself at the supreme and sovereign point of the Spirit.[262] Let me explain the truth of this by taking as an example a natural event. When a man or a woman is suddenly seized with fear of fire or of death, or some similar happening, that person is suddenly smitten in the depths of his spirit to cry out and beg for help. And he does this not in many words, or even in one word of two syllables. And this is because he feels that this would take too long to give vent to his need and the labouring of his spirit. So he breaks out in a loud and hideous scream, using a little word of one syllable, such as "fire!" or "out!"

Just as this little word "fire" suddenly beats upon and jars most effectively the ears of the bystanders, it is the same with the little word, whether spoken or thought or even ob-

---

260. De Balma: "This ascent ... is ... to be impelled directly by the ardour of love, without reflective knowledge of any creature *(sine omni creaturae speculo)*, without any preceding thought, without any accompanying impulse of the understanding" *(The Ascent to Contemplative Wisdom*, p. 244).

261. R. M.: "Contemplatives make use of vocal prayer, that is, prayer said out loud, in various ways according as they are led or acted upon by inspirations and infusions, as the apostle says: 'Those who are led by the spirit of God are children of God.' So their prayers willingly offered through grace are filled with contentment *(placor)* and fervour and sweet song *(canor)*. They are vocal in the sense that they are said out loud, or at least in the head, with or without movement of the lips."

262. De Balma draws an analogy between this infused prayer and the spontaneous movements of breathing—inhalation and exhalation, and emphasizes the Dionysian background: "... an exercise which cannot be properly expressed or explained in words, according to *Hidden Theology* (ch III) ... the higher one reaches in the ascent, the less the number of words. And when the ascent is complete, there will be no words at all" *(The Ascent to Contemplative Wisdom*, p. 247).

scurely conceived in the depth, or we may call it the height, of the spirit. (For in the spiritual realm, height and depth, length and breadth, are all the same.) And thus it bursts upon the ears of almighty God much more than any long psalm mumbled away in an inarticulate fashion.[263] And this is why it is written that a short prayer pierces heaven.[264]

CHAPTER XXXVIII

How and why their short prayer pierces heaven.

Why does this little prayer of one syllable pierce the heavens? Surely because it is offered with a full spirit, in the height and the depth, in the length and the breadth of the spirit of him who prays. In the height: that is with the full might of the spirit; in the depth: for in this little syllable all the faculties of the spirit are contained; in the length: because if it could always be experienced as it is in that moment, it would cry as it does then; in the breadth: because it desires for all others all that it desires for itself. It is in this moment that the soul comprehends with all the saints

---

263. Julian describes an aspect of her diabolic temptation as a conversation between two people speaking at once: "It was all low muttering ... they seemed to be mocking us when we say our prayers badly, lacking all the devout attention and wise care which we owe to God in our prayer" (*Showings*, pp. 315–16).

264. The traditional teaching on "short prayers" is to be found in the Patristic commentaries and references to the *Pater noster,* in the context of Matthew 6:7–13: "When you are at prayer, do not use many phrases. . . ." There is the additional teaching on ejaculatory prayer, which has its sources in Cassian's *Conferences* (X, 10), the rule of Saint Benedict (chap. 20), and especially Saint Augustine (*Epistola ad Probam* X, 20) who speaks of "very short prayers shot out *(iaculatas)* speedily." The Carthusian Dionysians Hugo de Balma and Guigues du Pont and our author, develop this teaching, referring it to the affective movement of the will in the exercise of dark contemplation. (Cf. Introduction, p. 81.) It would appear that the author is conflating texts here. Ecclesiasticus 35:17 says that "the prayer of the humble pierces the clouds"—"where God dwells," notes the *Bible de Jérusalem,* and refers us to Psalms 68:35, 104:3, etc. It is worth noting that a version of it occurs in *Piers Plowman,* (Passus X, 460–61) in an anti-intellectual context: "Souteres and sheperds, such lewed iottes/Percen with a *pater-noster* the paleys of hevene."

what is the length and the breadth, the height and the depth of the everlasting, all-loving, almighty and all-wise God, as Saint Paul teaches; not fully, but in some way and to some degree, as is proper to this work.

The eternity of God is his length; his love is his breadth; his power is his height, and his wisdom is his depth.[265] No wonder, then, that the soul which is so nearly conformed by grace to the image and likeness of God his maker is immediately heard by God.[266] Yes, and even if it were a very sinful soul, one which is, as it were, God's enemy, as long as it should come, through grace, to cry out with such a little syllable from the height and the depth, the length and the breadth of its spirit, it would always be heard and helped by God in the very vehemence of its shriek.

Let us take an example. If a man happened to be your deadly enemy and you heard him cry out with such terror, in the fulness of his spirit, this little word "fire!" or this word "out!" you would have no thought for his enmity, but out of the heartfelt compassion, stirred up and excited by the pain expressed in that cry, you would get out of bed even on a night in mid-winter, to help him put out the fire, or to bring him comfort in his distress.[267] O Lord, if a man can be moved by grace to such mercy and compassion for his enemy, his enmity notwithstanding, what compassion and

---

265. Ephesians 3:17. Walter Hilton's exegesis of this text is exactly the same: "... the length of the endless being of God, the breadth of the wonderful charity and goodness of God, the height of his almighty Majesty, and the groundless depths of the wisdom of God" (*Scale of Perfection*, I, chap. 12). The common source is Saint Bernard's *De Consideratione V*, chaps. 13–14.

266. The purpose of the contemplative exercise is this transformation, and one of the key texts of the medieval teaching on contemplation is 2 Corinthians 3:18: "We become transfigured into his likeness." So Augustine teaches: "The more the soul extends itself towards that which is eternal, the more it is reformed according to the image of God" (*De Trinitate*, 12, 7). This is the passage cited by Gallus in his treatment of the contemplative effort in *Divine Names*, chap. 1.

267. R. M.: "Good and devout contemplatives never rejoice over evil, but rejoice in truth (1 Corinthians 13:6). By this you may know if you are mortified and ready for this exercise, if you do not rejoice over the ill-fortune of your enemy, but are well-affected towards him from your heart and really love him because of Christ."

what mercy will God have for the spiritual cry of the soul welling up and issuing forth from the height and the depth, the length and the breadth of his spirit, which contains by nature all that a man has by grace, and much more! Surely he shall receive much more mercy, without comparison; since it follows that whatever belongs to a thing by nature is much closer to it than anything belonging to it by grace.

CHAPTER XXXIX

How the perfect contemplative must pray; the nature of prayer in itself; if it is vocal, it must be appropriate to the nature of prayer.

We must therefore pray in the height and the depth, the length and the breadth of our spirit; and not in many words but in a little word of one syllable. What shall this word be? Surely one which is most in accordance with the nature of prayer.[268] What word is that? First see what is the nature of prayer in itself; and then we can more clearly understand what word will be best in accordance with the nature of prayer.

Prayer in itself is nothing but a devout reaching out directly to God, in order to attain the good and to do away with evil.[269] And since every evil is comprehended in sin,

---

268. Gallus distinguishes three kinds of prayer: "Pure prayer is a petition for temporal things and for the removal of harmful things; purer prayer is a petition for spiritual things—'wash me from my iniquity ... create a clean heart in me' (Psalm 50); purest prayer is a petition not for his gifts but for himself." From the Prologue to the third commentary on the *Canticle*.

269. This is also the *Ladder*'s definition: "Prayer is the devout turning (ME 'entent', Latin *intentio*) to God to do away with evil and to attain the good" (p. 82). All prayer has within it the element of petition. Saint Augustine says, in the passage cited above (chap. 38, n. 264), that no bounds are to be set to this extension. Julian of Norwich also teaches that contemplative prayer is a continual seeking or beseeching (*Showings*, chap. 10). "... the fruit and the end of our prayer is to be united and like to our Lord in all things" (ibid., chap. 42, p. 251).

either as its effect or as sin itself, when we wish to pray with concentration for the removal of evil, we must neither say nor think, nor mean anything else, using no other words but this little word "sin." And if we desire with all our intent to pray for the attainment of any good, let us cry either verbally or in thought or desire, using nothing else, nor any other word, but this word "God." Because in God is contained all good, both as effect or as Being.[270]

Do not wonder why I set these words above all others. If I could think of any shorter words which so completely contained in themselves all good and all evil as do these two words, or if God taught me to use any other words, I would take them and leave these two; so I give you the same advice. But do not begin to reflect upon words, for if you do you will never achieve your purpose nor accomplish this work; for it is achieved not by reflection but only by grace. So take no other words for your prayer, although I give these two examples, except those to which God moves you. At the same time, if God does move you to take these, I advise you not to leave them: I mean if you must pray in words and not otherwise. Because these are very short words.

At the same time, although short prayers are highly recommended here, no bounds are being set on the frequency of prayer. For, as we have said, prayer is made in the length of the spirit. It must never end until what we long for is fully achieved. We have an example of this in the terror of the man or the woman of whom we have spoken before. We see that they never cease to cry out with this little word "out," or this little word "fire," until they have, by and large, been rescued from their affliction.

---

270. R. M., in his *Schola Amoris Languidi*, follows the author's advice: "And just as those who are terrified in the case of fire do not cry out, 'Fire has broken out in my house, come and help me,' but in their plight or rather deep distress can scarcely get out the word, Fire! Fire!, so it is in my situation" (MS TCC 1160 f. Fr.).

CHAPTER XL

During the time of this exercise, the soul must pay
no heed to any particular vice or virtue, or to the
nature of either.

So, in the same way, you are to fill your spirit with
the spiritual meaning of this word "sin," but without concentrating on any particular kind of sin, whether venial or
grievous: pride, anger or envy, covetousness, sloth, gluttony
or lust.[271] What does it matter to a contemplative what sin
it is, or how great a sin it is? For it seems to him, during
the time of this exercise, that every sin is as great as another,
since the smallest sin separates him from God and is an obstacle to his inward peace.

So feel sin as a lump, never mind what it is, it is nothing
else but yourself. Cry out spiritually, always with the same
cry, "Sin, sin, sin"; "out, out, out." This spiritual cry is better
taught by God by experience, rather than by the words of
man. Its perfection consists in pure spirit, when there is no
particular thought nor any word pronounced;[272] though it
can happen occasionally that because of the fulness of spirit
it bursts forth into words; for both body and soul are filled
with sorrow and the heaviness of sin.

Do exactly the same with this little word "God." Fill
your spirit with its spiritual meaning, without concentrating
particularly on any of his works, whether they be good, better
or best, physically or spiritually. Pay no regard either to any
virtue that can be effected in man's soul by grace, whether

---

271. The traditional list of the capital sins. Cf. Cassian, *Collationes* V, 10; Saint
Gregory, *Moralia* XXXI, 45.

272. De Balma, asserting that this is the method of spiritual prayer taught
in the Canticle of Canticles, adds: "So prepare your soul in such a way that when
the mind lifts itself up to God, it will find the sweetness wrapped up in the words
themselves; and thus your spirit will not be distracted by long narratives or wordy
utterances, but send them packing."

this be humility or charity, patience or abstinence, hope, faith or temperance, chastity or voluntary poverty.[273] What do all these matter to contemplatives? All virtues they find and experience in God; for in him is everything, both by cause and by being. And it seems to them that if they had God, then they would have all good. So they fix their desire on nothing in particular but only on the good God. You are to do likewise insofar as you can by grace. Have God alone for your intention and only God; let neither your understanding nor your will have any object except God alone.

But since you must always experience in some measure, as long as you are living in this wretched life, this foul, stinking lump of sin, as it were joined to and congealed with the substance of your being, you must fix your intention on one of these two words alternatively, "sin" and "God": with this vague knowledge, that if you had God then you would be without sin, and if you were without sin then you could have God.

Chapter XLI

Discretion applies to all other exercises except this.

If you ask me the further question, how you are to apply discretion to this exercise, I answer and say, "none at all!"[274] In all your other activities you are to have discretion, in eating

---

273. The first eight virtues seem to be drawn from Saint Paul's list of the fruits of the spirit in Galatians 5:22. But voluntary (ME wilful, H., 79/6) poverty clearly refers to the "evangelical counsel" and the profession a religious makes of it.

274. Cassian stresses that Antony the Hermit and all the other spiritual fathers maintain that discretion leads to God, and is the guardian of all virtues; it is the essential condition for reaching the highest point of perfection (*Collationes II*, 4). For the Dionysians, who teach that the reaching out to God (*consurrectio*, ME "nakid entent unto God") is the exercise of perfect love, it follows that it is the purpose of discretion, and is thus not governed by it. The teaching is elaborated in the letter *Discernment of Impulses*.

and drinking, in sleeping, and in protecting your body from the extremes of heat and cold, in the length of time you give to prayer or reading or to conversation with your fellow-Christians.[275] In all these things you are to observe moderation, avoiding excess and defect. But in this exercise there is no question of moderation; I would prefer that you should never leave off as long as you live.[276]

I do not say that you should persevere in it with the same vigour; for that is not possible. Sometimes sickness or other disorders of body or of soul, and many other necessities of nature, will greatly hinder you, and often pull you down from the height of this exercise. But I do say that you should always be either doing it or preparing for it; that is to say either actually or in intention. So for the love of God beware of sickness as much as it is possible for you. Insofar as you can, never be the cause of your physical weakness. For it is true what I say: this work demands a great tranquillity, and a clean bill of health as well in body as in soul.[277] So for the love of God, govern yourself wisely in body and in soul, and keep in good health as much as possible.[278] But if sickness comes to attack your bodily strength, have patience

---

275. De Balma points out the need for discretion in looking after the needs of the body, especially for those who spend some time in work in the fields, or in some spiritual work.

276. The will of the contemplative soul is to be fixed in one direction, never to be altered. Once the mind is purified and has passed above the sensible and material, there it must remain, never to descend, unless duty or necessity demand it: "Assiduously and when possible, continually; so that the mind's concentration is never in intention turned away, but only when necessity demands." So Gallus, Explanation on the *Divine Names*, chap. 1. His source is Augustine, *De Trinitate*, XV, 8.

277. Like all sound spiritual directors, the author insists that, all things being equal, the life of prayer is incompatible with poor health. Though in his teaching *Discernment of Impulses* he says that excess and defect are to be avoided precisely because virtue, which is God, is "hidden between them," he makes it quite clear that excessive penances and the rough treatment of body and mind ultimately lead the soul away from God.

278. The implication appears to be that the contemplative effort cannot normally be made during the time of sickness, when the soul will also be deprived, as a rule, of sensible consolation.

and wait in humility for God's mercy.[279] Everything shall then be well enough. What I say is true, that often patience in sickness, and in various other tribulations,[280] pleases God much more than any satisfying devotion[281] that you might have whilst you are in good health.

CHAPTER XLII

Through lack of discretion in this exercise, we achieve discretion in all things, and certainly in no other way.

Now perhaps you will ask how you shall observe prudence in eating and sleeping and everything else. My answer to this is brief enough: "Understand it as best you can."[282] Work at this exercise without ceasing and without moderation, and you will know where to begin and to end all your other activities with great discretion. I cannot believe that a soul who perseveres in this exercise night and day[283] without moderation should ever make a mistake in any of his external activities;[284] but otherwise it seems to me that he can never

---

279. Cf. Jude 21.

280. Cf. 2 Corinthians 6:4.

281. R. M. describes "satisfying devotions" as "the sentiments of the heart which draw it away from worldly vanities."

282. ME: "Gette that thou gette mayst" (H., 81/2). R. M. translates with an eye on Matthew 19:12 (Vulgate), *Cape quod potes capere.* The Bodley version paraphrases: "Learn something from what I say, if you can"—*Tu autem ex dictis meis adquiras aliquid si quid potes.*

283. R. M.: "Night and day: not always but when it is opportune; praying and meditating, not always but frequently; always exercise yourself fully in this work, in intention and habit."

284. In his *Letter to Hugh the Hermit*, R. M. writes: "Now thou mayst aske me how thou shalt be occupied day and night.... Fyve thinges there be accordyng for thee, that is to say, good prayer, medytacon that is callyd holy thinkyng, redying of holy englische bokes, contemplacyon that thou mayst come to by grace, and great devocyon, that is for to say to forget al maner of thynges but God ..." (MS Public Record Office S.P. 1/239, f. 267v.).

be free of error. If I could only concentrate with earnestness and a vigilance on this spiritual exercise within my soul, I would be completely heedless about eating, drinking, speaking and all other outward activities.[285] For I am sure that I would rather arrive at discretion in them by this heedlessness than by any earnest consideration of them, with the purpose of achieving a target or a degree of moderation in this respect. Indeed, I would never achieve it, no matter what I did or said. Other men may express different opinions, but experience is a true witness. So lift up your heart with this dark impulse of love; mean now "sin" and now "God." God you wish to have and sin you would avoid. You lack God; but you are sure you have sin. Now may the good God help you, for here you have need!

CHAPTER XLIII

All awareness and experience of one's own being must be done away with before the perfection of this exercise be truly experienced in this life.

Permit nothing to work in your understanding or in your will except God alone.[286] Try to destroy all understanding and awareness of anything under God and tread everything down deep under the cloud of forgetting. Understand that in this exercise you are to forget all other creatures besides yourself, or their deeds or yours; and in this exercise, you must also forget yourself and your own activities, as well as all other creatures and their activities, because of God.

---

285. R. M.: "He who has the Holy Spirit in his heart cannot err during that time; otherwise it is impossible or almost impossible always to keep the exact measure (*unguem*) of discretion."

286. In this and the following chapter, the author offers a psychological comment on the medieval interpretation of the Dionysian contemplative effort: *forti contritione et sensus derelinque* etc. (The Latin translation of John Sarracenus of the *Mystical Theology*; cf. *Hidden Theology*, chap. 1).

For the perfect lover's way is not only to love the thing
that he loves more than himself; he must also, in a sense,
hate himself for the sake of the thing that he loves.[287]

This, then, must be your attitude: Every object that exercises your understanding and your will you must account
as loathsome and wearisome, except God alone. For no matter
what it is, it is certainly between you and your God. So
it is no wonder that you should loathe and hate to reflect
on yourself, since you must always experience sin as some
sort of foul fetid lump between yourself and your God. This
lump is nothing else than yourself; it shall seem to you that
it is one with, congealed with, the substance of your being,
as though there were no division between them.

So you must destroy all knowing and feeling of every
kind of creature, but most especially of yourself. For on the
knowledge and experience of yourself depends the knowledge
and experience of all other creatures; compared with the self,
all other creatures can easily be forgotten. If you are willing
to make serious trial of this, you will find, after you have
forgotten all other creatures and all their works, yes indeed
and your own works as well, what remains between you and
your God is a simple knowing and feeling of your own being.
This knowing and feeling must always be destroyed, before
it is possible for you to experience in truth the perfection
of this exercise.[288]

---

287. De Balma: "Because it is difficult to abandon all those things, we are
directed to shear them away by contrition and a strong effort of the mind; for
the soul must as it were despoil itself of itself, and the affection must follow step
by step the love given from on high. So ... we are ordered to tread down and
leave behind all being, and the exercise of the knowing power itself" (*The Ascent*,
p. 246).

288. The source of the doctrine here is a passage of the *Divine Names*, chap.
7, as interpreted by Gallus: "Union passes beyond mind's nature, and by union
mind is joined to that which is above itself. By this power divine things are to
be understood; not according to our own powers, but when we are outside ourselves
and wholly deified." He also comments: "It is better to belong to God and not
to ourselves. So Job says that his soul chose *suspendium* for herself and his bones
chose death (Job 7:15). *Suspendium* is the extension of the mind to the divine light
... and when the mind withdraws from all things, and dismisses itself, it may
be said that it undergoes a certain death." The same scriptural text, with the same

Chapter XLIV

*How the soul must dispose itself to suppress all aware-
ness and experience of its own being.*

Next you will ask me how you can destroy this simple
awareness and experience of your own being. For doubtless
it seems to you that once it is destroyed, all other hindran-
ces will be destroyed as well. If this is what you think, you
are certainly right. My answer to you is this: Without a very
special grace which God gives out of his absolute bounty,
and along with it a corresponding capacity on your part for
receiving this grace, this simple awareness and experience of
your being can in no way be destroyed.

This capacity is nothing else but a strong and profound
spiritual sorrow.[289] With regard to this sorrow you need to
have this particular discretion: you must take care, whilst
you have this sorrow, not to put too great a strain on your
body or your spirit, but to keep very still, as though you
were asleep, all worn out and sunk deep in this sorrow.[290]
Here is true sorrow; here is perfect sorrow. He is fortunate
indeed who can come to this sorrow. All men have reason
for sorrow; but he who knows and feels that he exists has
a very special experience of sorrow.

In comparison to this, all other sorrows seem to be a
sort of pretence. Certainly, he who is aware and experiences
not only what he is but that he is can sorrow in earnest.
But he who has no experience of this sorrow, let him begin
to make sorrow, because he is not yet experienced in perfect
sorrow. This sorrow and the possession of it purifies a man's
soul, not only of sin, but also of the punishment that he

---

interpretation, is cited in the *Consuetudines Cartusiae*, concerning the acceptance of
a novice.

289. The author's own exegesis of his translation of the Latin rendering of
the *forti contritione* of the *Mystical Theology* of the Pseudo-Denis—"With an intense,
intelligent and loving contrition." Cf. *Hidden Theology*, chap. 1.

290. Cf. Luke 22:45.

has deserved because of his sin. It thus makes it possible for the soul to receive that joy which takes away all a man's awareness and experience of his own being. This sorrow, if we understand it aright, is full of holy desires.[291] Otherwise, in this life a man could never abide it or bear it. For unless a man were to be sustained in some way with some consolation in the true performance of this exercise, he would not be able to bear the pain which he has from the awareness and experience of his own being.[292] For often he desires to have a true awareness and experience of God in purity of spirit, as far as this is possible in this life; and as often he feels that he cannot, because he always finds that his awareness and experience are in a sense occupied and filled with this foul and fetid lump of himself. And because this lump must always be hated and despised and forsaken, if a man would be God's perfect disciple and taught by him on the mountain of perfection, he is nearly out of his mind with sorrow;[293] so much so that he weeps and wails, strives with himself, denounces and heaps curses upon himself.[294] In a word, it seems to him that this burden of himself which he carries is so heavy that he does not care what happens to him, as long as God is pleased.[295] At the same time, in all this sorrow

---

291. This is a most vivid and even classical description of compunction as traditionally taught by the Spiritual Masters of the Western Tradition. Cf. *The Love of Learning*, pp. 37–39; Julian of Norwich, *Showings*, pp. 51–58; and Introduction, supra, pp. 82-84.

292. The author is describing a particular aspect of what is traditionally accepted as "the gift of tears." The essence of it is this special interior grace, normally accompanied by the outward physical phenomenon of tears and sobbing, which often seriously affects the health of the recipient. Saint Ignatius Loyola attached great importance to this gift, but his eyesight was seriously damaged by the constant shedding of tears. The author's advice here is particularly shrewd. It would have been a great help to Margery Kempe, despite the expert counselling she received from Julian of Norwich (cf. *Revelations*, pp. 16–17, and *Showings*, p. 43).

293. Cf. Matthew 26:37–38.

294. R. M. remarks that the author is resorting here to hyperbole, "that is, exaggeration caused by overwhelming love."

295. De Balma uses similar language in a soliloquy on the same gift of compunction: "Lord, I cannot render you satisfaction for my sinfulness and for your

he has no desire not to be, because that would be the devil's madness and contempt for God. Rather he is very glad to be, and he is sincere in his heartfelt thanks to God for the noble gift of his being,[296] although he desires without seeking to lose the awareness and experience of his being.

Every soul must possess and experience in itself this sorrow and this desire, either in this way or in another way as God will grant in the teaching of his spiritual disciples, according to his good pleasure and their corresponding capacity, in body and in soul, in degree and disposition, before they can be perfectly united to God in perfect charity, in so far as this union can be possessed in this life, if God will grant it.

CHAPTER XLV

A detailed explanation of certain illusions that can occur during this exercise.

Let me tell you something else. During this exercise, it is very easy for a young disciple to be deceived, who is not yet accustomed to spiritual exercises, and is little experienced in them. Unless he is aware of this from the start and has the grace to stop and submit himself to spiritual direction, it is likely that his bodily strength will be seriously damaged, and he will become the victim of spiritual illusion. All this is due to pride and sensuality and false reasoning.[297]

---

goodness to me ... I dare not or cannot kill myself ... but I will do what in me lies, if it is not your will that I should die."

296. Julian of Norwich, after describing such a temptation of the devil, beautifully elaborates on "the noble gift of man's being." Cf. *Showings*, chaps. 66–68, pp. 310–15.

297. Our author is writing at the beginning of the period characterized by François Vandenbroucke as *La fièvre Satanique* (cf. *DSp* fasc. xviii, cols. 225ff.), in which, as the author's *Letter on the Discernment of Spirits* indicates, many factors gave rise to a certain pessimism concerning the undue influence of the "world, the flesh" and particularly the devil in monastic communities, especially those with

This illusion can happen in the following way. When young men or women who are beginners in the school of devotion hear this sorrow and this desire read or spoken about, how a man must lift up his heart to God and desire without ceasing to experience the love of his God; then, straight away, in their false reasoning they understand these words not as they are meant, spiritually, but carnally and physically, and they strive in their foolishness to raise up the heart in their breasts. And because grace is lacking to them, as they deserve for their pride and false reasoning, they strain themselves and their physical strength so roughly and so stupidly that within a short time they fall victim to weariness, or to a languid weakness in body and in soul, which tempts them to go out of themselves and to seek some false and empty sensible and physical comfort outside, for the relaxation of body and spirit.[298] Or, if they do not fall victim to this, through their spiritual blindness and the way in which they play on their sensations during the time of this false, animal and far from spiritual exercise, it is likely that their hearts will be inflamed with an unnatural fervour, due to the way in which they treat their bodies or to this false exercise, or else there is created in their imagination a false heat, the work of the devil, their ghostly enemy. And all this comes from their pride, their earthliness and their false reasoning.

Yet, like as not, they think that this is a fire of love produced and kindled by the grace and the goodness of the Holy Spirit.[299] From such illusions as these, and their rami-

---

a strong eremitical bias, like the Cistercians and the Carthusians. He is inveighing here principally against what today would be called psychological ignorance; hence the repeated insistence on the need for balanced spiritual direction. Cf. Introduction, supra, p. 85.

298. The author of *The Chastising* speaks in similar vein: "A foolish or negligent person in his indiscretion ... desires and seeks more than a moderate bodily ease and well-being.... Such people seek undue comfort and solace of men and women and other creatures" (p. 125, and cf. 130ff.).

299. "Also these men believe that whatever inward movements they experience, whether it is in accord with Christ's teaching or not, it all comes from the Holy Spirit" (*Chastising*, p. 145).

fications, come great mischief, great hypocrisy, great heresy and great error. For after the illusions in their feelings, there immediately follows a deception in knowing, which belongs to the devil's school; in the same way as a true knowledge in God's school follows immediately on a true experience.[300] For it is true that the devil has his contemplatives even as God has his.[301] This deceit and illusion in feeling, and in the awareness which follows upon it, has many different and remarkable variations, according to the different states and conditions of those that are deceived; as many as there are amongst those who, having true experience and awareness, are in a healthy state.

But I will not set down here any further examples of illusions; only those with which I believe you will be assailed whenever you set yourself to do this exercise. For what profit would it be to you to know how learned theologians, and men and women in other states of life than your own, suffer illusion? Truly, none. That is why I speak of no others than those which might happen to you when you set yourself to this exercise. And I am telling you about them so that you can be on your guard against them in your own exercise, if you are affected in this way.

---

300. "Some of these men have very little experience, intelligence or understanding, either by inward grace or theological learning; and yet they are clever in contradicting, in their explanations and expositions. . . . All these are wretchedly deceived by the devil, and anyone who knows his scriptures and is well acquainted with the teaching of holy Church, is well aware that they are steeped in error, and greatly fear that they may be the messengers of antichrist" (*Chastising*, pp. 143–44).

301. R. M., in his treatise on experiencing the truth (*Experimentum Veritatis*), explains that God has given everyone a bad angel as well as a guardian angel, so that "the bad angel has his own kind of ecstasy and rapture, offering fictitious sweetnesses to the senses of smell, taste and hearing" (MS *cit.*, f. 262).

CHAPTER XLVI

A careful instruction on how to avoid these illusions;
the exercise demands spiritual zest rather than bodily
exertion.

So for the love of God take very great care in this exercise
not to strain yourself immoderately or overtax the heart in
your breast. The exercise calls for spiritual skill rather than
brute strength. To work more skilfully means to work with
humility and in the spirit; if you force it, the work is merely
in the body and the senses. So take care. For indeed if one
should presume to draw near to the high mountain of this
exercise in a beastlike way, one shall be driven away with
stones.[302] It is the nature of stones to be dry and hard, and
where they strike, there one feels it sorely. These physical
exertions are very firmly fixed to the sensible feelings, and
they are very dry, in that they lack the dew of grace.[303] So
they hurt the foolish soul very sorely, and the illusion caused
by fiends makes the wound fester. So beware of these beastlike
efforts, and learn to love with true fervour, with a gentle
and peaceful disposition, both in body and soul.[304] And wait
patiently on the will of our Lord with courtesy and humil-

---

302. The reference is to the ascent of Moses to the top of the holy mountain
of Sinai, where he entered into the thick cloud in which God was hidden (cf. *Hidden
Theology*, chap. II). The people were not to approach the mountain or touch it
under pain of death, until the trumpet sounded (Exodus 19:12–22). The author takes
his spiritual exegesis from the reference in the Epistle to the Hebrews 12:18–24:
"If even a beast touches the mountain, it shall be stoned." Similarly, Gregory the
Great: "The beasts touch the mountain when the mind is overtaken with irrational
desires, and lifts itself up to the heights of contemplation" (*Moralia* VI, 58).
303. "Dew of grace." Scholars point out that R. M. has mistranslated the ME
"wetyng of grace," mistaking "weten" (OE woetan), to wet, for "witan," to know,
arguing that the reading should be "knowledge of grace." Internally, however, "heavenly dew" as a medieval metaphor for grace is a commonplace, both scriptually
and liturgically. Cf. the Advent antiphon *Rorate, caeli, desuper, et nubes pluant justum:*
"Rain down O heavens, your dew...." Cf. Isaiah 45:8.
304. Cf. Matthew 11:28–30.

ity,[305] and do not snatch at it hurriedly, like a greedy grey-hound, no matter how hungry you may be. And I advise you to play some sort of game, so that you can do all that is possible to contain these great and boisterous movements of your spirit: as though you did not wish him to know in any way how you desire to see him and have him or experience him. Perhaps you think this is somewhat foolishly and child-ishly spoken. But I am certain that whoever had the grace to do and feel as I say, he would find that this game was well worth playing with him, even as the father plays with the child, kissing and embracing it.[306]

CHAPTER XLVII

A careful instruction on the purity of spirit demanded in this exercise: how the soul must make its desire known to God in one way and to man in quite a different way.

Do not be surprised at my speaking in this apparently childish and foolish way, as though I were lacking normal discretion. I do it for several reasons; for I believe that I have been led for a long time now to feel and to think and also to speak in this way to others of my special friends in God as I am now speaking to you.[307]

---

305. Cf. Ecclesiasticus 13:9; Habacuc 2:3; Psalm 26:14.

306. The author offers a masculine version of the traditional image of the *ludus amoris*, where God is the mother. Cf. *Chastising*, 98:4. Julian of Norwich gives an especially felicitous version of it in her theological exposition of the Motherhood of God. Cf. *Showings*, chap. 61, pp. 299–302.

307. It would appear from the intimate tone of this passage that the *Cloud* is addressed, as it claims, to one disciple, by a man who enjoys a wide reputation as a spiritual counsellor, with many "spiritual friends in God." It is equally a "spiritual letter," in the accepted sense: having one particular addressee but written in the knowledge that it will become available in the *ex professo* contemplative milieu of the time, and in particular in those houses where Dionysian spirituality is enjoying a vogue. Cf. Introduction, supra, pp. 9–11.

One reason why I bid you hide the desire of your heart from God is this. I hope that by such concealment it may become more clearly known to him, to your advantage and for the fulfilment of this very desire, than it would be by any other way that I believe to be within your power of making it known to him. A further reason is that I wish, through this concealed showing, to bring you out of the ignorant state of sensible feeling into the purity and depth of spiritual feeling; and so finally to help you to fasten the spiritual knot of burning love between you and your God in spiritual oneness and union of wills.[308]

Of this you are well aware, that God is a spirit. And whoever wishes to be made one with him must live in the truth and depth of spirit, far removed from any bodily travesty of it. It is true also that everything is known to God and nothing can be hid from his knowing,[309] whether it be sensible or spiritual. But since it is also true that he is a spirit, then that which is hid in the depths of the spirit is known and shown to him more openly than anything which is in any way contaminated by the senses.[310] For in the natural order of things, that which is sensible is further from God than that which is spiritual. For this reason it appears that as long as our desire is contaminated with any kind of sensible thing, as it is when we strive and strain in spirit and body together, then for that time it is further off from God than it should be if it were done with more devotion and more zeal, in tranquillity, and in the purity and depth of the spirit.

---

308. For a full treatment of "union of wills" in the life and prayer of the contemplative tradition in the West, see P. Molinari, *Julian of Norwich* (London, 1958), pp. 94–103, and *Showings*, chaps. 5 and 6, 41–65; especially pp. 59–97.

309. Cf. the author's dedicatory prayer to the Holy Spirit, supra, p. 100. Cf. also Luke 12:2; John 21:17; and Psalm 43:22.

310. This is one of the author's own practical variations on the negative Dionysian theology. Cf. *Hidden Theology*, chap. III: "If we wish to designate him by doing away with all intelligible things, it is most fitting that we first do away with those things which are seen to be furthest from him."

This will help you to understand to some extent the reason why I ask you to conceal and to hide from God in this childish way the movement of your desire. But I do not bid you simply to hide it; for it would be the command of a fool to bid you do something that simply cannot be done in any way. I ask you to take every step that you can to hide it. And why do I command you thus? Simply because I want you to put it down into the depths of your spirit, far from any ignorant contamination with any sensible thing which would make it less spiritual,[311] and in that far, so much farther away from God.[312] I am sure as well that the more truly refined your spirit is, the less it is contaminated by the sensible and the nearer it is to God; the better it pleases him, and the more clearly it may be seen by him. This is not to say that his sight may be at one time or in respect of one object more clear than at another, for it is always unchangeable; but because, when the object is in purity of spirit, it is more like to him, who is a spirit.

There is another reason why I bid you to do all that in you lies to keep this desire hidden from him. You and I, and many others like us, are so inclined to conceive of the spiritual in a sensible way that perhaps had I directed you to show to God the movement of your heart, you would have showed it to him in a sensible way, either by a look or an exclamation or a word or some other ignorant sensible effort, as happens when you wish to reveal what is hidden in your heart to another man. And had this happened, your exercise would have been impure. For in one way must things be shown to man, and in another to God.

---

311. Cf. *The Ascent to Contemplative Wisdom*, p. 249.

312. The abstract doctrine lying behind this statement is perhaps to be found in the author's *Hidden Theology*, chap. III: "For in proportion as the things that we are considering are the highest, in that proportion the words spoken of them to correspond with our considerations show the limits of our understanding."

Chapter XLVIII

God wishes to be served with both body and soul,
and to reward man in both; and how we may know
when the sounds and sweetnesses affecting the bodily
senses in time of prayer are good, and when evil.

When I say this it is not my meaning that you should leave off at any time, if you are moved to pray in words or suddenly to break out because of the devotion in your spirit, to speak to God as to man and to speak, as you feel yourself moved to do, such good words as these: "Good Jesus, lovely Jesus, sweet Jesus," and so on.[313] No, God forbid that you should take it so, for I do not mean it in this way at all. God also forbid that I should separate what he has joined together, the body and the spirit; for it is God's will to be served both in body and soul together as is seemly, and to give man his reward, in bliss, both in body and in soul.

As a pledge of that reward, it is sometimes his will to set on fire the bodily senses of his devout servants here in this life, and not once or twice but perhaps very often, and according to his pleasure, with marvellous sweetness and consolation.[314] Such consolations as these do not come into our bodies from without through the windows of our senses, but they come from within, rising and springing up out of the abundance of spiritual gladness and of true devotion in the

---

313. Guigo the Angelic says that the contemplative soul "inflames its own desire for God with its own burning words, makes known its state, and by such incantations calls upon its Spouse" (*Ladder*, p. 87). Similarly, Gallus, in his *De septem gradibus contemplationis*, teaches that the fervour of prayer lifts up the soul itself to God. The author wishes to avoid saying anything which might depreciate the spontaneous nature of the prayer of the contemplative. Cf. supra, chap. 39, pp. 195–96.

314. Our author is very close here to the teaching of the *Ladder* (chap. 5), on the consolations granted in the midst of this spontaneous prayer: "He does not wait until their prayer is finished, but he breaks into the midst of the burning longing of that thirsty soul, and with the balm of heavenly sweetness, softens and comforts the soul, and overpowers it with delight and joy."

THE CLOUD OF UNKNOWING

spirit. Such comfort and sweetness should not be held suspect; and to be brief, I believe that he who has this experience cannot hold it suspect.

But the consolations, sounds, gladness and sweetness which come suddenly from outside, even though you do not know whence, I beseech you to hold all these suspect.[315] For they can be either good or evil. If they are good, they are produced by a good angel, and if bad, then by an evil angel. They cannot be evil as long as those illusions arising from false reasoning and immoderate effort of the heart and senses are removed, according to my instruction, or better instruction if you can get it. And why is that? Because of the cause of this comfort, which is the devout stirring of love which dwells in pure spirit. It comes from the hand of almighty God without any intermediary;[316] and therefore it must always be far removed from any illusion or false opinion that can come upon a man in this life.[317]

It is not my intention at this time to tell you how to distinguish whether those other comforts and sounds and sweetness are good or evil. And the reason is that I do not think that it is necessary, because you can find it written down in another place in another man's book, a thousand times better than I can say or write it.[318] And there you

---

315. Cf. the *Rules for the Discernment of Spirits* (second week) in the *Spiritual Exercises* of Saint Ignatius Loyola, 331–32.

316. De Balma: "This ascent by unknowing is nothing else than to be impelled directly by the ardour of love, without any mediate knowledge through creatures . . ." (*Ascent to Contemplative Wisdom*, p. 244).

317. "This is the truest and most certain knowledge, far removed from all error and opinion and deception in the imagination" (ibid., p. 245).

318. It is highly likely that "another man's book" is the *Scale of Perfection* I (chaps. 8–12). Hilton is speaking of the highest part of contemplation: the "knot of burning love" and the revelation of God. Such showing, he goes on to say, is not experienced in the bodily senses; and the next two chapters are entitled: "How revelations to the bodily senses, and the experience of them, may be both good and evil"; and "How you may know when revelations to the bodily senses and the experience of them are good or evil." A marginal annotation in a mid-fifteenth century *Cloud* manuscript (University College, Oxford 14) against this passage reads "*Hylton's*" (cf. H., p. 198). It is clear that the author is speaking not of those consolations which come to the newly converted, the sweet and satisfying meditations,

can also find what I am setting down here, said in a far better way than I do here. But I will not on that account forbear, nor shall it weary me, to fulfil the desire and the movement of your heart which you have previously shown me in your words, and now in your deeds.

This is what I say, then, about those sounds and that sweetness which come in by the window of your senses, which can be either good or evil.[319] Exercise yourself constantly in this simple, devout, zealous stirring of love of which I have been speaking. Then I have no doubt that this will be well able to tell you about them. Even if at first it is in some way or other dumbfounded by them, because it is not used to them, yet it will do this for you: it will bind your heart so strongly that you will not be able in any way to give any real credence to them, until you are assured of their authenticity by the spirit of God inwardly in wondrous manner, or else outwardly by the counsel of a spiritual father who has discretion.[320]

CHAPTER XLIX

The substance of all perfection is nothing else but a good will; and how all the sensible sounds, consolations and sweetness that affect us in this life are accidental to this perfection.

I pray you, then, to follow eagerly after this humble stirring of love in your heart. It will be your guide in this life,

---

but of spiritual consolations which accompany special contemplative graces—visions, locutions, and the like. He has in mind the passage from the *Mystical Theology:* "*Sonos et sermones derelinquunt celestes,*" which he translates: "(They) leave behind all the divine illuminations and all heavenly sounds and locutions." Cf. *Hidden Theology*, chap. I.

319. Cf., amongst other monastic fathers, Cassian, *Collationes* III, 19.

320. Gallus, in his commentary on this passage and elsewhere, says that their purpose is to help the soul in its ascent to the height of contemplation; but he

and will bring you to grace in the next. It is the substance of all good living, and without it no good work can be begun or ended. It is nothing else but a good will that is directed to God, and a kind of satisfaction and gladness that you experience in your will concerning all that he does.[321]

This good will is the substance of all perfection. All sweetnesses and consolations, sensible or spiritual, no matter how holy, are accidentals of this good will; they depend on it.

I call them its accidentals, for they can be present or absent without doing it much damage. I am speaking, of course, of this life. It is otherwise in the happiness of heaven; for there they will be united with the substance without any separation, even as the body in which they are experienced will be united with the soul. Their substance here is this good spiritual will. And I am sure that for him who experiences the perfection of this will, insofar as it may be possessed here, there is no sweetness nor consolation which can come to any man in this life, which he is as equally pleased and glad to do without, as he is to have it, in accordance with God's will.[322]

---

points out with Richard of St. Victor that their authenticity has to be tested by scripture and Catholic truth (cf Explanation on the *Mystical Theology*, ch. 1).

321. Walter Hilton writes in the *Scale of Perfection:* "The knitting and fastening of Jesus to a man's soul is by a good will and a great desire for him alone, to have him, and to see him in his spiritual bliss. The greater this desire, the more speedily is Jesus knit to the soul" (I chap. 12; cf. Underhill, p. 25). It is strange that Julian of Norwich should have been held in such suspicion by modern commentators for her teaching on this goodly (or godly) will, since she approaches it with much greater theological precision than either our author or Walter Hilton. See, for example, her definition of the contemplative prayer of petition: "Beseeching is a true and gracious enduring will of the soul, united and joined to our Lord's will by the sweet, secret operation of the Holy Spirit" (*Showings*, p. 149; and the introduction, pp. 26–27, 57, 67, 78).

322. Cf. Saint Augustine, *Ennarrationes in Psalmos* LXXII, 32.

Chapter L

*What chaste love is; and how sensible consolations
come very seldom to some creatures, but very often
to others.*

You can see, then, that we must focus all our attention
on this meek stirring of love in our will. And with regard
to all other sweetnesses and consolations, sensible or spiritual,
no matter how pleasing they are, no matter how holy, we
should have a sort of heedlessness, if this can be said without
failing in courtesy and seemliness.[323] If they come, welcome
them; but do not depend too much on them because of your
weakness;[324] for to continue for long in those sweet experiences and tears is a great drain on your strength. It may
be that you will be moved to love God simply for their sake.

---

323. John of the Cross will insist very strongly on the same doctrine in his
Ascent of Mount Carmel, books II and III: e.g., II, chap. XVII, 9: "These things
may be presented to the exterior senses, as are locutions and words audible to the
ear; or, to the eyes, visions of saints, and of beauteous radiance; or perfumes to
the sense of smell; or tastes and sweetnesses to the palate; or other delights to
the touch, which are wont to proceed from the spirit, a thing that very commonly
happens to spiritual persons. Or the soul may have to avert its eyes from visions
of interior sense, such as imaginary visions, all of which it must renounce entirely.
It must set its eyes only upon the spiritual good which they produce, striving to
preserve it in its works and to practise that which is for the due service of God,
paying no heed to those representations nor desiring any pleasure of sense. And
in this way the soul takes from these things only that which God intends and
wills—namely, the spirit of devotion—for there is no other important purpose for
which He gives them; and it casts aside that which He would not give if these
gifts could be received in the spirit without it, as we have said—namely, the exercise
and apprehension of the senses."

324. Cf. Walter Hilton: "If thou be stirred because of that liking that thou
feelest, for to draw out thine heart from the mind and the beholding of Jesus Christ
and from ghostly occupation, as from prayer, and thinking of thyself and thy defaults,
from the inward desire of virtues and of ghostly knowing and feeling of God, for
to set the sight of thy heart and thine affection, thy delight and thy rest principally
therein, weening that it should be a part of heavenly joy and of angel's bliss, and
for that thee thinketh that thou shouldst neither pray nor think nought else, but
all wholly tend thereto, for to keep it and delight thee therein, this feeling is suspect
and of the enemy" (Underhill, Scale I, chap. 11, pp. 21–21).

You will know that this is so if you grumble overmuch when they are withdrawn. If this is your experience, then your love is not yet either chaste or perfect. For when love is chaste and perfect, though it is content that the bodily senses be nourished and consoled through the presence of these experiences and tears, yet it does not grumble. It is well satisfied to do without them, if such be God's will.[325]

Some people are normally never without such comforts; but for others such sweetnesses and consolations occur very seldom. It depends entirely on the disposition and the ordinance of God, who looks to the different advantages and needs of his creatures. Some of them are so weak and so delicate in spirit that unless they were comforted somewhat by experiencing such sweetness, they could not at all abide or put up with the various temptations and tribulations with which they are burdened in this life, at the hands of their bodily and spiritual enemies.[326] There are some whose bodily health is so poor that they are unable to do penance for their own purification. It is the Lord's will to purify such people with his great graces in spirit, by these sweet consolations and tears. Again, on the other hand, there are some who are so strong in spirit that they have consolation enough interiorly, within their souls, in offering up this reverent and humble stirring of love and union of wills;[327] so that they scarcely need to be sustained with these sweet consolations in their bodily senses. Now which of these two kinds is holier or pleasing to God, God alone knows, and not I.[328]

---

325. A commentary on Psalm 91, sometimes attributed to Hilton, teaches the same. Cf. James Walsh and Eric Colledge, *Of the Knowledge of Ourselves and of God* (London, 1961), pp. 17–18.

326. The author of *The Chastising* makes the point in speaking of the analogy between God and the chosen soul, and the mother bringing up her child (p. 114, 4–20).

327. "No richer gift can be offered to God than the good will" (Saint Gregory, *Hom. in Evangelia*, V, 3).

328. It has been suggested that this chapter owes much to Hilton's Scale II, chap. 35 (Underhill, p. 387): "How some souls love Jesus by bodily fervours and their own virile affections which are moved by grace and reason; and how some

Chapter LI

We should be greatly on our guard not to interpret in a physical way what is to be understood in a spiritual way, and especially the words "in" and "up."

So follow humbly this simple stirring of love in your heart; I do not mean in your physical heart, but in your spiritual heart, which is your will.[329] And take great care that you do not construe in a material way what is to be understood spiritually. For what I say is true: that the material and sensual interpretations of those who go in for elaborate whims and fancies are the cause of much error.

One example of this you can see in my asking you to conceal your desire from God insofar as you can. For perhaps had I asked you to show your desire to God, you would have interpreted this in a more material way than you do now, when I have bidden you hide it. You are well aware that whatever is deliberately concealed is sunk deep into your spirit.

So it seems to me that we need to be greatly on our guard in the interpretation of words which are spoken with spiritual intent, lest we interpret them in a material way and not spiritually as they are meant. It is particularly important to be careful about this word "in" and this word "up," because the misinterpretation of these two words is the cause of much error and much illusion in those who set themselves to these spiritual exercises, or so it seems to me. I know this partly by experience, and partly by hearsay. And I would like to give you a brief description of these illusions.

The young disciple in God's school, newly converted from the world, may think that because he has for a short while given himself to penance and to prayer according to the advice

---

love Jesus more restfully, by spiritual affections only." If this is so, then our author shows considerably more refinement as a director.

329. Cf. Saint Augustine, *Ennarrationes in Psalmos* XCIII, 18.

received in confession, he is therefore able to take upon himself these spiritual exercises which he hears spoken about or hears read, or perhaps reads himself.[330] Now when he reads or hears these spiritual exercises spoken of, and particularly how a man must draw all his understanding within himself,[331] or how he should rise above himself,[332] then straightway, because of his soul's blindness and his sensuality and natural acumen, he misunderstands what is said. And because he has within him a natural desire to discover what is hidden, he concludes that he is called by grace to this exercise. The result is that if his spiritual director is unwilling to agree that he should undertake this exercise, immediately the disciple feels badly disposed to his spiritual director, and believes and perhaps even says to others who are in the same state as himself that he can find no one who can understand what he really means. And so, without any hesitation, because of the arrogance and presumption which comes from his intellectual pride, he abandons humble prayer and penance far too early, and sets himself, or so he thinks, to true spiritual exercises within his soul. Such exercise, if it be rightly understood, is neither the work of the senses nor of the spirit. In a word, it is an unnatural activity and the devil is its architect. Here is the quickest way to death both of body and of soul; for it is madness and not wisdom, and leads a man to madness. But the young disciple does not think in this way, for it is his intent in such an exercise to think of nothing except God.

---

330. P. H. reads: "of the whiche he herith men speke"; whereas R. M.'s translation reads *de qua me audit loqui*—"which he hears me speak about." Some scholars doubt whether the early ME *me*—"men," "one," could have survived as late as the last decades of the fourteenth century.

331. Saint Gregory on the degrees of contemplation: "The first degree is that (the soul) gather itself within itself; the second that it look over what is gathered; the third that it rise above itself, and give itself over with determination to the contemplation of the invisible Creator" (*Hom. in Ezech,* II, 5, 9).

332. In his commentary on the *Divine Names* (chap. 1), Thomas Gallus gives a list of terms that denote the exercise of dark contemplation: *ascensio, excessus, extensio, consurrectio, elevatio, suspensio,* etc.

CHAPTER LII

How young beginners in their presumption misinter-
pret this word "in," and the illusions which follow
from this.

The madness of which I spoke above comes about in
this way.[333] They read and hear it said that they are to leave
off the outward exercise of their senses and work interiorly;
and because they are ignorant of what interior working means,
they therefore work wrongly. They turn their bodily senses
inwards on themselves, physically, which is unnatural. They
strain themselves,[334] as though they could possibly see inwardly with their bodily eyes and hear inwardly with their
ears; and so with all their senses of smell, of taste and of
touch. And so they reverse the order of nature; they so overtax
their imagination with this fantastic behaviour and without
the least discretion, that finally they turn their brains in their
heads.[335] The result is that the devil has power to fabricate
false lights or sounds, sweet smells in their nostrils, wonderful
tastes in their mouths and many other strange ardours and
burnings in their bodily breasts or in their entrails, in their
backs and their kidneys, and in their private parts.[336] And

---

333. Hugo de Balma speaks of the many dangers attendant on the beginner
in this work. "He must watch himself much more carefully than those who are
practised in it, for they know the machinations of the enemy, and have the sagacity
to triumph over his wiles."

334. "If the person strains himself excessively in these impulses towards union
with the Spouse, the spirit cannot sustain itself through the overtaxing of the body"
(ibid.).

335. Walter Hilton, in his *Of Angels' Song*, uses very similar language of those
who "leave aside prayers, the reading of holy Scripture, meditations on the passion
of Christ, and the consciousness of their wretchedness; and before they are called
by God to it, they violently strain their senses ... to seek and behold heavenly
things ... they overtax their imaginations, forcibly and without discretion; they
turn their brains in their heads. And then because of this feebleness they imagine
that they hear wonderful sounds and songs. Or else it is the devil who fabricates
such sounds in their ears" (Horstman I, pp. 179–86).

336. It is the common teaching of the Western fathers that the enemy attacks

yet in spite of this illusion, they believe that they have a tranquil awareness of their God, without any hindrance of vain thoughts. And indeed they have, in a certain sense, because they are so filled with falsehood that idle thoughts cannot afflict them.[337] And why? Because the same devil, who would afflict them with idle thoughts were they in a good state, is the chief architect in this work; and you know well enough that he is in no hurry to hinder himself. He will not drive away the awareness of God from them, for fear that they should suspect that he is at work.

CHAPTER LIII

The various kinds of unseemly outward behaviour of those who have no experience in this exercise.

Those who are so deceived as to take up this false exercise, or any species of it, are addicted to much strange behaviour in comparison with those who are God's true disciples. These latter are always very decorous in their way of governing themselves, either physically or spiritually.[338] But it is not so of the others. Whoever might happen to catch sight of

---

a man through his senses. So Hilary of Poitiers, Leo the Great, and especially Augustine: ". . . Satan deceives the bodily senses" (*Enchiridion*, 60). Saint Thomas, with whose works the *Cloud* author is obviously familiar (cf., e.g., *The Letter on Prayer*), makes the point that the devils have power to work miracles "in the broad sense, in particular to influence the imagination and the bodily senses." Cf. *Summa Theologiae* I, 14, 4.

337. The author of *The Chastising* speaks at great length of this "falsehood"— the "natural" tranquillity that can have such dire consequences (chap. IX, pp. 130ff.).

338. R. M. is unwilling to accept that true contemplative graces always manifest themselves in exterior and interior decorum. The "always," he says, "depends on time, place and circumstances." He speaks of his own "spiritual drunkenness," which affected his bodily movements (in his Latin treatise *Refectorium salutis*). The *Cloud* author, though he may have known the ME version of Ruysbroeck's "Spiritual Espousals" in the *Chastising of God's Children* (p. 103), describing the "gostli drunkennesse" that is an extreme instance of intense spiritual consolation, is clearly very suspicious of any kind of "enthusiastic" behaviour.

them and of their behaviour at the time when their eyes are wide open will see them staring like madmen do, looking as though they were seeing the devil. And indeed they had better beware; for the devil indeed is not very far away.[339] The eyes of some of them are so set in their heads as though they were sheep suffering from the brain disease, and were near death's door.[340] Some of them hold their heads on one side as though a worm were in their ears. Some squeak instead of speaking normally, as though there were no breath in their bodies. Hypocrites tend to behave like this. Some again are so eager and quick to say what they think that they gurgle and splutter in their throats; which is what heretics are wont to do, and those who with their presumption and cleverness stubbornly hold fast to their error.[341]

Many disordered and unseemly gestures result from false opinion, as anyone can see. At the same time, some of them are so clever that they can for the most part control themselves when they are in anyone's company. But if you could see them in their own houses, then I am sure that they could not hide their faults. Nevertheless, I think that if anyone were to contradict their opinions they would see them react in some way or other. For in spite of everything they are sure that all they do is for the love of God and to maintain the truth. My expectation is that they are likely to go on loving God in this peculiar fashion until they go stark staring mad to the devil; unless, that is, he shows them his marvellous mercy and makes them put an end to this behaviour.

---

339. The author is not so concerned with "rules of modesty," such as we find, for example, in Hugh of St. Victor's treatise on the training of novices (*De Institutione Novitiorum* chap. 12), and which were a commonplace of the Western spiritual tradition, but with the fact that the external quirks of the "pious" are in reality signs of a hypocrisy that leads to obduracy, and eventually to heresy.

340. ME: "sturdy scheep betyn in the heed." The noun "sturdy" is still used to describe "vertigo in sheep caused by a tapeworm in the brain" (cf. *Concise Oxford Dictionary*, new edition, 1976).

341. Cf. Proverbs 6:12–13, "A man that is an apostate, an unprofitable man, walketh with a perverse mouth, he winketh with his eye ... speaketh with the finger."

THE CLOUD OF UNKNOWING

I am not saying that there is anyone so perfect a servant of the devil in this life as to be diseased and infected with all the fantasies that I write down here. Yet at the same time it could be that someone, and perhaps many, are infected with them all. What I do say is that there is no thoroughgoing hypocrite or heretic in this life who is innocent of all the fantastic behaviour I have mentioned, or will mention, if God gives me leave.

For some people are so burdened with quaint and unseemly posturing in their behaviour, that when they have to listen to anything, they waggle their heads from side to side and up and down most oddly. They gape with open mouths, as though they are listening with them and not with their ears. Others, when they have to speak, use their fingers, either poking on their own fingers or their chests, or the chests of those to whom they are speaking. Others yet can neither sit, stand, nor lie still; they have to be tapping with their feet, or doing something with their hands. Some make rowing motions with their arms whilst they speak, as though they were in for a long swim. Some are always laughing and smiling with every other word, as though they were girlish gossips or amateur jugglers unsure of their balance.

I am not saying that all this indecorous behaviour is in itself great sin, or even that the perpetrators of it are great sinners. What I do say is that these unseemly and inordinate gestures have such control over the man that makes them that he cannot stop them even when he wants to. So I maintain that they are signs of pride, of outlandishness, of exhibitionism and an inordinate desire for knowledge. In particular they are true tokens of moral instability and mental restlessness, and they indicate a lack of acquaintance with the exercises described in this book. The reason why I mention so many of these illusions here in these chapters is that he who undertakes this exercise can consider them, if he will, in order to put his own work to the test.

Chapter LIV

*By means of this work a man learns to govern himself
wisely and decorously in body and soul alike.*

If a man were practised in this exercise, it would give
him true decorum both of body and soul, and would make
him truly attractive to all men or women who looked upon
him.[342] So much so that the most ill-favoured man or woman
alive, if they could come by grace to work in this exercise,
would suddenly be changed in appearance to such graciousness
that all good people who saw them would wish and rejoice
to have them in their company, and would be convinced that
they had found spiritual peace and were strengthened in God's
grace through their presence.

So reach out for this gift, you who can do so by grace.
Whoever truly possesses it will know well how to govern
himself and all that belongs to him by its power. He would
be able to discern properly, at need, every kind of natural
behaviour and disposition.[343] He would know how to make
himself all things to all men who lived with him,[344] whether
habitual sinners or not, without any sin on his own part.[345]
He would be the wonder of all who saw him, and would
draw others by the help of grace to the work of that same

---

342. The author is not averse to using the language of courtly love, and "cur-
tesie" is a favourite word. It is not surprising, then, that he should take it for
granted, like his literary contemporaries Chaucer or the author of *Sir Gawain*, that
the love and practice of virtue should manifest themselves outwardly. Cf., for example,
the description in the *Prologue to the Canterbury Tales* of the "parfait gentil knight,"
who "loved chivalry/Truth and honour, freedom and courtesy."

343. R. M. cites Ecclesiasticus 7:14 in agreeing that, whilst the true contemplative is capable of governing all others, Christ himself, the perfect man, said to
the Jews: "My words have no place in you" (John 8:37), and "you have not the
love of God in you" (John 5:42).

344. Cf. 1 Corinthians 9:19.

345. The author seems to have Christ in mind, who, as Luke notes, exercised
a particularly attractive power on "publicans and sinners" (15:1). The current tradition, that Christ was a paragon of physical beauty, is well attested, and without
any self-consciousness, by Julian of Norwich. Cf. *Showings*, e.g., chap. 10, p. 195.

spirit in which he himself is exercised. His looks and his words would be full of spiritual wisdom, full of fire and of fruitfulness, spoken with truth and soberness, without any falsehood, far removed from any hypocritical showing-off or pretence.[346]

There are, however, others who study with all their might, inward and outward, how they can inflate themselves in their speech, and prop themselves up on every side with many humble-sounding words and gestures of devotion. Their aim rather is to seem holy in the sight of men, than to be holy in the sight of God and his angels.[347] Such people care more and sorrow more for a disordered gesture, or an unseemly and unfitting word spoken before men, than they do for a thousand idle thoughts and foul stirrings of sin deliberately accepted or carelessly committed in the sight of God and of the saints and angels of heaven. Ah, Lord God! whether or not there is any pride within, when such meek-sounding words are so plentiful without, I truly believe that it is fitting and seemly for those who are really humble within to show humble and seemly words and outward gestures which correspond to the humility within the heart. What I say is that this should not be shown in broken or in plaintive tones, contrary to the normal and natural voice of the speaker. Because if the words are true, then they will be spoken in a truthful way, in a round tone, coming from the hearts of those that speak them. Now if he who has a naturally round and resonant tone speaks poorly and pipingly, unless of course he has a physical defect or his way of speaking has to do with his relationship with God or with his confessor, then it is a true token of hypocrisy, whether the person be young or old.

What more must I say of these poisonous illusions? I truly believe that unless these people have the grace to leave

346. Cf. Paul's encomium on charity—1 Corinthians 13:3-5.
347. The author is likely to have derived his description of the religious hypocrite from Christ's denunciations of the Pharisees. Cf. Luke 11:42-43, 18:9-14.

off such whining hypocrisy, which is the link between the secret pride in their hearts within and their humble words without, their miserable souls will soon sink down into sorrow.

Chapter LV

To condemn sin without discrimination through excessive fervour is erroneous.

The devil deceives other men in the following way. In quite a remarkable fashion he sets their brains on fire for the maintenance of God's law and the destruction of sin in all other men. He never tempts them with anything that is openly evil. He makes them behave like busy prelates, who watch over various states of life of Christian men; or like an abbot over his monks. They reprove all men of their faults, just as though they had the pastoral care of their souls.[348] Indeed, they hold that they dare not act otherwise before God. So whatever faults they see in men they tell them about them, saying that they are moved to do this by the fire of charity and of God's love which is in their hearts; but they are liars, for it is rather by the fire of hell welling up in their brains and in their imaginations.[349] That this is true

---

348. The author may be referring to the wandering groups of self-appointed hermits and others who proved such a bane throughout the Middle Ages, and in particular to charterhouses from the time of Saint Bruno himself, who calls them *morbidum quorundam vanissimorum laicorum*—"a lethal band of vainglorious lay folk who abjure every kind of discipline and obedience, who calumniate good religious men, and think themselves praiseworthy when they blackguard those worthy of praise" (*Letters to the Brethren*, P.L. 152, 419; Cf. *Aux Sources de la vie Cartusienne* II, pp. 337–41). On the other hand, it may be an impersonal critique of the Lollards, "the Poor Preachers," in the initial stages of the movement, before it became the target of ecclesiastical severity. Cf. W. Pantin, *The English Church in the XIVth Century* (Cambridge, 1948), and his reference to the "good words" of Margery Kempe (p. 260).

349. It has been noted that a morbid curiosity for demonology infected the Western Church from the beginning of the thirteenth century, and died a lingering death only in recent times. The author is obviously affected by this *fièvre satanique*

may be gathered from what follows. The devil is a spirit, and according to his nature he has no body, any more than an angel has; but at the same time, whenever he or any angel by God's permission takes bodily appearance in order to minister to any man in this life, his body is in some way fashioned according to the work that he has to do. We have examples of this in holy Scripture. Whenever an angel was sent in bodily appearance, in the Old Testament and also in the New, it was always made clear either by his name, or by some function or quality of his body, what the spiritual matter of his message was. It is exactly the same with the devil. When he comes in bodily appearance, he shows in some bodily quality the spiritual nature of his servants.[350]

One example of this will stand for all others. I have learnt from students of necromancy[351] who make it their study to win the help of wicked spirits, and from others to whom the devil has appeared in bodily likeness, that no matter what bodily appearance the devil takes on, he always has only one nostril, which is large and wide.[352] And he will willingly turn it up, so that a man can see up it into his brain. His brain is nothing else than the fire of hell, for the devil can

---

(satanic obsession), as it has been called. Cf. François Vandenbroucke in *DSp.* 3, 225ff.

350. This is common doctrine, that demons are fallen angels, and are therefore purely spiritual beings. *Angeli non habent corpora sibi naturaliter unita* (*Summa Theologiae* 1, 51, 1) is very close to our author's original: "The devil is a spirit, and of his own kynde he hath no body, more than hath an aungele." In spite of our author's credibility, he stands firmly within the tradition. It is Thomas again who points out that in holy scripture the properties of intelligible things are described in images sensible in nature. In the same way, as the author says here, angels and demons take on the bodily appearance congruent with the spiritual or intelligible content of their representation (ibid., I, 51, 2, *ad* 2).

351. Father Aubrey Gwynn, in *The English Austin Friars in the Time of Wyclif* (London, 1940), p. 134, notes that John Erghome, prior of the Austin Friary of York in 1385, had a number of works on necromancy in his private library.

352. Thomas Gallus, in his commentary on Isaiah 6:1–6, assumes that the two nostrils of the body (like the two feet, hands, eyes and ears) are analogous to the organs of the spiritual senses: representing the intellect and the affect. Perhaps the destruction of the divine love in the fallen angel was meant to be represented by the one nostril.

have no other brain. And he seeks for nothing better than to make a man look into it; for in that sight he would lose his mind forever. But the perfect apprentice of necromancy knows this well enough, and can take the proper steps beforehand to avoid being harmed in this way.[353] It is for this reason that I say, and have said, that whenever the devil takes on any bodily appearance, he shows in some bodily quality what his servants are in spirit. He inflames the imagination of his contemplatives with the fire of hell, so that suddenly, without discretion, they give vent to their clever visionings, and without any sort of deliberation take it upon themselves immediately to blame other men's faults. This is because they have only one spiritual nostril. The division in the nose which separates one nostril from the other indicates that a man should have spiritual discretion, and be able to separate good from evil, evil from worse, good from the better, before he makes any considered judgment of anything that he hears or sees done or spoken around him. By a man's brain is spiritually understood the imagination; for it has its natural position and function in the head.

CHAPTER LVI

To pay more attention to intellectual acumen or to speculative theologians than to the ordinary teaching and counsel of holy Church is erroneous.

There are others who, though they are not deceived by the illusion which I have been mentioning, yet because of their pride and the cleverness of their natural understanding

---

353. R. M.: "Whether or not the devil always appears to his servants or to others in this guise, he has never shown himself to me like this." Richard says, in his *Experimentum Veritatis*, "Sometimes the evil angel *(angelus malus)* has appeared to me under a great variety of bodily guises. He has taken on the form of practically every kind of man, woman and beast." Cf. Julian of Norwich's vivid description of her own demonic hallucination, *Showings*, chap. 67, pp. 311–12.

and academic learning desert the common teaching and coun-sel of holy Church.[354] These and all their followers incline too much to their own opinion. Because they have not received the proper grounding in this humble, simple experience and virtuous living, it is their lot to have false experience fabricated and devised by the spiritual enemy; so that finally they break out and blaspheme all the saints, sacraments, laws and or-dinances of holy Church.[355] Men of the world who live ac-cording to the flesh, who think that the laws of holy Church are too hard to live by, incline themselves to these heretics very quickly and easily, and uphold them staunchly, simply because they believe that they will lead them by an easier way than that of holy Church.

My firm belief is that he who does not wish to go by the narrow way to heaven shall go the soft way to hell.[356] Let every man make test of this in himself.[357] And I believe that all these heretics and all their followers, if they could be seen as clearly as they will appear on the last day, would straightway appear burdened down by great and horrible sins of the world and their foul flesh, quite apart from their open presumption in maintaining error. Truly then are they called the disciples of anti-Christ; for it is said of them that in spite of their outward appearance, secretly they are foul lechers.[358]

---

354. This chapter is an extended commentary on 1 John 4:1–6: "... try the spirits if they be of God ... every spirit that dissolveth Jesus is not of God; and this is anti-Christ, of whom you have heard that he cometh ... He that knoweth God, heareth us ... By this we know the spirit of truth and the spirit of error." Bishop Challoner (1691–1781), who annotated the Douai version of the Vulgate from the ancient commentaries, says: *Try the spirits:* "by examining whether their teaching be agreeable to the rule of the Catholic faith and the doctrine of the Church." Cf. also *Chastising*, Introduction, pp. 61ff.

355. Probably a reference to the condemnation of the Beghards by Clement V in 1312. Cf. De Guibert, *Documenta Ecclesiastica*, p. 155.

356. Cf. Matthew 7:13–15. It is the false prophets, in sheep's clothing, who teach the softer way. The true teaching is "how narrow the gate and strait the way that leadeth to life ... broad is the way that leadeth to destruction."

357. Cf. 1 Corinthians 11:28.

358. Cf. Apocalypse 22:14–15: "... dogs and sorcerers, and unchaste ... and everyone that loveth and maketh a lie."

Chapter LVII

*Young disciples in their presumption misunderstand
this other word "up," and the illusions which follow
from this.*

Let us say no more about these people now, but get on
with our subject; how these young, presumptuous spiritual
disciples misunderstand this other word "up." For when they
read or hear read or spoken how men should lift up their
hearts to God, they look up to the stars as though they would
reach above the moon, and cock their ears as though they
could hear angels sing out of heaven. In their fantastic imagination they would pierce the planets or make a hole in the
firmament to look through it.[359] They would fashion a God
according to their own fancy, and dress him in rich clothes
and set him on a throne, far more fantastically than he was
ever painted on this earth.[360] They would fashion angels in
a bodily appearance and accoutre each one with different mu-
sical instruments, in far more curious detail than was ever
heard of or seen in this life.

Some of these the devil will delude in a remarkable manner. He will send down a sort of a dew, which they think
to be angels' food, which appears to come out of the air and
falls softly and sweetly into their mouths.[361] And so it is

---

359. The author's cosmology is Copernican, and in accord with the medieval
exegesis of Genesis: with the earth a flat disc resting on the ocean, and the firmament
or vault of heaven imagined as constructed of a thin metal plate, studded with
stars and planets; and above it the place of the other waters, rain, dew and snow.
But the "place" where God dwells is far "above" these heavens, in "inaccessible
light."

360. The author, with his main theme still in mind, is doubtless contrasting
the gospel simplicity and poverty with regard to the cenobitic clothing that symbolized
the following of Christ, and the sumptuous apparel of some religious—as satirized
by his contemporaries Chaucer and Langland. Cf., e.g., the Prioress of the *Canterbury
Tales*, Prologue, 151–62. There is no question that all the defects mentioned in these
chapters offend against the authentic monastic *sancta simplicitas*, interior and exterior.

361. Cf. Wisdom 16:20. It is interesting to compare the modern findings on

their habit to sit with their mouths open as though they were catching flies. Now all this is in truth delusion, however pious it might appear; for on these occasions their souls are void of any true devotion.[362] Great vanity and falsehood is in their hearts; and the cause of it is their outlandish exercises. So much so that very often the devil fabricates peculiar sounds in their ears, strange lights and shining in their eyes and remarkable scents in their nostrils; but all is false. Yet they do not think so. They believe that they are following the example of Saint Martin. He, in his exercises, looked upwards and saw, by revelation, God clad in his mantle amongst the angels;[363] and also of Saint Stephen, who saw our Lord standing in the heavens,[364] and of many others also; and of Christ himself who ascended, bodily, into heaven in the sight of his disciples.[365] And so they say that we should turn our eyes upwards. I certainly agree that if we are so moved in spirit, then in our outward behaviour we should lift up our eyes and our hands.[366] But I say that in our spiritual exercises we should not direct ourselves either upwards or downwards, or to one side or the other, or forwards or backwards, as one does in bodily matters. Because our exercise is a spiritual exercise, and not a physical one, nor is it to be performed in a physical way.

---

the "manna," the bread from heaven. Cf., e.g., J. L. McKenzie, *Dictionary of the Bible* (Chicago and London, 1966), p. 541.

362. Cf. Isaiah 29:8.

363. H. (p. 200) cites S. Baring-Gould, *Lives of the Saints*, vol. XIII (London, 1898), p. 242.

364. Cf. Acts 7:55.

365. Cf. Acts 1:9–11.

366. De Balma, in treating of the dispositions for unitive prayer, takes it as a principle that the bodily disposition should correspond to the exterior action. His model is Moses, who stood erect with his hands stretched up to heaven. Our author is anxious not to press the principle too hard, clearly because its ostentation can offend against the gospel principle "pray in secret." Cf. Matthew 6:5–6.

Chapter LVIII

*Saint Martin and Saint Stephen are not to be taken
as examples of straining upwards in our sensible imagination during the time of prayer.*

And though it is true what they say of Saint Martin
and Saint Stephen, that they saw such events with their bodily
eyes, these things were shown to them by a miracle, an au-
thentication of things spiritual.[367] For they are well aware
that the cloak of Saint Martin was never placed on Christ's
shoulders in reality, as though he had any need of it to keep
him from the cold,[368] but miraculously and in appearance,
for all our sakes who can be brought to salvation; for we

---

367. R. M.: "Whatever the facts in the case of St. Martin, I believe it to
be true of St. Stephen, that even if he saw the heavens opened in the literal sense—
which I neither deny nor affirm—his vision was not corporeal in the strict sense
of the term (and note that I say in the strict sense) but spiritual, which is also
called an imaginative vision. Such a vision appears to be corporeal, even though
it happens in the spirit. And more to the point, the mind is illumined by it."
Though he is alluding to the classical division of supernatural communication—
vision or locution—he is not as clear here as in his *Experimentum Veritatis*, where
he says, "Extasy and spiritual visions are those in which the 'forms' of things are
received by the spirit; rapture is a purely intellectual vision which excludes the
forms of visible things; a corporeal vision is one which is clear to the (physical)
eye" (MS P.R.O. S.P. 1/239, f. 263r.). Here, however, he is referring to his own
experience. The *Cloud* author is taking as read the current scholastic terminology,
deriving from Augustine (*De Genesi ad litteram* XII, 6): corporeal, imaginative and
intellectual visions. In corporeal visions there is real perception by the external
senses; in imaginative visions there is no such perception, God acting directly on
the imagination. It follows that it is extremely difficult in any concrete case to
prove that a vision is corporeal. The imaginative picture (or word) introduced into
the inner senses would be indistinguishable from those acquired through the perception of the exterior senses.

368. "One day in a very hard winter, during a severe frost, he met at the
gate of the city a poor man almost naked, trembling and shaking with cold and
begging alms ... Martin ... had nothing with him but his arms and clothes. So,
drawing his sword, he cut his cloak into two pieces, and gave one to the beggar....
That night, Martin in his sleep saw Jesus Christ dressed in that half of the garment
he had given away, and heard Jesus say, 'Martin, yet a catechumen, has covered
me with this garment' ... as a consequence of this vision he flew to be baptised"
(Butler's *Lives of the Saints*, ed. Thurston-Attwater [London, 1956], p. 310).

are made one with the body of Christ in spirit.[369] Those who clothe a poor man or who do any other good work, corporal or spiritual, for the love of God, to any who are in need, may be sure that they do it spiritually for Christ; and they shall be rewarded as fully as if they had done it to Christ in the flesh. He says this himself in the gospel.[370] Yet this was not enough for him; he felt that he must prove it by working miracles.[371] It is for this reason that he revealed himself as he did to Saint Martin.

All the revelations that were ever manifested in bodily likeness[372] to anyone here in this life have spiritual meaning. And my belief is that if they to whom they were shown, or we for whose sake they were shown, were spiritual enough, and were thus able to understand the spiritual meanings of these revelations, they would never have been manifested in bodily likeness.[373] So let us strip off the rough shell and feed on the sweet kernel.[374]

How are we to do this? Not as the heretics do, whom we may well compare to those wild men who, after drinking

---

369. Cf. Ephesians 4:4.

370. Cf. Matthew 25:39–40: ". . . when did we see you naked and clothe you? . . . as often as you did it to one of these least of my brethren, you did it to me."

371. The author is again stating the traditional doctrine concerning the purpose of private visions and revelations. For a modern statement, cf. Karl Rahner, *Les Révelations privées*, in R.A.M. 25 (1949): 506. The medieval author is not concerned to draw a distinction between scriptural and "historical" examples. It would not occur to the *Cloud* author that the Saint Martin story might be legendary; nor would it worry him if it were so. Cf. Introduction, supra, p. 90.

372. "Bodily likeness." It is noteworthy how much more theologically refined the analysis of Julian of Norwich is, when she uses this term. Cf. *Showings*, pp. 38–39, and Paul Molinari, *Julian of Norwich* (London, 1958), pp. 60–70.

373. The author is silently invoking the aphorism of his near-contemporary, the Franciscan William of Ockham (1280–1349), *Entia non sunt multiplicanda sine necessitate*, and applying it to the Divine Economy in the literal sense—all that God creates and provides has its purpose.

374. The ME version of *The Ladder* uses the same image, which is a commonplace drawn from the comparison between contemplative prayer as nourishing the soul as food nourishes the body. The source of the analogy in the West appears to be Augustine's *De Quantitate animae* 70. Cf. *Ladder*, pp. 28 and 146 n. 28. For English contemporary usage, cf. H., pp. 200–01.

from a beautiful cup, have the custom of throwing it against the wall and breaking it.[375] We should not imitate them, if we want to behave in a civilised fashion. We should not feed on the fruit, and then despise the tree; nor should we drink and then break the cup after we have drunk. By the tree and the cup are to be understood these miracles which are visible, and all those seemly bodily gestures which correspond with and do not hinder the work of the spirit. By the fruit and the drink are to be understood the spiritual meaning of these visible miracles, and those seemly bodily gestures, such as lifting up our hands and our eyes to heaven.[376] If they are done because the spirit so moves us, then they are well done; but otherwise they are hypocrisy and falsehood. If they are true and contain spiritual fruit within them, there is no reason why they should be despised. For men will kiss the cup on account of the wine which is in it.

What though our Lord, when he had ascended bodily into heaven, went his way upwards into the clouds, in the sight of his mother and his disciples? Should we therefore in our spiritual exercises continue to stare upwards with our bodily eyes,[377] to look and see if we can see him sitting in the flesh in heaven, or else standing as Saint Stephen saw him?[378] No, indeed, he did not reveal himself bodily in heaven to Saint Stephen in order to leave us an example that in

---

375. The analogy seems to be the author's own.

376. Hugo de Balma pays special attention to "the disposition of the body in time of prayer," and draws all his examples (apart from Moses in Exodus) from the N.T. He stresses, as does our author, that the one praying "with unitive desires" must bring his exterior and bodily dispositions into conformity with what is happening within.

377. R. M. notes that if our hearts are moved by devout desire to raise our eyes to heaven, well and good. Otherwise the gesture is incongruous, especially for this kind of contemplation. And cf. Acts 1:10–11.

378. The author begins here his long exegesis, allegorical in the strict meaning of the term, by referring to the literal sense of Acts 7:55: "... full of the Holy Ghost, he fastened his eyes on heaven, and saw ... Jesus standing at God's right hand." Cf. Introduction, supra, p. 90.

our spiritual exercises we should look up into heaven with our bodily eyes, in order that we might see him as did Saint Stephen, either standing or sitting or lying down. For no one knows how his body is disposed in heaven, whether standing or sitting or lying down. Nor is it necessary to know this, nor anything else, except that his body has been raised on high with his soul, without any division. His body and soul, which is his manhood, is made one with the godhead without any separation. We need know nothing of his sitting or his standing or lying down, but only this, that he is there present as pleases him, and he is so disposed in body as is most seemly for him to be. And if he shows himself lying down or standing or sitting in bodily fashion by revelation to any creature in this life, he does this for some spiritual meaning, not because of any disposition of body which he adopts in heaven.

Let us take an example. By standing is to be understood a readiness to help. So one friend is accustomed to say to another in time of battle: "Carry yourself well, man, fight hard and do not withdraw from the battle too easily; I will stand by you." By this is meant not merely a bodily standing by; for perhaps this battle is being fought on horseback and not on foot, and perhaps it is a running and not a standing fight. What he means, when he says that he will stand by his friend, is that he shall be at hand to help him.

This was the reason why our Lord showed himself in bodily appearance in heaven to Saint Stephen, when he was enduring martyrdom; and not to give us an example that we should look up into heaven. It was as though he said to Saint Stephen, as the representative of all those who suffer persecution for God's love: "See, Stephen, I am opening this physical firmament, which is called heaven, to let you see me, standing there; so you must trust steadfastly that as truly do I stand beside you spiritually, by the power of my Godhead, and am at hand to help you. Stand then bravely in the faith and endure steadfastly the severe buffetings of these hard stones. For your reward I shall crown you in bliss;[379] and not you alone, but all those who suffer persecution in any way for my sake."[380] So you can see that the purpose of these bodily showings was for their spiritual meaning.

CHAPTER LIX

The bodily ascension of Christ is not to be taken as an example of straining upwards in our sensible imagination in time of prayer. Time, place and the body are all to be forgotten during this spiritual exercise.

If you say, concerning the ascension of our Lord, that it took place bodily and for a bodily purpose, as well as for a spiritual one, because he ascended as true God[381] and true man; my answer is that he had been dead and was clothed in immortality,[382] as we too shall be at the last day. Then we shall be so subtle in body and soul together that we shall be able to move bodily wheresoever we wish, as swiftly as we can now move spiritually in our thoughts, whether up or down, to one side or the other, behind or in front. And I expect that then every movement will be equally good, as the theologians say.[383] But now you cannot come up to heaven bodily, but only spiritually; and this movement is to be so spiritual that it can have nothing to do with bodily movement,

---

379. Cf. James 1:12. Julian of Norwich makes much of this—cf. *Showings*, pp. 216, 230—as does the author himself in his *Letter on Prayer.*

380. Cf. Matthew 5:10ff; 2 Timothy 3:12.

381. R. M.: "He who says, 'I fill the heavens and the earth' is never subject in his divinity to any local movement. We are to understand our author to mean that he who ascended is true God and true man; and that this has a corporeal as well as a spiritual purpose. For it signifies that we, like him, are to ascend in body as well as in spirit."

382. Cf. 1 Corinthians 15:52–53.

383. The scholastic theologians list subtlety and agility *(subtilitas, agilitas)* as qualities attaching to the glorified body, which make the body able to obey every behest of the soul. Cf. *Summa Theologiae* 3a, Suppl. qq. 85 and 86.

neither up nor down, to one side or the other, behind or in front.

You must realize that all those who devote themselves to spiritual exercises, and particularly the exercises described in this book, even though they read the words "lift up" or "go in," and even though the exercise described in this book is called a movement, yet they must notice carefully that this movement is neither a bodily reaching upwards nor in the body, nor is it a local movement as from one place to another. And though it is sometimes called a rest, yet they are not to think that it is the sort of rest as is stopping in a place without moving away. For the perfection of this exercise is so pure and so spiritual in itself that when it is well and truly understood, it shall be seen to have nothing to do with any movement or any place.

It could reasonably be called a sudden change[384] rather than a local movement. As for time, place and body, all three must be forgotten in all spiritual exercises. So take care in this exercise that you do not take the bodily ascension of Christ as an example for straining up your imagination bodily in the time of your prayer, as though you wished to climb above the moon. For it could never be so, spiritually. Only if you were to ascend into heaven bodily, as Christ did, could you take it for an example; but no one can do that except God,[385] as he himself bears witness when he says: "There is no man who can ascend into heaven except he who descends from heaven,[386] and becomes man for the love of man." And even were it possible, as it cannot be, it would only be because of the abundance of spiritual working, simply through the power of the spirit, having no connection with any bodily stretching or straining in our imagination, either up or in

---

384. R. M.: "A sudden change does happen in this exercise, but I think it would be impossible for anyone to find the exact word to describe it."

385. R. M.: "No-one by his own power except he. But at the end of the world all the chosen will ascend with Christ, glorified in body and soul: though sometimes now the bodies of holy contemplatives are raised a little in the air."

386. Cf. John 3:13.

or on one side or on the other. So have nothing to do with such illusion. It could never be like that.

CHAPTER LX

The high road and the nearest way to heaven is measured not by yards but by desires.

And now perhaps you will ask how this can be right. It seems to you that you have clear evidence that heaven is upwards: because Christ ascended there bodily upwards and sent the Holy Spirit as he promised, coming in physical form from above, in the sight of all the disciples.[387] And this is our belief. And so, since you have this clear evidence, you do not see why you should not direct your mind upwards, bodily, in time of prayer.

I answer you as well as my feebleness permits, and say: Since it was so that Christ ascended bodily, and thereafter sent the Holy Spirit in physical form, it was appropriate[388] that it should be upwards and from above, rather than downwards and from beneath, from behind or in front or on one side or the other. But leaving aside what is seemly, there was no need for him to have gone upwards rather than downwards, from the point of view of distance to be travelled. For spiritually, heaven is as close down as up, and up as down, behind as in front, in front as behind, on one side as on the other; so much so that whoever has a true desire

---

387. This is a crux which H. (111/22) passes over. The majority of the MSS read "unseying alle his disciples," and R. M. translates *invisibilem omnibus discipulis.* It is the later MSS (including the Bodley translation, which reads *cernentibus corporeis oculis*) that correct to "seying" or "seeyng," thus resolving the contradiction with the later reference to the Holy Spirit's being sent in bodily form.

388. Hugo de Balma makes the same point with reference to the ascension and the Apostles praying with their faces turned upwards to heaven; but he also insists that it is the most appropriate posture for unitive (anagogical) prayer (cf. supra, chap. 58, note 376).

to be in heaven, then in that moment he is in heaven spiritually. For the high road and the shortest road thither is measured by desire and not by yards.[389] And so Saint Paul says about himself and many others: "Though our bodies are now on the earth, nevertheless our living is in heaven."[390] By this he means their love and their desire, which spiritually is their life. And indeed a soul is wherever it loves, as truly as it is in the body that lives by it, and to which it gives life.[391] So if we wish to go in spirit to heaven, we need not strain our spirit either up or down, or on one side, or on the other.[392]

CHAPTER LXI

All bodily things are subject to spiritual things; it is in the order of nature that they follow the rule of the spiritual, and not vice versa.

Nevertheless we need to lift up our bodily eyes and hands, as to the bodily heaven above, in which the planets are fixed.[393] I mean, of course, if we are moved by the work of our spirit;

---

389. The ultimate source is probably Augustine on Psalm 85, "I lift up my soul to you": "your strides are your affections, your way is your desire. If you love God you are in heaven, though you are standing on the earth" (*Enarr. in Psalmos* 85, 6; cf. H., p. 201). Our author is, however, very close to de Balma, when he speaks of the purified soul taking his place in the heavenly mansions by love and desire: "Where he loves, there is his true dwelling." Perhaps we have here a reminiscence of the hymn *Ubi caritas et amor*, sung at the Maundy Thursday Liturgy. Cf. J. Connelly, *Hymns of the Roman Liturgy* (London, 1957), pp. 88–89.

390. Philippians 3:20; cf. 2 Corinthians 5:6–8.

391. Cf. Luke 23:42–43; John 17:24; Galatians 2:20.

392. R. M.: "The soul is in the body until it leaves it at death; though in its working it can leave it for a while through excess of love or sorrow; unless it is someone like the apostle, who is so rapt that he does not know whether he is in the body or out of it" (Cf. 2 Corinthians 12:2).

393. The author seems unable to shake off the view of De Balma that this is the most appropriate posture for unitive prayer. Cf. supra, chap. 60, note 388. Doubtless the "third heaven" of Paul is in his mind (2 Corinthians 12:2).

otherwise not. For every bodily thing is subject to and ruled by spiritual things, and not the contrary.[394]

We have an example of this in the ascension of our Lord. When the appointed time was come in which it pleased him to go to his Father,[395] bodily in his manhood, which was never nor ever can be separated from his Godhead,[396] then the manhood with the body went up, in the unity of the person, mightily through the power of the spirit of God.[397] It was most seemly and fitting that this should be upwards in visible appearance.

The same subjection of the body to the spirit can truly be understood, in a sense, in the spiritual exercise described in this book, by the experience of those who undertake it. For whenever a soul disposes itself effectively to this exercise, then straight away and suddenly, and imperceptibly on the part of him who is making the exercise, the body, that perhaps before he began was a little bent over towards one side or the other in order to be more comfortable, comes upright by the power of the spirit, so that the body imitates and follows the work of the spirit, which is happening spiritually; and this is very appropriate.

It is because of this seemliness that man, who is the most seemly creature in body that God ever made, is not made bent downwards to the earth like all the other animals, but

---

394. Hilton, in his translation of the *Stimulus Amoris*, gives a lyrical rendering of this "baptised" Neoplatonic principle. Cf. Kirchberger, pp. 185–86.

395. Cf. John 13:1–3.

396. The author holds firmly to the teaching of the Council of Chalcedon: "We are to acknowledge one and the same Christ the Lord, the only-begotten son, immutably, unconfusedly, indivisibly, inseparably in two natures ... not separated or divided into two persons, but the one and only begotten son, God, the Word, the Lord Jesus Christ ..." (DS 302).

397. ME: "than miꝫtely, thy the vertewe of the Spirit God, the manheed with by body folowed in onheed of persone." Both R. M. and the Bodley translator are careful to offer theologically exact translations: *tunc potenter virtute spiritus Deus, humanitas concomitabatur in unitate personae; tunc virtute spiritus ipsum ascendentem in unitate personae copulata, indivisibiliter humanitas corporis sequebatur potenter.*

upright towards heaven.[398] This is because he must represent in bodily likeness the spiritual work of the soul, which must be spiritually upright and not crooked. Notice that I say spiritually, and not bodily. For how could a soul, which by nature has no bodily qualities, be strained bodily upright? No, it could not be. So take care not to interpret bodily what is meant spiritually, though it be spoken in bodily metaphor, as these words "up" or "down," "in" or "out," "behind" or "before," "on one side" or "on the other." For no matter how spiritual a thing may be in itself, yet when we come to speak of it, since speech is a bodily exercise performed with the tongue, which is an instrument of the body, it is necessary that bodily metaphors be used. But should it on that account be interpreted and understood bodily? No, spiritually.

CHAPTER LXII

How a man can know when his spiritual activity concerns what is beneath him or outside himself, when it is within him and on a par with himself, and when it is above him and under his God.

So that you may know how to understand spiritually words whose literal meaning is material, I intend to explain to you the spiritual meaning of certain words which pertain

---

398. The scriptural allusion here is doubtless Ecclesiastes 7:29: "God made man upright"; but a probable immediate source is the *De Bestiis et aliis rebus* of Hugh of St. Victor, III, 59, who, after quoting the same lines of Ovid (*Metamorphoses* I, 84–86) with which Dom James Grenehalgh glosses the passage in MS Douce 262, adds: "He who, intent on God, looks up to heaven in order to seek God must not bow down towards the earth like the beasts" (PL 177, 119). Saint Augustine expresses himself similarly in *De Trinitate* XII, 1: "As the body naturally stretches upwards, so the soul, which is a spiritual substance, is to be raised up to spiritual things."

to spiritual activity. Thus you will know clearly and unmistakably when your spiritual activity concerns what is beneath you and what is outside yourself, when it concerns what is within you and on a par with yourself, and when it concerns what is above you and under your God.[399]

Every kind of material thing is outside yourself and naturally below yourself. Yes, the sun and the moon and all the stars, even though they are above your body, are nevertheless below your soul.

All angels and all saints, no matter how they are reformed by grace, and adorned with virtues and therefore above you in purity, are nevertheless no more than equal with you by nature.[400]

Within yourself,[401] there are the natural powers of your soul. The three principal are these: mind, reason and will;[402] and the secondary, imagination and sensuality.

In nature, there is nothing above yourself except God alone.[403]

Wherever you read the word "yourself" in a spiritual context, this means your soul and not your body. The nature and worthiness of your work is to be judged according to

---

399. Cf. supra, chap. 8, pp. 137–38.

400. R. M.: "If you would avoid error, refrain from making obdurate statements about how in this life we are equal to the angels. There is a sense in which the author's statement is true, but it must be understood in that sense. We must work to be assimilated to them in their powers [purification, illumination, union?] especially if we would contemplate by this exercise."

401. R. M. reads "Below, in yourself." H. records no variant of the ME "Withinne in thyself." He may be interpreting rather than translating literally, since the author has just been speaking about "above" and "on a par" with oneself. Or else the copyist of his MS wrote *infra in te ipso*, instead of *intra*.

402. R. M.: Mind, reason and will have various names according to a variety of meanings. The author calls them "principal powers" because he is considering them with regard to the supreme point of the spirit *(supremo apice)*. They could in fact, from the point of view of the principal affection, all be called unitive wisdom.

403. R. M.: *except God alone.* "This must be understood in the strict sense," and he goes on to cite the Athanasian Creed—"wholly one, without any confusion of substance, but in the uniqueness of person."

the nature of the object upon which the powers of your soul are exercised,[404] whether the object is below you, within you or above you.[405]

Chapter LXIII

Of the powers of the soul in general. Specifically, how mind is a principal power, containing in itself the other powers and all their activities.

The mind is so great a power in itself that there is a sense in which it is true to say that it is never itself at work.[406] But reason and will are two working powers, and so are imagination and sensuality. The mind contains and comprehends within itself all these four powers and their activities.[407] The mind cannot be said to act in any way, unless this comprehension is itself activity.

I call some of the powers of the soul principal, and some secondary; not because the soul is divisible, for that is im-

---

404. Thomas Gallus notes that it is by the divine condenscension that the supreme point of the affection is united to the divine spirit itself. (Explanation on the *Mystical Theology*, Prologue.)

405. R. M.: "Note that in the future we shall also have a spiritual body, in place of our present fleshly one: granted, that is, that our loving is finally spiritualised by God's grace."

406. For the author, "mind" is distinguishable only from the nature of the soul itself, insofar as the former is a "power," i.e., dynamic. He has already said (supra, chap. 4, p. 123), that the "souls" of angels and men contain a "knowing" power and a "loving" power. He is developing this distinction in a more abstract way according to the triple distinctions of the previous chapter: "above, below and on a par with," and mind, reason and will.

407. For the Dionysian Gallus, using the medieval exegesis, the purified or "holy" soul is God's temple, with three mansions or "floors," and a foundation, which is the nature of the soul itself. The "mansions" consist in the operations of reason and will, which eventually find union in the "deified or spiritual intelligence," whose apex is "the affection in the supreme point of the spirit." Cf. his Explanation on the *Angelic Hierarchy*, chap. X.

possible,[408] but because all the objects on which they are exercised are separable. And some of these objects are principal, as are all spiritual things, and some secondary, as are all material things. The two principal working powers, reason and will, work entirely by themselves with regard to all spiritual things, and without the help of the two secondary powers.[409]

With regard to material things, whether these are bodily present or absent, the imagination and sensuality work as the animals do, with the bodily senses. But it is not possible for the soul, by means of these two powers, to come to know the source of activity and mode of being of material creatures, nor the cause of their being and their creation, without the help of reason and will.[410] It is because of this that reason and will are called principal powers; the field of their activity is purely spiritual and never material. Imagination and sensuality are called secondary, for they work in the body with bodily instruments, which are our five senses.

Mind is called a principal power because it contains in itself spiritually not only all the other powers, but also all the objects on which these powers work. Let me explain.

CHAPTER LXIV

Of the other two principal powers, reason and will,
and their activity before and after original sin.

Reason is a power by means of which we can distinguish the evil from the good, the bad from the worse, the good

---

408. This is the classic scholastic doctrine, following Saint Thomas. Cf. *Summa Theologiae* I, q. 75, a. 5.

409. Here, as McCann has pointed out (p. 149), the author begins to rely heavily on the *Benjamin Minor* of Richard of St. Victor (chaps. 3–6). Cf. *A Study of Wisdom*.

410. It is Augustine in his *De Trinitate* (chap. XII) who makes the distinction between the *ratio superior* and the *ratio inferior*, on which Richard and our author elaborate in turn.

from the better, the worse from the worst, the better from the best. Before man sinned, reason could do all this naturally.[411] But now it is so blinded with original sin that it can do this work only if it is enlightened by grace.[412] Both reason itself and the object upon which it works are comprehended and contained in the mind.

Will is a power by means of which we choose the good when this has been ascertained by reason. Through the will we love God, we desire God, and finally come to rest in God with full liking and full consent.[413] Before man sinned, will could never be deceived in its choice, in its loving or in any of its works; for then it had the natural power of appreciating everything at its true worth. But now it can do this only if it is strengthened by grace; for very often, because of the infection of original sin, it accepts a thing as good when it has only the appearance of good, and is really evil.[414] The mind contains and comprehends in itself both the will and the object of its willing.

---

411. ME has "Byfore er man synned," here and again in chaps. 65 and 66. H. (117–18) records no variant. "Adam" may simply be R. M.'s interpretation, in the light of the immediate reference to the original "blinding" of the reason, but this is unlikely.

412. R. M. makes the point that God is the author of all good, and that neither the angels nor Adam before the fall "could stand without God's help." "But the author of this book is here speaking of a special grace."

413. There is more than an echo of the opening of Augustine's *Confessions* here: "... our hearts are restless until they rest in thee." For, as the author says earlier, the "spiritual heart is the will."

414. The author is rather more refined in his psychology than is Hilton, who equally depends on Augustine. Cf. J. Walsh, ed., *Revelations of Divine Love*, pp. 28–29.

Chapter LXV

*Of the first secondary power, whose name is imagi-
nation; its activity and its obedience to reason, before
and after original sin.*

Imagination is a power by means of which we make all
our images of things, whether they are absent or present.
The imagination itself and the images which it makes are
contained in the mind. Before Adam sinned,[415] imagination
was so obedient to the reason—it was, in a manner of speaking,
its servant[416]—that it never presented to the reason any unseemly image of any bodily creature, or any fanciful image
of any spiritual creature. But now it is not so. For unless
it is restrained by the light of grace in the reason, the imagination never ceases, whether we are asleep or awake,[417] to
present various unseemly images of bodily creatures, or else
some fanciful picture, which is either a bodily representation
of a spiritual thing or else a spiritual representation of a bodily
thing. Such representations are always false and deceptive,
and compounded with error.[418]

This disobedience of the imagination can clearly be seen
in those who are recently converted from the world to a
life of devotion, in the time of their prayer.[419] For until their

---

415. Richard of St. Victor (loc. cit., chap. 2) introduces his allegory on reason
and imagination, affection (will) and sensuality, with a chapter on the nature and
the desire of justice, which our author omits in his *Study of Wisdom*. Here, however,
he seems to extend Richard's thoughts on perfect justice to "original" justice, and
refers it to Adam's state before the fall.

416. In the allegory, imagination and sensuality are the maidservants of reason
and will. "Imagination is always on hand to assist reason, nor does it cease its
servitude, even for a moment" (ibid., chap. 5).

417. R. M.: "When the author says, *it never ceases,* he is speaking about its
activity at least in dreams."

418. R. M.: "When he says, *compounded with error,* we must not understand
this of the representation itself, but of the phantasy."

419. Gallus, in his Explanation on the *Ecclesiastical Hierarchy,* speaks of those
who easily fall prey to the "stings of inordinate affections and the fantasies of impure
thoughts." They are those who are not yet purified of the memory of their past

imagination is, in great measure, controlled by the light of grace in the reason, as it is in continual meditation on spiritual things: for example, on their wretched state, on the passion and the humanity of our Lord God, and so on,[420] they cannot get rid of the elaborate variety of thoughts, fancies and images which are served up and imprinted on their minds by the light and the curiosity of the imagination.[421] All this disobedience is the painful result of original sin.

CHAPTER LXVI

The other secondary power which is called sensuality;
its activity and its obedience to the will, before and
after original sin.

The sensuality is a power of the soul whose sphere of activity is in the bodily senses;[421a] through it we have knowledge and experience of all bodily creatures whether they please us or not. It has two functions: one through which it looks to our physical needs, the other through which it ministers to the pleasures of our senses. It is this power which complains when the body lacks what is necessary for it and, when we are seeking what the body needs, impels us to take more than is necessary in order to satisfy and minister to our pleasure. It complains when we are deprived of creatures which

---

lives, and the fantasies that insinuate themselves into their thoughts, and titillate them (chap. 2).

420. Thomas Gallus, this time in his first commentary on the Canticle, speaks of a "contemplative meditation of the crucified Christ, when the soul looks upon him with the eyes of a reformed imagination" (Pez, p. 674).

421. In the "work" of Dionysian contemplation, we have to "tread down not only inordinate affections or thoughts, but the roots of the vices and thoughts" (*Ecclesiastical Hierarchy*, chap. 3).

421a. Julian of Norwich has a much more optimistic and concrete view of the "sensuality" than our author or Richard of St. Victor (cf. *Benjamin Minor*, chap. 5, and *The Study of Wisdom*). Cf. *Showings*, chaps. 45, 6, 55; and J. Walsh, "A Note on Sexuality and Sensuality," in *Supplement to The Way* 15, pp. 88–92.

please us, and greatly delights in the presence of such creatures. The presence of creatures which displease it annoys
the sensuality, and it is greatly delighted by the absence of
such creatures. This power itself and the object of its working
are contained in the mind.

Before man sinned, the sensuality was so obedient to the
will—it was its servant in a manner of speaking—that it never
presented the will with any inordinate pleasure in or repugnance for bodily creatures, or with any spiritual counterfeit
of pleasure or pain, induced by spiritual enemies in the bodily
senses. But now it is not so; for unless it is ruled by grace
in the will, so that it can accept meekly and measurably the
pain of original sin—which it experiences in the absence of
pleasant things needed by the body, and in the presence of
unpleasant things beneficial to the spirit—and also can refrain
from lusting after those pleasant and necessary things and
from rejoicing excessively in the absence of those unpleasant
but beneficial things, it will, in its wretchedness and wan-
tonness, wallow like a swine in the mud[422] in the pleasures
of this world and the foul flesh; so much that all our living
becomes beastly and carnal instead of being human and spiritual.

CHAPTER LXVII

*Unless we know the powers of the soul and their way
of working, we may easily be deceived in our understanding of spiritual words and spiritual activity;
and our soul is made godlike by grace.*

You can see then, my friend, into what a wretched state
we are fallen because of original sin. It is hardly surprising
that we should be like blind men and be easily deceived in

---

422. Cf. 2 Peter 2:22. The author's reflection here is similar to that in *The
Ladder*, p. 98.

our understandings of spiritual words and spiritual activities, particularly those of us who are ignorant of the powers of the soul and the way in which these powers operate.

So whenever your mind is occupied with any material thing, no matter how good the end in view may be, you are still beneath yourself in this working, and outside yourself. And whenever you are aware that your mind is occupied with the intricacies of the powers of your soul and the way in which they operate in spiritual matters, such things as your own vices or virtues or of any spiritual creature who is on a par with you by nature, to the end that by this activity you may learn to know yourself and advance in perfection; then you are within yourself and on a par with yourself.[423] But whenever you are aware that your mind is occupied with no created thing, whether material or spiritual, but only with the substance of God himself, as indeed the mind is and can be in the experience of the exercise described in this book; then you are above yourself and under your God.[424]

You are above yourself because you are striving by grace to reach a point to which you cannot come by nature; that is to say, to be made one with God in spirit and in love and in oneness of wills.[425] You are beneath your God; for though it can be said that during this time God and yourself are not two but one in spirit,[426] then insofar as you or any other who experiences the perfection of this work, "because of this oneness and by witness of holy scripture, may truly be called a God,"[427] nevertheless you are still beneath him.

---

423. Julian of Norwich puts the matter of this long digression simply and pithily in the context of the divine indwelling, "... I understood truly that our soul may never have rest in anything which is beneath itself. And when it comes above all creatures into itself, still it cannot dwell in the contemplation of itself" (*Showings*, pp. 313–14).

424. The author at last returns after sixteen chapters to "the exercise described in this book."

425. Cf. Philippians 3:7–15—a capital text for the author here.

426. Cf. 1 Corinthians 6:17.

427. "I say you are Gods and all of you sons of the most High" (Psalm 81:6; cf. John 10:34).

For he is God by nature from without beginning; and there was a time when you were nothing in substance, and even afterwards when you were by his power and love made something, then deliberately by sin you made yourself worse than nothing.[428] It is only by his mercy and without any merit of yours that you are made a god in grace, united with him in spirit without any division between you, both here and in the happiness of heaven without end.[429] So though you are one with him in grace you are yet far, far beneath him in nature.

So you can see, my friend, from what I say, at least in part, that he who is ignorant of the powers of his own soul, and the way in which these powers operate, can very easily be deceived in his understanding of words which are set down with a spiritual meaning.[430] You can also see in some way the reason why I did not dare to bid you openly to show your desire to God; but I bade you do all that you could to hide it and to conceal it like a child. And I still do so, for fear that you should understand bodily what is meant spiritually.

---

428. Cf. *The Ladder*, pp. 97–98: "When you did not exist I created you, when you sinned ... I redeemed you, when ... I let you find favour in my sight, you gave me nothing but contempt ... you turned away in pursuit of your own desires."

429. R. M.: "If the author is speaking of prevenient grace and condign merit, then he is inaccurate. And when he says *united with him ... without any division*, what is meant is the charity which never falleth away. He is referring to the divine power and man's aptitude for union, which, for the time being, nothing can defeat or destroy."

430. Cf. *The Ascent to Contemplative Wisdom*, p. 247.

CHAPTER LXVIII

What is nowhere to the bodily senses is everywhere spiritually; our outward nature reckons nothing of the work of this book.

Similarly, where someone else would direct you to gather together all your powers and faculties within yourself, and worship God there,[431] I am not happy with such counsel, for fear of deceit and lest these words be taken in a bodily way, even though they are well and truly said, and none more true if they are properly understood. My counsel is to take care that you are in no sense within yourself. To put it briefly, I would have you be neither outside yourself, above yourself, nor behind, nor on one side or the other.

"Where then," you will say, "am I to be? According to your reckoning, nowhere!" Now indeed you speak well, for it is there that I would have you. Because nowhere bodily is everywhere spiritually. Take good care, then, that your spiritual exercise is nowhere bodily. Then, wherever the object is on which you set yourself to labour in the substance of your mind, truly you are there in spirit, as truly as your body is in the place where you dwell bodily.[432] And though all your bodily faculties can find there nothing to feed on, because they think that what you are doing is nothing, carry on, then, with that nothing, as long as you are doing it for God's love. Do not leave off, but press on earnestly in that

---

431. The process known in the Western spiritual tradition as "recollection" and "introversion": the proximate preparation for contemplation. See, for example, the well-known autobiographical passage from Augustine in the *Confessions*, book X: "Too late have I loved thee. For behold thou wert within"; and Gregory the Great in his *Homilies on Ezechiel* II, V, 9: "The first step is for the soul to collect itself within itself; the second that it consider what its nature is so collected; the third, that it ... yield itself to the intent contemplation of its invisible maker." Cf. C. Butler, *Western Mysticism, passim*; and *DSp.* fasc. l, *Introversion*, 1904–18.

432. R. M.: "In the practice of this exercise, the soul is essentially in the body *(in corpore)*, but by the movements of the mind it is there with the object of its exercise."

nothing with an alert desire in your will to have God, whom no man can know.[433] For I tell you truly that I would rather be in this way nowhere bodily, wrestling with this blind nothing, than to have such power that I could be everywhere bodily whenever I would, happily engaged with all this "something" like a lord with his possessions.

Leave aside this everywhere and this everything, in exchange for this nowhere and this nothing. Never mind at all if your senses have no understanding of this nothing; it is for this reason that I love it so much the better. It is so worthy a thing in itself that they can have no understanding of it. This nothing can be better felt than seen; it is most obscure and dark to those who have been looking at it only for a very short while.[434] Yet to speak more truly, a soul is more blinded in experiencing it because of the abundance of spiritual light than for any darkness or lack of bodily light.[435] Who is he that calls it nothing? It is surely our outward man, not our inward. Our inward man calls it All,[436] for because of it he is well taught to have understanding of all things bodily or spiritual, without any specific knowledge of any one thing in itself.

---

433. R. M.: "When he says *whom no-one can know*, he is speaking of the fulness of knowledge, for even in heaven we shall be seeing One who is incomprehensible, immense and infinite."

434. So De Balma: "In the beginning of the exercise, the sovereign point of the affections rises with difficulty ... and the intellect is overcast and obscured by a thick cloud of darkness".

435. The ultimate source is again Gallus, in his exposition on the *Letter of the Pseudo-Dionysius to Gaius:* "By darkness and ignorance I mean the divine light, not because of the deprivation of light ... but because of the excess of all illumination and knowledge." Cf. J. Walsh, in AHDLMA 30 (1963): 204. De Balma cites the letter to Dorotheus in the translation of Sarracenus: "The divine darkness is the inaccessible light in which God is said to dwell (1 Timothy 6:10), invisible indeed, because of the superabundant light."

436. Cf. 2 Corinthians 6:16.

CHAPTER LXIX

How a man's affections are marvellously changed in the spiritual experience of this nothing, which happens nowhere.

A man's affection is remarkably changed in the spiritual experience of this nothing when it is achieved nowhere.[437] For the first time that he looks upon it, he finds there imprinted all the particular sinful acts that he ever committed since his bodily or spiritual birth,[438] in secret or in darkness. And no matter what way he turns, they will always appear before his eyes, till such time as he shall have in great part rubbed them away with much hard labour, many sore sighings and many bitter tears.[439]

It seems to him, sometimes, in this labour, that to look upon it is like looking upon hell.[440] He despairs of ever winning, out of that pain, to the perfection of spiritual rest. Many arrive so far inwardly, but because of the great pains that they experience, and because of the absence of consolation they go back to behold bodily things,[441] to seek fleshly com-

---

437. R. M.: "He does not say that nothing is something, since nothing is nothing, that is, no thing. But because next to nothing *(quasi nihil)* is something, a man labours to cut away everything that exists that he might be purified and naked, according to that knowledge which is unknowing *(cognitionem incognitam).*" Cf. also Augustine Baker, "on that mystic saying—nothing and nothing make nothing," quoted by McCann, ed. cit., p. 217; and St. John of the Cross, on "everything and nothing," in *Ascent of Mount Carmel* I, XIII (ed. cit., p. 59).

438. The ME text is ambiguous: "... specyal dedes of sinne þat ever he did sithen he was borne bodely or goostly ..." (H., 122/21). Is the author referring to sins of the flesh or of thought, or to physical or baptismal birth? The latter is obviously more likely, as R. M. renders: *ex quo corporaliter vel spiritualiter natus fuit*—"from the time when he was physically or spiritually born."

439. Cf. *The Ascent to Contemplative Wisdom*, p. 248.

440. Cf. Julian of Norwich: "And therefore it often seems to us as if we were in danger of death and in some part of hell, because of the sorrow and pain which sin is to us" *(Showings,* chap. 72, p. 120).

441. Teresa of Avila sums up this constant teaching of the Western tradition when she says: "... it is most important—all-important, indeed—that they should begin well by making an earnest and most determined resolve not to halt until

forts without, because of the absence of spiritual consolation that they have not yet deserved, and which they would have deserved if they had endured a while.

He that has patience sometimes experiences consolation, and has some hope of perfection.[442] For he feels and sees that many of the particular sins committed in the past are in great part rubbed away by the assistance of grace. But always in the midst of the consolation he feels pain; but now it seems to him that it shall have an end, for it is growing less and less. So he calls it not hell but purgatory. Sometimes he does not find any particular sin written upon it, but it seems to him that it is a lump of sin: and somehow or other nothing else than himself. And then it is to be called the ground and the pain of original sin. Sometimes it seems to him that it is paradise or heaven, because of the many wonderful sweetnesses and consolations, joys and blessed virtues that he finds in it. Sometimes it seems to him that it is God, because of the rest and the peace that he finds in it. But let him think what he will, he shall always find that it is a cloud of unknowing which is between him and his God.[443]

---

they reach their goal, whatever may come, whatever may happen to them, however hard they may have to labour" (*Way of Perfection* XXI, ed. cit.). Cf. also Walter Hilton, *Scale II*, chap. 18, ed. cit., p. 292.

442. This true contemplative attitude to the absence of spiritual consolation is summarized in the *Commentary on Psalm 91* commonly attributed to Hilton. Cf. Walsh and Colledge, *The Knowledge of Ourselves and of God*, pp. 17–18. The point is also stressed in *Private Direction*.

443. The experience of the alteration of extreme consolation and desolation during the contemplative exercise is the author's ultimate concern in *Private Direction*.

CHAPTER LXX

The silencing of our bodily senses leads most readily to the experience of spiritual things; similarly, the silencing of our spiritual faculties leads to such experiential knowledge of God as is possible by grace in this present life.

Work hard in this nothing and this nowhere, and desert your outward bodily senses and the objects of their activity. For I tell you truly that this exercise cannot be understood by them.[444]

With your bodily eyes you cannot comprehend anything except by its length and breadth, its smallness and greatness, its roundness and squareness, its farness and nearness, and its colour; by your ears, nothing except noise or some manner of sound; by your nose, nothing except stench or savour; by taste, nothing except sour or sweet, salty or fresh, bitter or pleasant; and by touch, nothing except hot or cold, hard or tender, soft or sharp.[445] And truly neither God nor spiritual things have any of these qualities or quantities. So leave your outward senses and do not work with them, neither exteriorly nor interiorly. For all those who set themselves to be spiritual workers inwardly, and yet think that they ought either to hear, smell, see, taste or touch spiritual things, either within or outside themselves, surely they are deceived and are working wrongly, against the course of nature. For by nature it is ordained that through the bodily senses men should have knowledge of all outward bodily things, and not that they should come to the knowledge of ghostly things through them.

---

444. The author is here summarizing the directives of Denis's *Mystical Theology*, chap. 1; and especially the key text, which has been his main concern throughout the whole book: *Forti contritione derelinque sensus et operationes intellectuales*—the Latin translation of Sarracenus. Cf. Chevalier, I, p. 507, and the author's own *Hidden Theology*.

445. Hugo de Balma gives us a similar list of the apprehension of the exterior senses or their objects; but he transfers them to the interior senses.

I am speaking of their positive activity. For we can come to the knowledge of spiritual things through their lack of activity. When, for example, we read or hear of certain things, and realise that our bodily senses cannot inform us what these things are through their qualities, then we can certainly be assured that these things are spiritual and not bodily things.

The same is true spiritually of our spiritual powers, when we are labouring concerning the knowledge of God himself. For no matter how much spiritual understanding a man may have in the knowledge of all created spiritual things, he can never, by the work of his understanding, arrive at the knowledge of an uncreated spiritual thing, which is nothing except God. But by the failing of it, he can.[446] For where his understanding fails is in nothing except God alone; and it was for this reason that Saint Denis said, "The truly divine knowledge of God is that which is known by unknowing."[447] And now whoever cares to examine the works of Denis,[448] he will find that his words clearly corroborate all that I have said or am going to say, from the beginning of this treatise to the end.[449] But I have no mind to cite him to support my views on any other thing than this, at this moment, or any other doctor either. For at one time men believed that it was humility to say nothing out of their own heads, unless they corroborated it by scripture and the sayings of the fathers.

---

446. The author is not here contrasting the bodily senses with the "spiritual senses" as traditionally interpreted in Western mysticism, but with the spiritual powers of mind, reason and will. Rather he is again drawing attention to the crucial need for discernment in distinguishing the essential object of the exercise—union with God—from any accidentals that may accompany its process. He is not concerned to condemn the doctrine of the spiritual senses.

447. Gallus, commenting on the citation from the Pseudo-Denis, says that to know by unknowing is to know "by suspending all rational and intellectual operations and knowledge."

448. This is the only explicit text of the Pseudo-Denis cited by the author. It is again a rendering of the Latin of Sarracenus, *Divine Names*, chap. VII: *et est rursus divinissima Dei cognitio quae est per ignorantiam cognita* (cf. Chevalier, op. cit., I, p. 406). Most MSS translate *divinissima* as "goodly" or "goostly" (H., 125/11).

449. It is difficult to estimate just how familiar the author is with all "the works of Denis." Cf. Introduction, supra, pp. 26–27.

But now this practice indicates nothing except cleverness and a display of erudition. You do not need it and so I am not going to do it. He who has ears, let him hear;[450] and he who is moved to believe it, let him do so; otherwise he will not.

CHAPTER LXXI

Some may experience the perfection of this exercise during rapture, but some can experience it whenever they will, in their normal conscious state.

Some people believe that this work is so difficult and so awesome that they say it cannot be undertaken without great toil preceding it;[451] that it can be achieved only very seldom, and this during the time of rapture.[452] To these I wish to answer as well as my feebleness permits. I say that it depends on the ordinance and the disposition of God, and the spiritual capacity of those to whom this grace of contemplation and spiritual working is given. There are some who cannot reach it without long and frequent spiritual exercises; and even then it is only very seldom that they will experience the perfection of this exercise, at the special calling of our Lord; this is what is meant by rapture.[453]

---

450. Matthew 13:9.

451. The author has already explained at length wherein lies the labour of this exercise (cf supra, chap. 26, p. 173). He will return more directly to its alleged difficulty in *Private Direction*. Cf. Introduction, supra, pp. 71–72.

452. Walter Hilton, in his version of the *Stimulus Amoris* (ed. cit., p. 154), defines rapture as being "ravished from the use of thy bodily wits so that all manner phantoms of bodily likeness be withdrawn from thy soul, and thy mind overpass the common and reasonable manner of thinking of this life."

453. The author here uses rapture in the sense of "mystical trance," in which the normal consciousness and the use of the faculties are suspended. But the essence of contemplative perfection is that the affection leaves the understanding behind, so that the mind is said to go out of itself. This *excessus mentis* does not necessarily involve trance.

But there are some who are so refined by grace and in spirit, and so familiar[454] with God in this grace of contemplation, that they may have the perfection of it whenever they will, in their ordinary state of soul: whether they are sitting, walking, standing or kneeling. And at the same time they have the full command of all their faculties, bodily and spiritual, and can use them if they so wish: not without a certain hindrance, but one not hard to overcome.[455] We have an example of the first type in Moses, and of the second in Aaron, the priest of the Temple.[456]

This grace of contemplation is prefigured by the Ark of the Testament in the Old Law; and those who exercise themselves in this grace are prefigured by those who are most concerned with this ark, as the story bears witness. This work and this grace is rightly said to resemble that ark. For just as in that ark all the jewels and relics of the Temple were contained, in the same way in this little love, when it is offered, are contained all the virtues of a man's soul, which is the spiritual temple of God.[457]

Before Moses could come to see this ark, and to know how it had to be made, he climbed up to the top of the

---

454. The "familiar loving" of God is a fundamental theme of Julian of Norwich. Yet, in spite of her considerable theological learning, she never names, in her deep consideration of the union of wills, the *via negativa* of dark contemplation. Cf. *Showings*, Introduction, *passim*, and especially chap. 5, p. 184. Cf. Introduction, supra, pp. 24–25.

455. R. M.: "To be rapt purely into God for the sake of himself alone is only possible through the divine bounty. But to be lifted up to the Cloud of Unknowing, or even further, to some sort of state of glory, even though the senses are not fully but only partially suspended, can happen by human industry with the co-operation of grace after long labour. Ultimately there will be almost no labour at all, for it happens in what might be called a natural way." Saint Teresa of Avila has much to say about the various phases of rapture and suspension. Cf. Index to *Complete Works*, ed. cit., especially the *Spiritual Relations*, vol. 1, p. 331.

456. Cf. Exodus 24:15ff. The immediate source is Richard of St. Victor's *Benjamin Major*, IV, 22–23 and V, 1 (P.L. 195, 461–69). For an English translation, cf. C. Kirchberger, *Richard of St. Victor* (London, 1957), pp. 175–83.

457. This is a summary of Gallus's teaching on the "hierarchies of the mind." Cf. Introduction, supra, pp. 72–73.

mountain and dwelt there and worked in a cloud for six days with hard and long labour, until the seventh day, when our Lord would deign to show him the way in which the ark should be made. By the long labour of Moses, and the delay in the revelation to him, we are to understand those who cannot come to the perfection of this spiritual exercise unless long labour precedes it, and even then only very seldom, and when God will deign to show it.

But what Moses could only come to see very seldom, Aaron, because of his office, had it in his power to see in the Temple within the veil, as often as it pleased him to enter. By Aaron's power we are to understand all those of whom I spoke above, those who by their spiritual skill and the help of grace can make the perfection of this exercise their own as often as it pleases them.

CHAPTER LXXII

He who habitually practises this exercise must not take it for granted that other contemplatives have his precise experience.

You can see then, that the man who can only come to see and experience the perfection of this work with heavy toil, and even then only seldom, can easily be deceived if he speaks, thinks and judges of other men according to his own experience: that they too cannot come to it except seldom and only then with hard labour.[458] Similarly, he also can be deceived who has it whenever he wishes, if he judges all others by his own experience, and says that they can have it when they wish. Forget this; for certainly no one must

---

458. The author constantly insists that the grace of contemplation is completely gratuitous, but that it is always given as an individual grace according to the capacity of each one, and to fit the circumstances of each time; and that it belongs to discretion to understand all this.

think in this way. If such be God's pleasure, it may be that those who at first can have it only seldom, and even then at great cost, may later on come to have it when they will and as often as they like. We have an example of this in Moses. On the mountain he saw the form of the ark very rarely and after heavy toil. But later on, within the veil,[459] he saw it as often as it pleased him.[460]

CHAPTER LXXIII

This grace of contemplation is prefigured in the Ark of the Covenant: in the sense that Moses, Beseleel and Aaron, in their dealings with the ark, are three types of how we exercise ourselves in this grace.

There were three men who were chiefly concerned with this ark of the Old Testament: Moses, Beseleel and Aaron. Moses was taught how it should be made on the mountain of our Lord.[461] Beseleel fashioned and made it in the valley, according to the directions which were revealed on the mountain.[462] Aaron had it in his keeping in the Temple, to touch it and see it as often as it pleased him.

According to the example of these three, we make progress in this grace of contemplation in three ways.[463] Sometimes

---

459. Methley translates *infra velum vidit*, meaning within the veil of the Tabernacle. "Vaile" is the reading of several manuscripts, but the rest read "Vaale" (H., 128/5).

460. Cf. Exodus 33:7–11.

461. Cf. Exodus 25:8–27: 21.

462. Cf. Exodus 36:1–38:31. R. M. comments: "At the end of Exodus we read: when he had brought the Ark into the Tabernacle, he hung the screen before it, in order to fulfil the Lord's command [40, 21]. We must note that the author says Beseleel here, because it was he who fashioned and made the Ark in the vale which was afterwards placed behind the veil." Another hand (James Grenehalgh?) has added in the margin of the Latin MS: "In the english original we read: 'Beseleel fashioned the Ark, and he made it in the valley etc.'"

463. This is the division in the *Benjamin Major*, where Richard postulates three

we make progress by grace alone, and then we are like Moses who, for all the hard cost of the mountain climb, could only come to see it seldom; and that sight was only through the revelation of our Lord, when it pleased him to show it; and not as a reward which Moses deserved. Sometimes we make progress in this grace by our own spiritual skill, supported by grace; and then we are like Beseleel, who could not see the ark before he had fashioned it with his own skill, helped by the pattern which was revealed to Moses on the mountain. And sometimes we make progress in this grace by other men's teaching; and then we are like Aaron who had it in his keeping, and could regularly see and touch the ark whenever he liked, after Beseleel had fashioned and made it ready for him.

So, my spiritual friend, though I am a wretch, unworthy to teach any creature, in this exercise I hold the office of Beseleel. Perhaps I am speaking childishly and foolishly; for in a way I am fashioning and making plain on your behalf the nature of this spiritual ark. But you can work far better and much more worthily than I do, if you will take on the office of Aaron: that is to say, to exercise yourself continuously in it for yourself and for me as well. Do so, I beseech you, for the love of God Almighty. And since we are both called by God to work in this exercise, I beseech you, for God's love, to fill up on your part what is wanting in mine.[464]

---

kinds of contemplation, *dilatatio, sublevatio* and *alienatio*. "The first kind involves human labour, the third proceeds from grace alone, and the middle one from the interaction of the other two" (P.L. 196, 170).

464. Cf. Colossians 1:24. Note the author's clear implication that both he and his disciple are called to the same "singular" state of life. Cf. supra, chap. 1, pp. 116–17, and Introduction, supra, pp. 3–11.

Chapter LXXIV

A man is rightly disposed to the contemplation which is the subject matter of this book when he cannot read or speak about it, or hear it read or spoken about, without feeling that he is really suited to this work and its effects. A repetition of the directives given in the prologue.

But if you think that this way of working is not according to your bodily or spiritual disposition, you can leave it and take another safely and without reproach, as long as it is with good spiritual counsel.[465] And in that case I beseech you that you will hold me excused. For truly my purpose in writing this book was to help you to make progress according to my own simple knowledge. That was my intention. So read it over two or three times; and the oftener the better, and the more you shall understand of it; so that, perhaps, if some sentence was very difficult for you to understand at the first or second reading, it will then seem to you easy enough.

Yes, indeed. It seems impossible to my understanding that any soul who is disposed for this exercise should read the book, privately or aloud, without feeling during that time a true affinity for the effect of this exercise. So if it seems to you that it does you good, thank God heartily, and for God's love pray for me.

Do this, then. I also pray you, for God's love, not to let anyone examine this book, except those whom you believe to be disposed for it—as you find written at the beginning of the book, where it says what men may undertake this exercise, and when they should do so. And if you do let any such person examine it, then I beg you to bid them take

---

465. This is a clear indication that the author is concerned with *one* method of prayer proper to the *ex professo* contemplative state, and that there are others equally praiseworthy. Cf. Introduction, supra, p. 25.

the necessary time to examine it right through. For it may happen that some question occurs at the beginning or in the middle which depends on what follows, and is not fully explained in that place. If it is not explained here, it will be so a little later on, or else at the end. Hence, if a man were to read one section and not another, it might easily happen that he would fall into error. So I beg you to do as I say. If you think that there is any point here that you would wish to have clarified in greater detail than it is, let me know what it is, and what you think about it, and I shall amend it to the best of my simple ability.[466]

But as for the chatterboxes, the rumour-mongers, the gossips, the tittle-tattlers, the fault-finders of every sort, I would not want them to see this book. It was never my intention to write on these matters for them. I would refuse to have them interfering with it, those clever clerics, or layfolk either. For no matter how excellent they may be in matters pertaining to the active life, my subject is not for them.[467]

Chapter LXXV

Of definite signs whereby a man may test whether or not one is called by God to take up this exercise.

All those who read the subject-matter of this book, or listen to it read or spoken about, and in their reading or listening think that this is good and congenial to them, are not on that account called by God to undertake this exercise, simply because of this congenial feeling that they have in

---

466. Though the author expects *The Cloud* to be read or heard by others as well as by the addressee, it is different with the letters *Prayer, Discernment* and *Private Direction.*

467. This last paragraph, repeated word for word in the prologue (cf. supra, p. 102) gives every indication of an addition—either by the author or by another, probably from this chapter to the prologue.

the time of their reading.[468] It can happen that this feeling comes more from a natural intellectual curiosity than from any calling of grace.

If, however, they wish to discover whence this feeling comes, they can find out in this way if they so wish. First let them see to it that they have first done all that in them lies to prepare themselves for it by the cleansing of their conscience according to the judgment of holy Church, and with the approval of their spiritual director.[469] So far, so good. But if they wish to know more, let them see if this impulse is always pressing on their minds more regularly than is so with any other spiritual exercise. And if it seems to them that nothing that they do, bodily or spiritually, is of any value according to the witness of their conscience except this little secret love, directed in a spiritual way as the chief of all their exercises: if that is their feeling, then it is a token that they are called by God to this exercise; otherwise, not.

I do not say, for those who are called to undertake this exercise, that this stirring will always exist and dwell in their minds continuously. No, it is not so. For often the actual experience of this impulse is withdrawn for various reasons from the young spiritual apprentice in this exercise: sometimes in order that he might not become too familiar with it, and so consider that it is for the most part in his own power to have it when he pleases and as he pleases.[470] Such a belief would be pride. Whenever the experience of this grace is

---

468. The chapter has all the appearances of an *arrière-pensée*, and is an additional argument for the view that the whole work is primarily intended as a letter to an individual. Its subject matter is developed at length in *Private Direction*. Cf. Introduction, supra, p. 9.

469. The author is adamant that a general auricular confession is a *sine qua non* for entry into the *ex professo* contemplative life, and in particular for what he has called "singular." Cf. Introduction, supra, pp. 37–38. He equally takes it for granted that the individual is subject to regular spiritual direction.

470. The warning here on the withdrawal of contemplative graces, which is common doctrine, may have its immediate source in the *Ladder:* "For this grace the Spouse bestows when he pleases and to whom he pleases" (ed. cit., chap. X, pp. 90–91).

withdrawn, pride is the cause. That is to say, not actual pride, but the pride that would be there unless this experience of grace were withdrawn. And often young people in their folly think that God is their enemy when he is their best friend.

Sometimes the experience is withdrawn because of their carelessness; when this happens, they experience immediately a very sharp pain that afflicts them very sorely. Sometimes our Lord deliberately delays the experience, because it is his will, by such delaying, to enlarge the experience and make one care more for it when it is found again and experienced afresh, after having been lost for a long time. This is one of the clearest and simplest signs that a soul can have to know whether he is called to undertake this exercise or not: if he feels, after such a delay and a long absence of this experience, when it comes suddenly, as it does, achieved without any intermediary, that he has a greater fervour of desire and a greater longing to get on with this exercise than he ever had before; so much so that often, I believe, he has more joy in the finding of it than ever he had sorrow in the losing of it. If it is thus, then it is truly a most authentic token that he is called by God to undertake this exercise, whatever his state is or has been.

Because it is not what you are nor what you have been that God looks at with his merciful eyes, but what you desire to be.[471] And Saint Gregory is witness that "all holy desires grow by delay; and if they diminish by delay then they were never holy desires."[472] And he who experiences less and less joy in the new experiences and sudden presentations of his own desires, though they all must be called natural desires

---

471. This beautiful paraphrase of the aphorism "to take the will for the deed" has its counterpart in *The Book of Margery Kempe:* "I take no heed of what a man has been, but I take heed of what he will be" (ed. cit., chap. 21, p. 49). It clearly has its affinities with Philippians 3:13–14. R. M. adds: "The author is speaking of the exercise of this book, upon which God, from whom nothing is hid, looks with loving eyes; so that he will help you to this greater perfection more than you could ever imagine or desire."

472. Gregory the Great, *Homilia in Evangelia* II, 25 (PL 76, 1190).

for the good, nevertheless they were never holy desires. Of this holy desire Saint Augustine speaks, when he says that "the whole of life of good Christian men is nothing else but holy desires."[473]

Farewell, spiritual friend, in God's blessing and mine. And I beseech almighty God that true peace, sane counsel and spiritual comfort in God with abundance of grace, always be with you, and with all those who on earth love God.[474]

Amen.[475]

---

473. Saint Augustine, *In Epistolam Joannis ad Parthos*, IV, 6.

474. Concerning the opinion that this blessing and prayer is proof that the author is a priest, cf. Introduction, supra, p. 3.

475. R. M. ends his translation with the following *envoi:* "Brother Thurstinus, it was for God and for your sake, and at your request, that I undertook the labour of this work; and with God's help I have brought it to the desired conclusion as you asked me to do: Anno Domini 1491, on the second day after the feast of Saint Lawrence [12th August]. I submit this work and all my previous works to our holy mother the Catholic Church, if there is any need for scrutiny."

BIBLIOGRAPHY

Manuscripts Consulted

MS Bodleian Library, Oxford: Douce 262 *(Cloud)*.
MS Bodleian Library, Oxford: 856 (Anonymous Latin Translation).
MS British Library, London: Harleian 674 and 2373 *(Cloud)*.
MS British Library, London: Royal 17C xxvi *(Cloud)*.
MS Cambridge University Library: Kk, vi, 26 *(Cloud)*.
MS Pembroke College, Cambridge: 221 (Richard Methley's Translation).
MS Public Record Office, London: 1/239 (Methley's Letter to Hugh the Hermit).
MS Stonyhurst LXVIII (Guigues du Pont's *De Contemplacione*).
MS Trinity College, Cambridge: 1160 (Methley's other Latin works).

Books

Allison-Peers, E. (ed. and trans.) *The Complete Works of St. Teresa of Avila.* (3 vols.) New York/London: Sheed and Ward, 1946.
———— (ed. and trans.) *The Complete Works of John of the Cross.* London: Burns & Oates, 1953.

BIBLIOGRAPHY

Anselm, St. *Meditationes*, Ed. F. S. Schmitt, *S. Anselmi Opera*, III, Edinburgh: Nelson, 1946.

Augustine, St. *De gratia et libero arbitrio*, P.L. 44, 881–912.

──── De Civitate Dei, P.L. 41, 13–804.

Aux Sources de la vie cartusienne. Grande Chartreuse: 1960.

Barbet, J. *Thomas Gallus: Commentaires du Cantique des Cantiques*. Paris: Vrin, 1967.

Bazire, J. and E. Colledge (eds.) *The Chastising of God's Children and the Treatise of Perfection of the Sons of God*. Oxford: Basil Blackwell, 1957.

Bernard of Clairvaux, St. *Sermones super Cantica*. Ed. J. Leclercq, A. Talbot, H. Rochais. Rome: *Editiones Cistercienses*, 1946. *De Gradibus humilitatis*. Ed. B. Mills, Cambridge Patristic Texts. *Treatise on Consideration*. Dublin: Browne & Nolan, 1922.

Bonaventure, St. *'Itinerarium mentis in Deum,'* Ed. E. Cousins, *The Soul's Journey Into God*. N.Y.: Paulist Press, 1978.

Bruno, St. *Letter to the Brethren at Chartreux*, P.L. 152, 48–49.

Butler, C. *Western Mysticism* (2nd ed.) London: Constable, 1951.

Cassian, John. *Institutions and Collations*. Ed. E. C. S. Gibson. Library of Nicene and Post-Nicene Church Fathers, 2nd series, 2, XI, Oxford: 1894.

Caplan, H. (ed.) *Cicero ad C. Herennium de ratione dicendi*. London: Loeb Classical Library, 1954.

Chevalier, P. (ed.) *Dionysiaca*. Paris: Descleé, 1937.

Clay, R. M. *The Hermits and Anchorites of England*. London: Methuen, 1913.

Combes, A. *La théologie mystique de Gerson*. Rome: Vrin, 1963–64.

Colledge, E. and J. Walsh. *The Ladder of Monks and Twelve Meditations by Guigo II*. New York/London: Image/Mowbrays, 1978.

Colledge, E. and W. Evans. "Piers Plowman," in *Pre-Reformation English Spirituality*. (ed. J. Walsh, S.J.) London/New York: Burns & Oates/Kennedy, 1964.

──── and J. Walsh. *Julian of Norwich: Showings*. New York: Paulist Press, 1978. London: S.P.C.K., 1979.

Connelly, J. *Hymns of the Roman Liturgy*. London: Longmans, 1955.

Deanesly, M. *The Lollard Bible*. Cambridge: University Press, 1920.

Déchanet, J. M. *Guillaume de St. Thierry*. Paris: Beauchesne, 1978.

──── "John Scotus Erigena," *Spirituality Through the Centuries* (ed. J. Walsh). London/New York: Burns and Oates/Kennedy, 1964.

BIBLIOGRAPHY

De Guibert, J. (ed.) *Documenta Ecclesiastica Christianae Perfectionis.* Rome: Gregorian University Press, 1931.

De Lubac, J. *Exégèse Médiévale.* Paris: Aubier, 1959.

Denzinger, H. and A. Schönmetzer. *Enchiridion Symbolorum.* Freiburg-im-Breisgau: Herder, 1967.

Dickens, A. G. *Clifford Letters of the Sixteenth Century.* Surtees Society 172: 1957.

Dumontier, P. *S. Bernard et la Bible.* Paris: Descleé, 1953.

Erigena, John Scotus. *De Predestinatione Liber.* P.L. 122, 355–440.

Glorieux, P. *Répertoire des Maîtres en Théologie de Paris au XIII* *Siècle,* tome I. Paris: Vrin, 1933.

Gregory the Great. *Homilies on Ezekiel.* P.L. 76, 785–1072.

Gwynn, A. *The English Austin Friars in the Time of Wyclif.* London: Oxford University Press, 1940.

Harvey, W. W. (ed.) *Sancti Irenaei libri quinque adversus haereses.* Cambridge: University Press, 1858.

Hodgson, Phyllis. *The Cloud of Unknowing.* London/New York: Early English Text Society, 1944.

———— *Deonise Hid Divinite.* London/New York: Early English Text Society, 1955.

Holmes, J. D. *More Roman than Rome.* London/Shepherdstown, W. Virginia, 1978.

Hope Allen, Emily. *Writings Ascribed to Richard Rolle.* London: Oxford University Press, 1927.

Horstman, C. *Richard Rolle of Hampole and His Followers.* London: Sonnenschein, 1895.

Hugh of St. Victor. *De Sacramentis Fidei Christianae,* P.L. 176, 173–616. *Homilia in Ecclesiasten,* P.L. 175, 113–251. *De Arca Noë Morali,* P.L. 176, 618–80.

Johnston, William. *The Mysticism of the Cloud of Unknowing.* New York: Desclee, 1967.

Kirchberger, C. (ed. and trans.) *Walter Hilton: The Goad of Love.* London: Faber and Faber, 1952.

———— *Richard of St. Victor.* London: Faber and Faber, 1957.

Knox, R. A. *Enthusiasm.* London: Oxford University Press, 1950.

Leclercq, J. *Études sur le vocabulaire monastique du Moyen Age.* Rome: Studia Anselmiana, 1961.

Lonergan, B. *Grace and Freedom: Operative Grace in the Thought of St. Thomas Aquinas.* New York: Herder, 1971.

BIBLIOGRAPHY

Ludolph of Saxony. *Vita Jesu Christi*. (ed. Rigollot, L. M.) Paris: Palmé, 1878.

Maisons de l'Ordre des Chartreux. Parkminster: Chartreuse de St. Hugues, 1919.

Meech, S. and E. Hope Allen. (eds.) *The Book of Margery Kempe*. London: Early English Text Society, 1940.

Mittelalterliche Bibliothekscataloge. München: C. H. Beck'sche, 1928.

Molinari, P. *Julian of Norwich: The Teaching of a 14th Century English Mystic*. London: Longmans, 1958.

McCann, J. *The Cloud of Unknowing*. (2nd ed.) London: Burns and Oates, 1936.

O'Rahilly, A. *Fr. William Doyle, S.J.* London: Longmans, 1931.

Pachôme, S. et ses disciples. *Oeuvres*, tome 24. (Ed. L. Th. Lefort) Louvain: Imprimerie Orientaliste, 1956.

Pantin, W. A. *The English Church in the Fourteenth Century*. Cambridge: University Press, 1955.

Parry, D. *Households of God*. London: Darton, Longman & Todd, 1980.

Pez, B. *Thesaurus Anecdotorum Novissimus*. Augustine Vindelicorum, 1721.

Powicke, Maurice. (ed.) *The Legacy of the Middle Ages*. London: Oxford University Press, 1926.

Progoff, Ira. *The Cloud of Unknowing*. London: Rider, 1959.

Richard of St. Victor. *Benjamin Minor; Benjamin Maior*. P.L. 196, 1–64; 63–202.

Routledge, D. *Cosmic Theology: The Ecclesiastical Hierarchy of Pseudo-Denys*. London: Routledge & Kegan Paul, 1964.

Salu, M. B. *The Ancrene Riwle*. London: Burns & Oates, 1955.

Shewring, W. (trans.) *The Golden Epistle of William of St. Thierry to the Carthusians of Mont-Dieu*. London: Sheed and Ward, 1930.

Théry, G. *Thomas Gallus: Grand Commentaire sur la théologie mystique*. Paris: R. Halova, 1934.

Thomas Aquinas, St. *Summa Theologiae; De Veritate; Commentarium in Epistolam ad Romanos; In Divinis Nominibus S. Dionysii, Commentarium in Sententiis; Contra Gentiles*. Turin/Rome: Marietti Editions, n.d.

Thompson, E. M. *The Carthusian Order in England*. London: S.P.C.K., 1930.

Thurston-Attwater. (eds.) *Butler's Lives of the Saints*. London: Burns & Oates, 1956.

BIBLIOGRAPHY

Thurston, H. *The Physical Phenomena of Mysticism*. London: Burns & Oates, 1952.

Underhill, E. (ed.) *Walter Hilton: Scale of Perfection*. London: Watkins, 1923.

Walsh, J. (ed.) *Revelations of Divine Love*. Wheathampstead: Anthony Clarke Books, 1973.

———— and E. Colledge. *Of the Knowledge of Ourselves and of God*. London: Mowbrays, 1961.

Wenzel, S. *The Sin of Sloth: Acedia in Medieval Thought and Literature*. Chapel Hill: University of North Carolina, 1967.

Wilmart, André. *Auteurs spirituels et textes dévotes du moyen âge latin*. Paris: Bloud et Gay, 1932.

ARTICLES

Callus, D. "The Date of Grosseteste's Translations and Commentaries on the Pseudo-Dionysius," *RTAM*, xiv, 1947.

Chevalier, P. "Denis L'Aréopagite (Pseudo)," *DSp*, fasc. xviii, 318–23, 1954.

Debonguie, P. 'Dévotion moderne,' *DSp.*, fasc. xx, 727–47, 1955.

Doyère, P. "Erémitisme," *DSp.* fasc. xxviii–xxix, 1960.

Gardner, Helen. "The Authorship of *The Cloud*," *Medium Aevum*, xvi, 1947.

Grausem, J. P. "Le 'De Contemplatione' de Guigues du Pont," *RAM*, X, July 1929.

Knowles, D. "The Excellence of *The Cloud*," *Downside Review*, Vol. lii, January 1934.

Lesage, Germain. "Sacred Bonds in the Consecrated Life," *Supplement to the Way*, 37, Spring 1980.

Olphe-Galliard, P. "Cassien," *DSp.* fasc. vii, 214–276, 1953.

Rahner, K. "Les Révélations privées," *RAM*, 25, 1949, p. 506.

Roques, R. "Denys L'Aréopagite (Pseudo)," *DSp.* fasc. xviii, 244–286, 1954. Jean Scot (Érigène), *DSp.* fasc. lix, 735–61, 1973.

Russell-Smith, J. (ed. and trans.) "Walter Hilton's Letter to a Hermit," *The Way*, VI, July 1966.

Sudbrach, J. "Jean de Kastl," *DSp.* fasc. liv, 592–94, 1973.

Thery, G. "Thomas Gallus, Aperçu Biographique," *AHDLMA*, xii, 1939.

BIBLIOGRAPHY

Tugwell, S. "Intellectualism and Anti-Intellectualism," *The Way*, Vol. 20, October 1980.

Vandenbroucke, F. "Fièvre Satanique," *DSp.* fasc. xviii.

Van Elswick, H. C. "Victorine Spirituality," *NCE*, Vol. 14.

Walsh, J. "The Ascent to Contemplative Wisdom," *The Way*, Vol. 9, July 1969, pp. 243–50. (trans. from *Exposicio super quedam ver ba libri beati Dionysii de Mystica Theologia* in MS Douce 262 Bodleian Library, Oxford).

Walsh, J. "The Expositions of Thomas Gallus on the Pseudo-Dionysian Letters," *AHDLMA*, 38, 1964.

Walsh, J. "A Note on Sexuality and Sensuality," *Supplement to the Way*, 15.

Walsh, J. "Thomas Gallus et l'effort contemplatif," *Revue d'Histoire de Spiritualité*, tome 51, 1975.

For manuscripts and published works of Thomas Gallus cited in the Introduction and Notes, cf. this article, p. 18, note 4.

SCRIPTURAL CITATIONS AND ALLUSIONS

BIBLIOGRAPHY

273

BIBLIOGRAPHY

BIBLIOGRAPHY

7, 55	90	6, 4	200
17, 34	43	3, 18	194
		12, 4	174
Romans		1, 2–4	3
5, 12–21	171	5, 13	28
7, 21–25	75	12, 2–4	28, 239
13, 11	118	1, 2	79
6, 6	145	5, 15–17	86
19, 16	39	6, 16	252
8, 17	57		
8, 14	40, 59	**Galatians**	
8, 2–17	86	2, 20	71, 239
2, 4	56	5, 22	198
		5, 22	168
1 Corinthians			
6, 17	249	**Ephesians**	
9, 19	224	4, 4	233
13, 3–5	225	3, 17	194
11, 28	229	6, 18	81
15, 52–53	236	3, 19–20	122
13, 6	194	3, 14	87
1, 28	181	5, 13	86
13, 8	179	5, 23	172
4, 3	179	6, 10	115
2, 2	172	6, 23–24	3
13, 8	162	3, 9	43
10, 12	145	4, 12	55
13, 3	146	4, 15	62
16, 23–24	6	3, 1–21	72
2, 13–16	281	3, 19	81
1, 25	299	6, 18	81
2, 10–16	63		
3, 9	57	**Philippians**	
12, 30–31	59	3, 3–14	265
13, 8–13	59	3, 7–15	249
13	63	3, 20	239
13, 4–8	64	2, 5ff	152
		2, 9–11	147
2 Corinthians		2, 6–8	118
5, 6–8	239	3, 13	118

BIBLIOGRAPHY

INDEX TO FOREWORD, INTRODUCTION AND NOTES

INDEX

INDEX

24, 25, 29, 35, 38, 42, 57, 63, 64, 71, 81, 85, 93, 129, 130, 149, 173, 174, 202; will of, xii, 31, 32, 39, 72.
The Good, 31, 32, 40, 74, 81, 82, 122.
Grace, actual, 32, 39; cooperative, 30, 31, 32, 36, 39, 258; and contemplation, 14, 23, 24, 36, 55, 81, 86, 87, 88, 93, 94, 95, 135, 139, 146, 148, 150, 183, 184, 185, 190, 200, 214, 221, 259, 264; and desire, xii; effect of, 30, 31; gratuitous, 35, 39, 84; habitual, 31, 36, 38, 40; impulse of, 56, 58; and justification, 30, 31, 33, 35, 36; and nature, 84, 93; operative, 30, 31, 32, 36; prevenient, 30, 40, 250; sacramental, 38, 66; sanctifying, 35; and scholasticism, 22, 30, 31, 44; and sin, 32–34, 38, 40, 74, 75, 84, 92, 120; subsequent, 30, 40; and virtue, 26–42; and will, 37, 40, 76, 87, 92.
Grant, R.M., xvi.
Grausem, J.P., 23, 25, 26, 131.
Grenehalgh, James, 2, 99, 167, 187, 241, 260.
Gregory of Nyssa, 48, 51, 55.
Gregory the Great, 10, 11, 22, 37, 40, 61, 65, 70, 72, 81, 83, 84, 119, 132, 158, 171, 188, 197, 208, 217, 219, 251, 265.
Griffiths, Bede, xxi.
Guigo I, 4.

Guigo II (the Angelic), xiii, 7, 10, 20, 44, 73, 115, 171, 187, 185, 212.
Guigues du Pont, 19, 23–26, 60, 81, 129, 131, 156, 163, 169, 174, 193.
Gwynn, Aubrey, 227.

Habacuc, 2:3, 209.
Harvey, 70.
Hebrews, 4:11ff., 77; 4:12, 182; 5:11–14, 43; 10:1–3, 76; 12:18–24, 208.
Henry III, 46.
Hermits, 3, 6, 15, 16, 70, 101, 102, 116, 206, 226.
Hilary of Poitiers, 221.
Hilton, Walter, 2, 14, 15, 79, 120, 122, 144, 149, 159, 179, 188, 191, 194, 213, 215, 216, 217, 220, 240, 245, 257.
Hincmar, 48.
Hinduism, xxi.
Hodgson, Phyllis, 2, 4, 8, 9, 10, 15, 19, 20, 21, 27, 28, 58, 79, 91, 99, 100, 120, 122, 126, 147, 159, 165, 168, 169, 180, 187, 188, 198, 200, 213, 219, 233, 238, 242, 245, 253, 256.
Holmes, J. D., 95.
Holy Spirit, 154; coming of, 90; gifts of, 33, 35, 43, 59, 93, 141, 168, 206; and grace, 35, 50, 103, 138; instruments of, 75; and virtue, 41, 201; work of, 12, 47, 103, 179, 215.
Homer, 1.
Honorius II, 49.
Hope Allen, Emily, 6.

INDEX

Kirchberger, C., 155, 240, 258.
Knowledge, 18, 38, 78, 81, 87,
    140, 162, 186, 191, 208, 256.
Knowles, Dom David, 22, 96.
Knox, R. A., 89.

Langland, 230.
Lateran Council IV, 153.
Leah, 61.
Le Clercq, Jean, 70.
Lectio divinia, 26, 40, 65, 79, 96.
Leo the Great, 221.
Lesage, Germain, 13, 101.
Leviticus, 19:18, 169.
Lewis, C.S., xiii, xvi, xviii.
Life, active, 13, 14, 40, 41, 61, 70,
    101; Christian, 30, 69, 147;
    contemplative, 8, 9, 13, 17,
    20, 21, 40, 44, 61, 62, 68, 69,
    70, 73, 77, 79, 101, 103, 115,
    119, 135, 168, 210, 264; and
    grace, 30; and love, 72;
    mixed, 41, 45, 61, 158; and
    nature, xx; purgative, 132;
    religious, 95, 97, 144; of sin,
    37; solitary, 13, 15, 16, 28,
    51, 53, 54, 62, 63, 64, 67, 68,
    75, 82, 83, 85, 89, 91, 93, 94,
    95, 101, 116, 158, 159;
    spiritual, xiii; state of, 61,
    69; two kinds of, 25, 61, 67,
    136, 156, 157, 158, 163;
    virtuous, xix, 30.
Light, 24, 58, 72, 148, 174, 202,
    252; Father of, 61.
Liturgy, 3, 12, 86, 239.
Locutions, 87.
Lollards, 11, 21, 51, 226.
Lonergan, Bernard, 30–34, 36, 37,
    40.

Love, cf. also God;
    contemplative, 33, 71, 129,
    163; courtly, xviii, 88, 224;
    and ecstasy, 29; and
    intellect, xiv, 81; and
    longing, 17, 18, 83; ordered,
    xvii; of neighbor, 35; and
    understanding, 72, 81; and
    union, 5, 74, 81, 163; and
    will, xiv.
Love, Nicholas, 21.
Ludolph of Saxony, 23.
Luke, 61; 1:28, 125: 1:46–53, 169;
    6:27–36, 171; 7:36, 67;
    7:36 ff., 166; 7:37–38, 154;
    7:47–48, 153; 10:21–24, 65;
    10:27, 169; 10:27 ff., 55;
    10:38–43, 67, 156; 10:39–42,
    155; 10:42, 162, 168;
    11:42–43, 225; 12:2, 210; 15:1,
    224; 15:10 ff., 54; 15:18, 154;
    15:31, 125; 18:1, 81; 18:9–14,
    225; 18:13–14, 154; 22:43, 93;
    22:45, 203; 22:61–62, 154;
    24:31–32, 94.
Luke, 115.
Luscote, John, 8.

Man, end of, 12; faculties of, xix,
    32, 58, 61, 72, 80; and Fall,
    xxi, 48, 56, 73, 92; nature of,
    xvi-xvii, 32, 33, 82, 85, 86,
    90, 93, 154, 177; perfection
    of, 69; restored, 56; state of,
    56, 80, 92–93, 122; and
    supernature, 33; and time,
    32, 56; will of, 31, 32, 33, 37, 44.
Mark, 2:27, 124; 14:3, 166.
Martha, 61, 62, 67, 68, 156, 157,
    160, 168.

284

INDEX

St. Martin of Tours, 90, 232, 233.
Mary, 59, 66.
Mary of Bethany, 61, 62, 67, 68,
 145, 156, 157, 162, 166, 168.
Mary Magdalen, 38, 67, 166, 171,
 184.
Matthew, 5:10 ff., 236; 5:11–12,
 167; 5:48, 153; 6:5–6, 231;
 6:7–13, 193; 6:31–33, 167;
 6:44–48, 170; 7:1, 178; 7:12,
 161; 7:13–15, 89, 229;
 11:25 ff., 72; 11:25–30, 65, 76;
 11:27, 174; 11:27–30, 150;
 11:28, 119; 11:28–30, 55, 208;
 13:9, 257; 16:25, 77; 19:6, 86;
 19:12, 146, 166, 200; 19:21,
 144; 20:16, 75; 22:39, 70;
 25:35–36, 164; 25:39–40, 233;
 26:37–38, 204; 26:38, 83; 28:1,
 166.
McGann, Dom Justin, 2, 53, 91,
 188, 244, 253.
McKenzie, J. L., 231.
Mechtild of Hackborn, 89.
Meditation, xiii, xviii, 6, 14, 24,
 26, 60, 62, 64, 68, 79, 92, 129,
 132, 133, 136, 137, 138, 188,
 189, 220.
Meekness, 5, 65, 85.
Meerseman, P. G., 49.
Mercy, Father of, 79, 174; of
 God, 42, 184; of Lord, 39,
 149, 170; and sin 71; works
 of, 14, 62, 68, 101.
Methley, Richard, 7, 11, 14–19,
 74, 99, 100 101, 115, 116,
 119, 125, 130, 131, 132, 136,
 138, 139, 140, 141, 142, 143,
 144, 145, 148, 149, 151, 152,
 154, 157, 158, 159, 160, 163,
 165, 176, 178, 179, 180, 183,
 184, 187, 189, 191, 192, 194,
 196, 200, 201, 204, 207, 208,
 219, 221, 224, 228, 232, 234,
 236–240, 242, 243, 245, 246
 250–253, 258, 260, 265, 266.
Molinari, P., 210, 233.
Monasticism, 3, 10, 13, 28, 42, 47,
 55, 70, 73, 74, 79, 89, 101,
 188, 230.
Mortification, 83, 87, 194.
Moses, 57, 58, 94, 134, 157, 172,
 208, 231, 234.
Mystery, of Christ, 24, 26, 86, 93;
 divine, 24, 37; of God, xvi,
 xvii, xx, 24, 29, 72; of
 redemption, 56.
Mysticism, 97; false, 89;
 Franciscan, xviii; German,
 xix; and rules, xx; sensory,
 17; and trances, 257; and
 union, 23, 24; Western, 51,
 256.

Nature, of Christ, 240; of God,
 xxii, 57, 122; of man, xvi–
 xviii, 32, 33, 82, 85, 86, 90,
 93, 154; of soul, 251.

St. Odo, 70.
Olphe-Galliard, P., 75.
O'Rahilly, Alfred, 121.
Origen, xiv, 48, 51, 87, 146, 171.
Otto, Rudolf, 96.
Ovid, 241.

Pachomius, Abbot, 13.
Pantin, W. A., 6, 14, 28, 226.
Parry, Dom David, 47.
St. Paul, 27, 28, 29, 49, 52, 59, 64,

285

INDEX

INDEX

Roques, René, 43, 48, 50.
Russhbroke, 15.
Ruysbroeck, 221.

Sabellianism, 12.
Sacraments, 37, 38, 79, 87, 96, 152.
Salvation, 12, 30, 59, 70, 71, 184.
Salu, 168.
Sarracenus, John, xxv, 19, 28, 45, 46, 56, 201, 252, 255, 256.
Saux, Henri le, xxi.
Schroedel, W. R., xvi.
Self, -awareness, xx, xxi, xxii, xxiii, 64; -control, 56; -forgetfulness, 18, 58, 67, 75, 83; -hatred, xv, 83, 147; -knowledge, 65, 66; -love, 33, 63; -renunciation, 36, 77.
Senses, 27, 73, 86, 87, 92, 94, 132, 142, 227.
Shewring, W., 7, 53.
Sin, actual, xxi, 184, 190; capital, 64, 144; and Christ, 66; forgiveness of, 34, 71, 153; and grace, 32, 33, 34, 38, 40, 74, 75, 84, 92, 120; grievous, 34, 35, 132, 142, 151; habitual, 34, 39, 76, 189; and Holy Spirit, 47; impulse to, 63, 79; original, 63, 93, 176, 184, 190; recollection of, 75, 82, 132, 149, 154, 176; sorrow for, 154, 253; venial, 34.
Solomon, 151.
Soteriology, 70.
Soul, and contemplation, 23, 24, 25; essence of, 23; and God, 54, 93, 122, 137, 145; and grace, 32.

Spirituality, Christian, xiv; and *Cloud*, 28, 76; Dionysian, 18, 47–51, 209; and directors, xi, 3, 11, 22, 79, 264; English, 49; Franciscan, 84; monastic, xxi; Western, xi, 47–51.
St. Stephen, 90, 232.
Sudbrach, Josef, 28.

Tauler, xix.
Tears, gift of, xxi, 84, 204.
Temptation, 64, 75, 88, 89, 143, 193, 205.
Teresa of Avila, 94, 253, 258.
Theology, apophatic, 10, 82; Christian, xiv, xix; and controversy, 5, 6, 47; cosmic, 50; heretical, 88; "infused", 21; medieval, xvi; monastic, 28, 29, 42, 51, 147; mystical, 7, 20, 23, 82; negative, 210; scholastic, 21, 28, 29, 42, 49, 50, 89, 93, 95–96, 126, 147, 236; symbolic, 21.
St. Thérèse, xix.
Théry, G., 45, 46.
2 Thessalonians, 3:18, 3.
Thomas Aquinas, xiii, xiv, xix, 6, 14, 22, 29–42, 44, 49, 51, 55, 60, 65, 70, 80, 86, 89, 145, 186, 221, 227, 244.
Thomas Gallus, cf. under Gallus.
Thompson, E. M., 8, 21, 168.
Thurston, Herbert, 89.
Timothy, 27, 52.
1 Timothy, 1:5–7, 52; 6:10, 252; 6:15, 118.
2 Timothy, 3:12, 236; 4:3–4, 52.
Titus, 3:15, 3.

287

INDEX

INDEX TO TEXT

INDEX

290

INDEX

INDEX